MIND BODY & SPIRIT

Nancy Deville

Let Knowledge Spread

Published by
Vitasta Publishing Pvt. Ltd.
2/15, Ansari Road, Daryaganj,
New Delhi - 110 002

ISBN 978-93-80828-55-8

© Nancy Deville 2012

First published in 2011 as Healthy, Sexy, Happy by Greenleaf Book Group Press, Austin, Texas

All Rights Reserved.

This book is intended as a reference volume only, not as a medical manual. The information given here is designed to help you make informed decisions about your health. It is not intended as a substitute for any treatment that may have been prescribed by your doctor. If you suspect that you have a medical problem, you should seek competent medical help. You should not begin a new health regimen without first consulting a medical professional.

No part of this publication may be reproduced, stored in a retrieval system, or transmitted, in any form, or by any means—electronic, mechanical, photocopying, recording or otherwise—without the prior permission of the publisher.

Cover Design and Layout by Vitasta Publishing Pvt. Ltd.
Printed by Vits Press, New Delhi

Marketed and Distributed exclusively in India & Sub-Continent by:

Times Group Books
(A division of Bennett, Coleman and Company Limited)
Times Annexe, Express Building
9-10 Bahadur Shah Zafar Marg, New Delhi-110 002

For
Nadine, Heini, and Jitka

contents

India Introduction vii

Foreword ix

Preface: Defining the Rest of Your Life xiii

1 Redefine Health, Sex, and Happiness 1

2 Ultimate You Skill No.1: Get Educated About Weight Loss and Aging 9

3 Ultimate You Skill No. 2: Stop Eating All Factory-produced Food 22

4 Ultimate You Skill No. 3: Eat a Balanced Diet of Real, Whole, Living Food 36

5 Ultimate You Skill No. 4: Properly Care for and Feed Your Big Dumb Pet—Your Brain 73

6 Ultimate You Skill No. 5: Quit Addictions 81

7 Ultimate You Skill No. 6: Supplement Your Diet 96

8 Ultimate You Skill No. 7: Live a Detox Lifestyle 121

9 Ultimate You Skill No. 8: Flush, Rinse, and Nourish 130

10 Ultimate You Skill No. 9: Use Bioidentical Hormone Replacement if You Need It 141

11 Ultimate You Skill No. 10: Sleep Eight Hours a Night 171

12 Ultimate You Skill No. 11: Practice Self-compassion Meditation 187

13 Ultimate You Skill No. 12: Exercise Regularly 207

Conclusion 232

Appendix One: Toxins in Factory Food Products 233

Appendix Two: Supplements and Herbs 238

Appendix Three: Therapeutic Herbal Teas 257

Appendix Four: Environmental Toxins 261

Appendix Five: Self-care Toxins 266

Appendix Six: Home-care Toxins 273

Appendix Seven: Medical Toxins 277

Appendix Eight: Carbohydrate Counter 294

Acknowledgments 299

Endnotes 301

India Introduction

In 1968, I had just left Japan where I was living as a "Navy brat," modeling in Tokyo and otherwise being a typical 18-year old American teenager. After high school I decided to meet my new boyfriend, a Swiss German hippie, in Europe and go to India with him. We traveled across the Middle East on foot, ferry, hitchhiking, by train, and on windowless Mercedes buses that dated back to WWII, and then we arrived in India, on eighteenth century coal fueled trains. It was, in the parlance of the day, "a trip." My life changed on that journey in more ways than I can relay in short note here. But one very significant change was my attitude about food.

I was raised on factory-produced food as you'll read shortly. Forty years ago in India, you could buy a Coke but that was the only American product on the market. After several months of eating curry I would lie awake on my rope bed in the hostel garden where I was living in New Delhi and gaze at the stars thinking cheeseburger, French fries, cheeseburger, French fries. It would go on for hours.

I returned to Europe and a few years later to the US. By then I had no taste for factory-produced food, and would much rather eat curry and rice than a cheeseburger and fries. I was lucky to have lived outside of the US at a time when other cultures ate real food. Today, no one really has that luxury because American corporations have invaded the entire planet. The American factory food diet, as well as toxic drugs, self and home care products have caused a worldwide epidemic of accelerated aging: obesity, disease and the outward signs of aging like wrinkles, cellulite, hair loss and so on.

My beloved India has not been exempt. Even though India is a mere 15 per cent of the world's population, 60 per cent of the heart disease patients in the world are in India. India has the most diabetics worldwide with one million Indians dying every year from this disease. Eighty to 90 per cent of Indians have suffered from depression. Morbid obesity has reached 5 per cent of the population. In short, Indians are aging in an accelerated way.

Now that we live in a global village, though we may stem from different cultures we are all in danger of accelerated aging, largely due to the American corporate invaders. The reason people are aging faster than they have to is because their bodies are breaking down faster than they are building back up again. My Mind Body and Spirit program can be summed up simply as building up more than you break down.

In India you know a lot about building up. India is exploding in exciting ways. I'd like to see your bodies building up too, and Indians getting off the accelerated aging track. From what I know about Indians, I have no doubt that when you get the correct information, you will waste no time putting it to good use. It's my honor and privilege to stand in front of the American corporate invaders and hand you that information.

Nancy Worries
Santa Monica, California

foreword

When I reviewed Nancy Deville's previous book, *Death by Supermarket*, I realized she is a person who understands what many physicians and highly educated professionals do not understand, and that is that our diets are killing us. This is not an exaggeration. It is something that is increasingly recognized by those who have spent their lives carefully researching nutrition and toxicology.

During my medical training and neurosurgery residency, few of my colleagues understood the relationship between what we eat and our health. They looked upon nutrition as something that was just a matter of balancing calories with a proper mix of proteins, carbohydrates, and fats. Such matters, in their view, was relegated to the dieticians, the women who noted this intake on patients' progress sheets.

Like Nancy, it has taken me decades to come to a full understanding of the relationship among good nutrition, avoiding environmental toxins, and health. We hear a lot of talk about lifespan and ways to extend it, but not enough about healthspan, the number of years we spend in good health.

People often ask me, "If our diets are so poor and we are exposed to so many toxins, why are people living longer than ever?" It's a good question and one that illustrates that sometimes what we see is an illusion. Yes, people are living longer, but they are sicker than ever. What modern medicine has learned to do is to keep people alive, often barely alive, with an array of medications, surgical techniques, and medical technology. Pacemakers and medications, for example, force worn-out heart muscles to keep pumping, even if they barely work. Yet, little is done to prevent the heart from failing in the first place or to protect the brain from degenerating.

Our nursing homes are filled with frail, debilitated elderly residents who can barely see, are either wheelchair bound or using walkers, and who struggle to perform the simplest tasks. Worse still, diseases that were once confined to the elderly are now appearing in the young, even children. The "metabolic syndrome" (insulin resistance/obesity/type 2 diabetes, hypertension, and abnormal blood lipids), for instance, was a disease of middle age, and now we are seeing an epidemic rise in this devastating syndrome in children. Many children are grossly obese, weak, sick, and getting sicker. They are in essence aging faster than ever before.

People living in developed countries, the United States being one of the worst, are exposed to a growing number of toxins and environmental hazards, such as pesticides, herbicides, fungicides, industrial solvents, microwave radiation, toxic metals, and vaccinations that are responsible for a growing number of sick and dying people. All of these stresses require a body that is healthy and able to deal with this unprecedented toxic load.

Instead, we are eating processed foods that are deficient in nutrients and contain a vast array of toxins, including toxic metals, endocrine-disrupting chemicals, excitotoxins, and metabolic poisons. We eat fats known to promote inflammation, stimulate cancer development and growth, interfere with brain function, weaken our pulmonary and immune systems, and impair detoxification. Incredibly, our diets, designed by the medical establishment, actually promote heart disease and atherosclerosis.

We feed our children an array of food dyes, brain toxic metals, inflammatory fats, harmful sugars, and excitotoxic food additives and wonder why so many have behavioral problems, learning difficulties, and impaired language skills. When they are stressed by excessive vaccinations, infections, injuries, or the stresses of life, they fall apart. The medical establishment's answer is to put them on mind-altering drugs, tranquilizers, and other harmful pharmaceuticals that lead to increased mental problems, suicides, homicides, and a rise in chronic depression. As a result, we hear cries for more medical intervention and more drugs.

Recently, researchers have disclosed that our children are sicker than ever and the rising life expectancy discussed earlier is now reversing. We can expect the next generation to live shorter lives and experience diseases of aging earlier in life. Ironically this is all occurring at a time when our nutritional science is showing, in dramatic ways, that nutrition plays a critical part in health and longevity.

We know more now about how diet, exercise, and stress affect us than at any time in history. Yet, it's as if we live in two worlds. One in which we are learning that diet and eliminating toxins play the most critical part in our health and another in which the answer to health is more surgery, pharmaceutical combinations, and medical technology. The two groups ignore each other. You would think that nutritional science was voodoo. Ironically, nutritional science is significantly more scientific than medical "science." We now know, down to a molecular and cellular level, how nutrition affects our health. Today, scientists better understand why nutrition affects the way we develop, resist disease, and protect ourselves from environmental toxins than ever before.

The science of nutrition now understands the complex way nutraceuticals affect cures of many disorders. It is no longer a mystery why curcumin, for example, inhibits the development of cancer, protects the brain against neurodegeneration, and relieves inflammation. We know that it directly affects the signaling mechanisms in cells that are responsible for inflammation, and unlike chemotherapy, affects numerous mechanisms cancers use to grow and invade and does so selectively, that is, it has no harmful effects on normal cells. Likewise, we know on a molecular level how silymarin improves detoxification.

Despite mountains of new evidence concerning the beneficial effects of nutrition, exercise, and stress relief, the medical profession remains in the dark. Therefore, people must take protecting their health into their own hands. Books such as *Mind Body and Spirit* allow you to benefit from what we now know about nutrition and health. Practicing good nutrition is really not that hard—it just takes discipline and dedication. This book shows you how to reach your goal of good health by following some well-demonstrated techniques that are backed up by centuries of experience and good science. Nancy Deville has done the hard work by researching this technique; all you have to do is follow her advice.

—Russell L. Blaylock, M.D., CCN
Theoretical Neurosciences Research, LLC

preface

Defining the Rest of Your Life

While working on *Mind Body and Spirit*, I spent the summer in a beach house on Martha's Vineyard, an island off the coast of southern Massachusetts. There I finished writing the manuscript and celebrated my birthday with friends from Santa Barbara, Ojai, Los Angeles, San Diego, Boston, New York, São Paulo, and Prague. Before my guests arrived, I went into town to have a mani-pedi. As I talked about my birthday party, a women seated next to me said sympathetically, "I'm going to turn forty pretty soon, too." I was flattered to say the least.

The truth is I've lived through sixty revolutions around the sun. "Sixty" conjures up images of old age, but that's not me, my life, or my daily experience. I don't feel much different than I ever have. In fact I feel healthier than I have in my entire life. I'm still planning trips to India and far away places like I always have. I'm into yoga, hiking, and biking. I wear a size two to four. And when I walk down the street, I still get compliments. Of course I love it. What woman wouldn't?

I'm not a medical professional. I'm also not a celebrity with a staff of personal trainers, cooks, researchers, and ghostwriters at my beck and call. Initially, I was lucky to have had several significant positive influences that helped define the way I eat and live. Beyond that, everything I've accomplished in my health, fitness, and career as a health-book writer and real-food advocate I've done on my own.

My career writing health books began in 1996. My latest, an exposé, *Death by Supermarket: The Fattening, Dumbing Down, and Poisoning of America*, triggered a landslide of questions, the most prevalent being, "What do you do to look like you do?" At first I was confused. I thought, *Didn't you just say you read my book? You should know what to do.* After a while, I realized that it took me fourteen years of research, not to mention my own personal journey of struggle, experimentation, and discovery to develop my personal program. Getting educated is the first step, but then you need to pull all the pieces together. We live in a toxic wasteland of factory food, chemicals, scams, and bad medicine, and so accelerated aging (obesity, outward signs of aging, and disease) could have been my legacy, but it's not. I feel so grateful that I wrote *Mind Body and Spirit* to share what I've learned.

I was born in 1950 at the dawn of the age of factory-produced food and chemicals. Like everyone else, I have a story that's not all fun. Mine begins in utero. Like other women of her era, my mother smoked when she was pregnant. She didn't quit smoking until I was twelve. It was normal to ride in a car with the windows closed in what was essentially an iron lung of tobacco smoke. We were a cat family and consequently existed in a cloud of Raid Flea Foggers. My childhood was saturated in chemicals. It was no big deal to sit down at a picnic table that was dusted with DDT. My mother was on a tight budget as a military widow, and one of her hobbies was redecorating by repainting our asbestos-insulated house with lead-based paint. In the summer we'd run screaming out to a truck that sold candy and buy little wax bottles of "Coca Cola" that were filled with gooey colored syrup. We'd drink the blue and green fluids and then chew on the wax bottles. Candy cigarettes were the rage, but the be-all and end-all were the big wax red lips that we'd hold between our teeth until they got too melty, and then we'd chew and swallow the wax even though it tasted like sugary chemicals. Growing up in the 50s and 60s "Better living through chemistry" was introduced, and my family warmly embraced the concept in every way.

My mother hated to cook, but she loved that food could be purchased ready to eat. She wasn't concerned that the food had been made in a factory. She went grocery shopping once a month at the Navy commissary, so you can imagine the artificial foodstuffs we were served. I ate Trix for breakfast, baloney on Wonder Bread, Kool-Aid and chips, margarine, and Kraft Macaroni & Cheese. I never ate a green vegetable at home during my entire childhood, unless you count iceberg lettuce. Ironically, we only ate Hostess Twinkies on occasion as they were too expensive for my mother's budget.

I guess it's no surprise that I was chronically sick with tonsillitis. In the fourth grade I morphed overnight. One day I was a cute little kid of normal weight, the next I was ballooning. Although that period only lasted two years, it established a self-image that stuck in my head for many decades. And when I look at old photos I feel for that little girl in the dirndl dresses with the tieback bows and chopped-off hair, just like I feel for overweight kids today.

My paternal grandma Stella was my first influence on health. Her family emigrated from Poland in 1911, escaping an unavoidable future as impoverished farmers. Stella suffered from malnutrition and ended up losing all her teeth as a young woman. In 1942, at age thirty-nine, she accidentally wandered into a "health" lecture and was converted. From then on she had a very strong point of view about health matters, in particular the perils of processed food, going so far as to accuse a friend of murdering her husband by feeding him nothing but hot dogs.

She was regarded as a "health nut" and a "kook" in our family, but she ignored the slights and went about her business staying healthy and dispensing advice. After her night shifts cleaning offices at General Motors ended, she came home and juiced and canned homegrown vegetables. She'd lie in the basement in the darkness on her slant board, blood rushing to her brain to improve circulation as she meditated. She regularly guzzled olive oil from the bottle to "Fix herself up," and she knew how to deal with myriad conditions using various supplements and foods. Unfortunately my grandma was only a part of my childhood until age eight when my widowed mother remarried and moved my brother and sister and me from Michigan to California. So I missed a lot of the direct influence she could have had on my early health.

My family moved to Japan when I was fifteen, and by sixteen I was modeling in Tokyo. Being skinny was crucial to my success as a model and to my self-esteem. I'd chain smoke cigarettes and eat a chocolate chip cookie before going to bed, feeling virtuous for starving all day. But still, my grandma's voice stuck in my head when I saw that the Japanese ate only real food—sushi and veggies. I couldn't help but think she was right about food, because most Japanese were thin.

After graduating from high school I went back to the states for a few weeks to wait for my eighteenth birthday. There Grandma introduced me to the books of Adelle Davis, who was the very first real-food advocate: *Let's Get Well*, *Let's Eat Right to Keep Fit*, and *Let's Cook It Right*.

After my birthday, I left the states and flew to Europe. I toted Adelle Davis's books with me to India for ten months. While I pondered my newly hatching philosophies about healthy eating, I smoked a lot of hashish and even more cigarettes. With less than one dollar a day to live on, I had very little choice about food, so my diet was the same subsistent diet of the street-vending untouchables, India's poorest caste. When I returned to Europe I was malnourished and my hair was thin and brittle. But I was young and recovered quickly by eating the real-food diet Europeans ate. My Swiss-German boyfriend taught me about real food: "This is asparagus," and "This is yogurt," and so on. His mother showed me how to make my first recipe—olive oil, vinegar, and mustard salad dressing. I lived in Switzerland for two and a half years and learned how to eat the way Europeans ate.

When I returned to the United States at age twenty-one, factory food made my mouth burn. It was a shock to be back in a culture where people put anything into their mouths, dousing the consequences with over-the-counter (OTC) drugs.

When I was twenty-four, I stopped smoking, which was a major milestone. Like many who quit smoking, I gained ten pounds. That instigated another turning point for me. I remember the moment I looked at my butt in a mirror and thought, *Ohhh no, that is not going to work for me!* Then I started jogging. I still remember the agony of running after a lifetime of being sedentary. It actually felt like my lungs were going to burst into flames and explode. But I kept at it, and lo and behold my body transformed. I was a runner for twenty years, six miles a day.

Because of Grandma's influence and having lived out of the country all those years, I'd learned that eating real food equaled good health. Even back then I understood that being fat was a symptom of bad health and that one of the benefits of good health was an attractive body. I wanted that. So I rarely ate sugar and ate mostly real food. I didn't have one cold or flu for that entire twenty years. I was healthy. My body was fit and toned, and my hair was thick and shiny.

By the time I was in my midforties my knees were giving me clear signals that running on asphalt for two decades had consequences. I had to quit running. It was traumatic because it was a big part of my identity. To make matters worse, a little bit of fast food had crept into my diet. I put on a few pounds and couldn't get them off. I was feeling frantic about it all when a doctor I trusted told me I was experiencing sex hormone decline and pitched bioidentical hormone replacement therapy (BHRT) to me. It all sounded plausible—staving off aging by beginning early BHRT—but instead of feeling better and losing those few pounds, I crashed and burned into a hormonal tailspin, gaining twenty-five pounds (going from size 4 to size 10) and suffering numerous health problems.

From then on, I was on an obsessive journey. I hadn't been overweight since my chubby elementary school years, and I literally felt trapped in someone else's body. Twenty-five pounds might not seem like that much, but the problem was that I couldn't lose it no matter what I did. It took me years of research to finally put it together. Although bioidentical hormone replacement is one component of antiaging I'm going to share with you, estrogen, like any other hormone, needs to be replaced in physiologic doses—that is, only the equivalent of what your body has stopped producing should be replaced. Abnormally high levels of estrogen can damage the thyroid gland, and that's what happened to me.

Because my thyroid was down-regulated, so was my metabolism, and I couldn't shed the weight. Plus, I had other health issues related to hormonal imbalance, like insomnia. I was determined to find the answers. I went all out seeing the crème de la crème of specialists in Santa Barbara, Los Angeles, Las Vegas, New York, and Brussels, as well as on labs, hair and other analyses, food allergy testing, heavy metal testing, chelation, neurofeedback therapy, Chinese medicine, supplements, and hormone replacement. I took up yoga, learned how to cook, and became a humble student of Buddhist Metta meditation. You name it, I did it. I read, read, read, and researched, researched, researched. I connected the dots. I learned the facts about nutrition. I learned how to determine which BHRT doctors and practitioners were trustworthy, thoughtful, and knowledgeable, and those to avoid. I learned how to distinguish between truths and fads, and I learned a lot about bad medicine.

Like my grandma, I've experienced disdain and eye rolling over my views about health and wellness. I've also had an avalanche of requests from people who want to know about my personal program. My book differs from other how-to books on the market because I'm not going to promise eternal youth, unreal weight loss per week, or instant happiness. Anyone who knows me knows that I only sell the truth. Many people read self-help books to find out the magic secret to weight loss. The secret is *Mind Body and Spirit*. It's about total health. By achieving optimal health something magical is going to occur. Just like I did, you're going to recapture your unique physical and mental gifts and propensities, shrink to your optimal body weight, be sexy, and increase your chances of living a long, healthy, happy life. It won't happen in a week or two. You have a choice to keep buying into the quick-fix promises or to reframe your life so that you actually do become healthy. How you act on the state of your health now will define the rest of your life. And when you arrive at optimal health, you'll know, just like I knew when people began complimenting me on my appearance.

Obesity, chronic illness, disease, and outward manifestations of aging are symptoms of accelerated aging. There is no way we can stop aging because we are all headed to the same end: death. After living a healthy, sexy, happy life, dying peacefully is important to me. People are dying in droves from cancer, heart disease, and autoimmune conditions. Modern death means dying drugged up in impersonal hospital rooms, tethered to monitors with beepers going off, with strangers walking in and out. If I do nothing more in my career than to bring awareness to the way we're dying and effect even a small shift, I'll be happy. I'd like to see more people healthy enough to die of old age peacefully in a celebratory experience at home, surrounded by loved ones. That's the way we are meant to leave this world.

We're living way below our health ideals and then dying cold and ugly deaths because we've been duped into eating and living in ways that have been extremely destructive to our health. My program centers on taking care of what I call our "big dumb pets"—our brains—as brain health is the linchpin of optimal health. With a healthy, happy brain, you can do anything in life. You're more likely to be thin and healthy, have better relationships, and enjoy all the benefits in life that come to happy people, including dying a peaceful death. My program also focuses on the GI tract because that is where all nutrition enters, and right now our GI tracts are taking a major beating. I also place a lot of emphasis on adrenal health, as adrenal fatigue is the unhappy companion to all other conditions. Accelerated aging can be slowed way down, and you can live a happy life and increase your chances of dying a peaceful death by honing these twelve Ultimate You Skills:

1. Get educated about weight loss and aging.
2. Stop eating all factory-produced food.
3. Eat a balanced diet of real, whole, living food.
4. Properly care for and feed your big dumb pet—your brain.
5. Quit addictions.
6. Supplement your diet.
7. Live a detox lifestyle.
8. Flush, rinse, and nourish.
9. Use bioidentical hormone replacement if you need it.
10. Sleep eight hours a night.
11. Practice self-compassion meditation.
12. Exercise regularly.

From the many conversations I've had over the years with people of all ages about health, fitness, and appearance, it's clear that everyone experiences moments when they realize something about themselves has changed. It's always an unpleasant revelation. Health, fitness, and appearance do change with age, especially with accelerated aging. But you don't have to age in an accelerated way.

No matter if you're twenty and physically fit and want to stay that way, or you're thirty and you're scratching your head about that fat roll that you want to get rid of, or you're forty, sixty, or seventy or older and have gotten to the point where you feel that recovery is beyond your capabilities. It's all possible. I believe that the human body, mind, and spirit desire equanimity and that you can have those forces working with you.

I said earlier that I'm not a Ph.D. or an M.D., nor am I a Buddhist scholar. Even though my mantra is "get educated," I'm not formally educated. Actually, I skipped school so much to spend my days in Tokyo that when graduation rolled around I didn't have enough attendance days to graduate. I have my mother to thank for my diploma, since she begged the counselors to allow me to graduate. I completed one year of college at age thirty-nine before I started my writing career. *Mind Body and Spirit* is the result of my own life experience, study, and research. I also said that everything I've accomplished I've done on my own. I want to emphasize that, because I want you to understand that even if you're not a celebrity with a personal trainer and a cook, you can still achieve health.

If a child of a smoker, raised on sugar and chemicals, who smoked for ten years, and whose endocrine and immune systems were trashed by irresponsible hormone replacement can recover to be healthy, sexy, and happy at age sixty, you can too. Of course, it takes sacrifice, determination, and persistence just like any other major life accomplishment.

People have the idea that living a healthy lifestyle is drudgery and that the food you are required to eat is dull and unappetizing. On the contrary, healthy eating is likely the polar opposite of what you think it is, and the journey to the ultimate you is going to be the most enjoyable, most incredible, most addicting journey you will ever embark on. Getting healthy is such a fun ride.

Let's get started, now.

one

Redefine Health, Sex and Happiness

My mission is to inspire health for the mind, body, and spirit. Being healthy is sexy. And being healthy and sexy contribute greatly to your quality of life (i.e., happiness). These are not commodities that can be purchased over the counter or online in pill form. Attaining the Ultimate Healthy, Sexy, Happy You, is a process that begins with a new understanding. We've been sold a fake model of health based on toxic food, bad medicine, and scams. We've been convinced of a confectionary ideal of sexuality with images from TV, movies, gossip magazines and so forth, which has nothing to do with real life. We've bought into an ideal of happiness that is based on wealth, power, and acquisitions that ultimately equates to more insecurity, yearning, and unhappiness.

Health

Part of the reason some people have given up on their health is because the expectations are so unrealistic. Americans are crazy for thin. But face it, very few can look like the adolescent (or prepubescent) girls and boys who are constantly shoved down our throats by the neurotic machinery of the fashion industry. I'd like you to reject the false ideals of beauty as thinness and youth, and instead redefine beauty as optimal health.

An important aspect of becoming healthy is being realistic about your optimal body weight. This is a huge hurdle for many people. For example, I recently heard that a certain celebrity has proudly starved down to his "high school weight" on an extreme diet. I'm not going to say who it is, but only that he used to be attractive and sexy and he now looks like a skeletal old man. Remember in Tom Wolfe's novel *Bonfire of the Vanities* when he referred to the bone-thin socialites as "X-rays"? Maybe he was trying to tell us something—being emaciated isn't attractive or sexy. If I wasted down twenty-five pounds to my high school weight we could have titled this book *Prison Camp Thin!* Becoming realistic about body image is crucial in your quest for the Ultimate You.

And beauty is relative, too. The greatest fictional heroine of all time was described on page one of Margaret Mitchell's masterpiece *Gone with the Wind*: "Scarlett O'Hara was not beautiful, but men seldom realized it when caught by her charms." The real-life femme fatale Cleopatra was said to be short, dumpy, and squat, her appearance unremarkable, yet she scored Julius Caesar and Mark Antony. Anne Boleyn, who was not at all a true beauty, so enchanted King Henry VIII with her magnetism that to marry her he broke from the power of the Roman Catholic Church to have his first marriage annulled. Do you think these real-life women sat around and compared themselves to others? No, of course not. They accepted who they were and made the best of what they had going for them. Not everyone can be thin. Not everyone can be movie-star gorgeous. But you can make the most of what you have by achieving your optimal health.

I'm talking to men here too. Physical appearance, confidence, and sexual prowess hinge on optimal health, not on your car, your designer sunglasses, your cowboy boots, or your bank account. Of course it's easier to impress when you are wealthy, powerful, and connected, but you also want to live long enough with strength and vitality to enjoy these things if you are so privileged. A very wise man recently said to me, "Never underestimate the ability of men to be oblivious about their appearance." So if you're a guy reading this and you're in denial about the state of your health, please take a realistic look in the mirror because what you see on the outside (without mental Photoshopping) is a barometer of what's going on inside you. If you're not optimally healthy, things can only go downhill from there.

That said, when it comes to health, no one is perfect either, especially me. We all have health issues, things we wish were different about our health, and regrets that we didn't do things differently in the past. Although I intentionally do not point out my flaws, I will say that I've personally come to terms with physical changes and have made a lot of adjustments in my attitudes about myself, my appearance, my fitness level, my total health, my age, and so on. One of my favorite sayings is "Nothing lasts forever." Thus I'll have to make more attitude adjustments in the future. There may be attitude adjustments you need to make too. The Buddha taught that self-compassion is at the heart of true spiritual transformation. And what better way to begin your quest for transformation than with a little bit of self-compassion.

Our globe has entered an apocalyptic time of science fiction food and government-approved toxins and drugs. In response, people have divided into two classes that have less to do with money and more to do with personal choice. (Okay, I'm generalizing, because there are gray areas, but you'll get the point as you read these two descriptions.) One group eats nothing but factory-made or -raised products. Every self- and home-care product they use is toxic, from weed, roach, and ant killer, to chemical-infused room fresheners, dryer sheets, cosmetics, toothpaste, and on and on. They take OTC and prescription drugs every day—even babies and little kids, and especially the elderly. Midlife right of passage initiates men into the club of antidepressants, statins, sleeping pills, beta blockers, antacids, and impotence pills. Middle-aged women take antidepressants, statins, sleeping pills, beta blockers, antacids, and osteoporosis drugs and believe that hormone replacement will kill them. Both genders pop cheap industrial vitamins that they stock up on at the pharmacy, supermarket, or Big Box. They're constantly dieting with the endorsement of their doctors, but remain overweight, or becoming prison-camp thin. They're aging rapidly, depressed, and chronically or acutely sick. They don't remember when they last had sex.

Members of another group are ostracized from the government/doctor-approved group, including the doctors who've defected. This group eats organic, real, living food whenever possible. They don't go on diets. They take high-quality vitamins/minerals, herbs, and nutraceuticals. They've made a point to become educated about bioidentical hormone replacement, and they use drugs extremely judiciously. They fork over the extra cash for organic home- and self-care products, or they do without. While this group (due to ubiquitous environmental toxins and unavoidable eventualities) can get sick, they are generally healthy, sexy, and happy.

You may be thinking, *Okay, I can buy into all of this but I still want to lose weight. So how do I do that?* Along with being realistic about what weight would actually look good on you, it's important to adjust your mentality about how to arrive at that weight. When people think of weight loss, they think of deprivation and suffering in the form of calorie, fat, and/or carb restriction. I don't believe in any form of dieting, as I know from all my reading and research that ninety percent of diets fail, fail, fail. And at this point in my life I've lived through my own dietary debacles and have witnessed the consequences for others around me. Dieting perpetuates malnutrition, because it deprives the body of the nutrition it needs for ongoing building and replenishing (which is covered in the following chapter). Like the celebrity above, people who starve themselves ultimately look much older than they would had they provided their bodies with the necessary nutrition to rebuild along the way. You simply cannot starve the human machine—it needs operating materials. I will go into greater detail about the pitfalls of dieting shortly. For now all you need to know is that your dieting days are over, because dieting is not healthy. Achieving your optimal health will cause your body to naturally shrink to its optimal body weight.

Sexy

When I arrived in Hollywood I was twenty-eight years old, barely keeping it together financially to pay rent, so I didn't have any money left over for clothing or jewelry. I'd been a runner for four years, and even though I ate modestly, I ate all real food. I was nervous about forays into Hollywood and Beverly Hills because at that time the term "beautiful people" had just been coined, and I was insecure. Eventually the moment came when I made my first visit to a Beverly Hills restaurant. I drove up in my white Lincoln Capri wearing a cheap dress and the only pair of cork-wedged sandals I owned. I'll never forget walking inside that restaurant, expecting a Dionysian display of Olympic beauty and virility. My first thought, however, was, *Where are all the beautiful people?* I was surrounded by unhealthy-looking people with extreme plastic surgery, big stomachs, sun-baked tans, glitzy clothing, and lots of flash. At first I was surprised that heads turned when I walked through the restaurant. It didn't take me long to figure it out: Being healthy is sexy.

I hate to say it, but for a very long time, being healthy has been unusual, as our society has deteriorated health-wise because of factory food, diets, and drugs. Like those Beverly Hills people I remember from way back then, people attempt to mask bad health with too much plastic surgery, tanning beds, a revolving wardrobe, makeup, and so on.

The term "magnetic" conjures up images of sex gods or goddesses. To me, magnetic means that you attract into your life all the people and circumstances that will make your life tick in ways that further your goals, dreams, and aspirations. Being optimally healthy is such a turn-on and generates the magnetism that creates the milieu for sex and happiness. In other words, being healthy gives you confidence, and with self-confidence, you can do and achieve anything in your life. Since my Beverly Hills "beautiful people" epiphany, I've always considered my health first, and flash a fun but not imperative second. And that's what I'd like for you. Instead of being victims of the food, fashion, cosmetic, self-care, and medical industries, get healthy if you want to be sexy.

This program is not just about *looking* sexy, it's about feeling sexy and having a sex drive. I also want to say that I'm not condemning anyone who was a victim of psychological trauma, or those who were injured in an accident or one of the wars, who for various reasons can't have sex. Those are different subjects. This is about the fact that so many people have lost their sex drive. Sex makes the world go around, and a sexless life is not very interesting. Even the Dalai Lama was quoted as saying that he has "women in his dreams."[1] His Holiness has to deal with having sex on the brain because he's a celibate lama. But what is shocking to me is when women and men tell me, "Oh, I'm done with sex." Even if you feel that you're done with sex because you have no drive or don't experience sexual pleasure anymore, you don't have to deny your human desire for sexual fulfillment. You can get desire, endurance, and satisfaction back.

There are three major contributing factors to a tanking sex drive: malnutrition, adrenal fatigue, and endocrine imbalances. Healing from these three is definitely possible by honing the Twelve Ultimate You Skills, and I will talk more about this as we go.

Happy

Anyone who has had health problems understands how important health is to happiness. Aside from physical illness, given the number of prescriptions written every year for antidepressants it's pretty clear that there are a lot of unhappy people walking around. Our medical community focuses on plastering Band-Aids on brains in the form of antidepressant drugs, even though the vast majority of people (borne out by studies) are not made any happier by taking these drugs.[2] The truth is that you can't pick up a bottle of happiness at your local pharmacy. The only way to achieve happiness and to rid your life of depression is to build a healthy brain.

When your brain is healthy, you will have the wherewithal to go after your goals, dreams, and aspirations. We're going to talk a lot more about brain health soon.

There is also a mind/spirit aspect to happiness. When I first went to India all those years ago, it opened my eyes to the fact that Westerners basically have no idea what it means to be happy. I saw extremely impoverished people smiling and laughing. I'm not saying that being poor is a happy state of being. But as an Indian friend once said to me, "The villagers only started getting discontent when they got TV antennas on their roofs and started watching *Dynasty* and *Dallas*." Dazzling riches are seductive. But real happiness comes from letting go of grasping, and clinging, and accepting yourself and your circumstances.

Establishing your goals, dreams, and aspirations is a way to chart the course to your new life of health, sex, and happiness. It's important to visualize where you want to be six months from now, a year from now, and for the rest of your life. The Sanskrit word drishti means "gazing point." In yoga, if you gaze at the appropriate drishti you'll eventually experience the full expression of the pose. The same is true for life. If you establish your drishti—your gazing point at where you want to go—you'll eventually experience the full expression of your life. Read over the following lists and check the changes you'd like to occur in your mind, body, and spirit:

Mind

- ☐ End cravings.
- ☐ Stop being controlled by nicotine, sugar, caffeine, and other stimulants.
- ☐ Stop being a victim of temper tantrums and emotional meltdowns.
- ☐ Feel healthy and vital.
- ☐ Be more creative and productive.
- ☐ Feel more pleasure and satisfaction.
- ☐ Feel as if life is worth living.
- ☐ Feel able to accomplish your goals, dreams, and aspirations.
- ☐ Exude more self-confidence.
- ☐ Enjoy better relationships.
- ☐ Be able to chill out and stop sweating the small stuff.

- ☐ Sleep deeply and restfully every night.
- ☐ Improve concentration and mental clarity.
- ☐ Restore short-term memory.

Body

- ☐ Halt and reverse accelerated aging.
- ☐ Improve metabolic function.
- ☐ Lose weight without dieting to achieve an ideal body composition.
- ☐ Burn away the fat roll or big belly.
- ☐ Minimize cellulite.
- ☐ Grow thicker and shinier hair and stronger nails.
- ☐ Have softer and smoother skin.
- ☐ Prevent premature wrinkling.
- ☐ Minimize the dark circles under eyes.
- ☐ Become more fertile (men and women of childbearing age).
- ☐ Rely less on prescription and OTC drugs.
- ☐ Restore and improve immunity.
- ☐ Reduce occurrence of flu, cold, and bronchitis.
- ☐ Have fewer allergies—or get rid of them completely.
- ☐ Reduce arthritic pain.
- ☐ Reduce the risk of cancer, heart disease, stroke, osteoporosis, neurological, autoimmune disorders.
- ☐ Heal from medical modalities of treating cancer, heart disease, stroke, osteoporosis, neurological, autoimmune disorders.
- ☐ Heal from osteoporosis.
- ☐ Live longer with quality of life and increase chances of dying a tranquil death.
- ☐ Have a hot sex life again.

Spirit

- ☐ Feel emotionally stable.
- ☐ Feel safe and secure.
- ☐ Feel connected and grounded.
- ☐ Have a spiritual foundation to be able to deal with life's pain.
- ☐ Feel optimistic and positive about life, and be self-compassionate.
- ☐ Feel happy and well-adjusted.
- ☐ Stop obsessing, worrying, and feeling anxious.
- ☐ Have more patience and compassion for self and others.
- ☐ Feel calm and at peace and live life more easily.

Now that you've listed all your mind, body, spirit desires, keep the list to refer to in the future. You're about to embark on a thrilling journey to the Ultimate You.

The following chapter is your first Ultimate You Skill: Get Educated About Weight Loss and Aging. It's probably the most complicated chapter in the book and I don't want to scare you off! If it's too much, just skim it and come back to it later. Learning about how the body operates, however, will help you in your quest for understanding. Being the Ultimate You is not about being perfect; it's about doing your best to achieve a healthy, sexy, happy you while living in a world of factory-produced food, chemicals, scams, and bad medicine. This is where the road to optimal health—that fun ride I've been talking about—begins.

two

Ultimate You Skill No. 1: Get Educated About Weight Loss and Aging

A year after my thyroid crash, I found myself in a Hollywood restaurant with three girlfriends from the film industry. They were all thin, and for most of our friendship, they had known me as super thin. They ordered salads for dinner with the dressing on the side. When the waiter turned to me, I said, "I'll have the house salad and the steak." The needle screeched discordantly over the record and the music stopped. It was almost as if I could see an actual bubble with my friends' thoughts hovering over their heads, *Why is she ordering so much food when she's fat?*

It was mortifying. But even though I was fat, I wasn't going to stop eating. By then I had come to understand several key factors of physiology, which had crystallized my dietary philosophy.

My nutritional views were formed by three influences: my grandmother; living abroad for seven years in Japan, India, Spain, and Switzerland; and the research of Weston A. Price, a dentist. Dr. Price traveled the world for ten years (1930–40) and analyzed the effects of nutrition on health by studying people who were then deemed "savages." Dr. Price documented incontrovertible proof that people who ate a balanced diet of real, whole food, especially cholesterol-laden fat from the meat and milk of grass-grazing animals, were free of disease and had perfectly beautiful teeth and bodies. Not a single one suffered from depression. Those who strayed off to eat "white man's food" (sugar, flour, pasteurized milk, vegetable oil, and other factory-produced food), suffered from obesity, infertility, horrid teeth, depression, and disease.

My influences have one thing in common: They all point to a balanced diet of real, whole food that people historically ate until 150 years ago, specifically organically raised or caught meat, poultry, fish, dairy, vegetables, fruits, grains, legumes, seeds, and nuts that could (in theory) be picked, gathered, milked, hunted, or fished, that were grown or raised in a clean environment, and that have not undergone any processing.

You may be scratching your head at my references to eating meat and fat because your doctor and the media advise a low-fat diet, and moreover you've read celebrity books on the miraculous weight loss and health benefits of eating low fat, especially a vegetarian, vegan, and/or soy-based diet. We've all seen the documentaries about the grisly plight of factory-raised animals. And here I'm stomping all over what at least a certain segment of our culture reveres as sacrosanct. But the fact is that just because we're no longer involved in the actual slaughtering of animals, and we live so far removed from the procurement of food doesn't mean that our human physiology has evolved to eat a different diet than our ancestors. The DNA, biochemistry, and endocrinology of human beings haven't changed since the dawn of humankind. In the twenty-first century this can be either our doom or our salvation, depending on how we choose to eat and live.

Although my nutritional philosophy was inspired by Grandma, living abroad, and Dr. Price's research, my entire program came together by developing an understanding of some of the key factors of aging. (When I say "aging" I mean obesity, disease, as well as the outward signs of aging like wrinkles, cellulite, flab, tooth loss, thinning hair, and so on.)

Consequences of Accelerated Aging

As I said in the Preface, your brain, your GI tract, and adrenals are major focal points of health and healing. When you starve and otherwise neglect and trash your brain, GI tract, and adrenals, you jump onto the accelerated aging path, a slippery slope to depression, obesity, illness, and all the outward signs of aging. It's also important to understand the underlying processes that direct accelerated aging on a cellular level:

- Metabolic breakdown
- Hormone imbalance
- Mitochondrial degeneration
- DNA oxidation
- Insulin resistance (getting fat)
- Inflammation
- Adrenal burnout

Metabolic Breakdown

When I ate that dinner in Hollywood, I already knew that metabolism is a complicated orchestration of biochemical reactions that are essentially divided into two functions: breaking down and rebuilding. Our bodies are made up of dynamic tissues that are constantly disposed of and replaced. The breaking-down process clears out the old cells and cellular material (enzymes, hormones, neurotransmitters), and then the rebuilding process begins. Your body breaks down on a cellular level and rebuilds 24/7/365. This intricate replacement process requires that we eat the same biochemicals that we're made up of—plants and animal foods.

You want to provide your body with the best-quality building materials available. If you don't eat a balanced diet of real, living food, but instead eat soy products or other factory-produced food—or even a diet comprised of nothing but veggies—it's like remodeling your house with deficient and/or inferior materials. If you choose to remodel your body year upon year with deficient or inferior materials, your metabolism will begin to falter. Your body will break down more than it will rebuild, and you will be on a speedway toward aging. During my recovery—and still—I provide my body with the best-quality building materials available, because my entire program can be summed up as *building up more than breaking down*.

Hormonal Imbalance

In that Hollywood restaurant, my girlfriends sat in embarrassed silence picking at their salads as I mashed butter into my baked potato. I reminded myself that a key component of the breaking down and rebuilding process is the communications system. Our endocrine system is the chemical communication system of our bodies. Nothing happens—from breathing to assimilating food—without hormones. You need all your hormones operating at a normal level, interactive and balanced at all times for this communication system to operate efficiently. We have the same physiology that humans have always had, which depends on proteins and fats, like butter, to produce and regulate hormones.

Mucking with your hormonal communication system by depriving your body and brain of proteins and fats is like arbitrarily removing a part from your computer. You wouldn't do that now, would you? When a hormone tanks then all other hormones get dragged over the cliff. Then you have faulty communications and its code-red bedlam in your body. If you tamper with your hormonal communication systems by not eating proteins and fats, your body and brain will break down faster than they can rebuild. You'll age very quickly. It will be obesity (or prison-camp thin), disease, brain issues, and all those not so lovely outward manifestations of aging.

Free Radicals

At dinner, my girlfriends ordered Diet Cokes. Aspartame (among other things) generates free radicals in your system. Free radicals are molecules with an odd or unpaired electron. Molecules consist of a positively charged nucleus and negatively charged electrons that orbit the nucleus in pairs. When an electron is added or lost, the molecule becomes extremely reactive and is referred to as a "free radical" because it frantically seeks electrons to join with its unpaired electrons. Free radicals ravage the molecules in your body, stealing electrons from complete molecules. This process of stealing electrons creates a domino effect whereby molecules become free radicals and further rampage to obtain paired electrons, causing more free radicals.

In very simple terms, free radicals destroy cellular membranes and impair cellular function (cells' ability to use nutrition, communicate, and coordinate with one another). One very important aspect of free radical damage is called "lipid peroxidation," which is when free radicals steal electrons from the lipids (fats) in cells, called oxidation (think of a rusting piece of metal in the sun). Cells become brittle and stiff. Imagine a little boy and girl playing with free and fluid movements. Then imagine an elderly woman and man doddering on canes. The kids' bodies are comprised of fluid, fatty cells. The elderly people's bodies are made of dried-up, inflexible cells. Inside your body, free radicals damage tissues and organs, beginning the process in which tumors grow; damage blood vessels, initiating the buildup of plaque; and on the outside, free radical damage to the skin causes wrinkles and premature aging. Free radical damage is also associated with cataracts, autoimmune diseases such as arthritis, and neurological disorders such as Parkinson's disease, Lou Gehrig's disease, and Alzheimer's.

Free radicals are generated by normal metabolic processes, but in a normal, healthy body with a healthy diet, your body is equipped to neutralize these free radicals. It's the bombardment of free radicals from artificial sources that we need to worry about. Free radicals are generated in your body and brain via seemingly innocuous sources. A cheeseburger and a Diet Coke introduce toxins into your digestive track. The dryer sheet scent emitting from your laundry introduces toxins into your lungs. Petting a kitty that's wearing a flea collar introduces toxins through your skin. All of these toxins generate free radicals.

In the past fifty years, because of the proliferation of toxins, aging due to free radical damage has snowballed and placed the majority of people on this planet on an accelerated aging path. At that dinner—and every day of my recovery and onward—I ate vegetables to continually bombard my body with antioxidants. (More about antioxidants later.)

Some Free Radical Generators

Anything that activates your immune system
Drugs (prescription, OTC, recreational)
Environmental toxins and chemicals
Excitotoxins (MSG and aspartame)
Exposure to heavy metals
Extreme exercise
Factory-produced food
Flavorings
Fluoride
Fragrances
Grilled meat (heterocyclic amines)
Infection

Inflammation
Normal metabolic processes
Pesticides/herbicides/insecticides
Preservatives
Processed vegetables oils
Radiation
Stimulants (see page 82)
Stress
Tobacco smoke
Trauma
Ultraviolet radiation (too much sun exposure and tanning beds)

Mitochondrial Degeneration

Eating the balanced diet of real, living food that I advocate also protects your mitochondria. Every single cellular structure in your body and brain requires energy to perform its function. A cell's mitochondria are energy factories that do the actual work of converting incoming carbs into usable cellular energy, the universal energy molecule called adenosine triphosphate (ATP), which is used to fuel every facet of your being. The production of ATP requires sugar and oxygen.

When you're young, each of your hundred trillion cells contains more than a thousand mitochondria. As you age, mitochondrial degeneration reduces those energy factories by half. Mitochondrial degeneration is a normal process of aging. In the normal metabolism of food, as oxygen enters your cells to assist in energy production, free radicals are also created. These free radicals damage mitochondria. And so, even in a perfect world, mitochondria would decay as one ages.

However, mitochondrial decay is accelerated when your cells are required to overwork due to high sugar and/or stimulant consumption, as well as exposure to toxins, all of which are typical of our modern lifestyles.

When mitochondrial energy factories inside your cells have been destroyed by free radicals, each cell is much less efficient at deriving energy from the food you eat. This accounts for the "slowing" of your metabolism (which I'd like you to rethink as "inefficient" metabolism). Your cells simply don't have enough little energy factories to process incoming food into energy and so some of the food must be shunted off to fat production and stored. This inefficiency (gaining fat) is often the first symptom of aging. In fact, the more mitochondrial degeneration you have, the less efficient your metabolism and the more overweight you are likely to be. And because your cells are generating less energy, you're going to feel less energetic and much more fatigued.

DNA Oxidation

People don't get old overnight, rather it's a cell-by-cell process that's caused in part by free radical oxidation of our DNA. The main role of a DNA molecule is to store information, which is why it's referred to as a blueprint. This blueprint contains genetic instructions used in the development and functioning of all known living organisms—including the instructions needed for the replacement cells that will be replicated during the breaking down and rebuilding. As DNA is oxidized, we age on a cellular level, and that means that every time a cell replicates, it's a little less functional that the one before it. It's like xeroxing something a zillion times. The copies are going to be less and less readable. At a certain point, obviously, the game is over. When I ate with my girlfriends whose disdain for what I was eating was thinly disguised, I already knew about DNA oxidation and was eating for prevention. I was also eating and living to reverse insulin resistance.

Insulin Resistance

While free radicals are destroying mitochondria and DNA, another phenomenon is occurring. You'll notice a visible symptom developing (a big belly or fat roll), courtesy of insulin resistance. Insulin has gotten a bad rap, but it's a hormone that keeps us alive. What's not good is eating and living in a way that overproduces insulin, which is harmful to cells. Prolonged high insulin levels are implicated in every degenerative disease. The goal of eating and living is to keep insulin levels balanced.

Things That Raise Insulin Levels

- Aspartame
- Being sedentary
- Caffeine or any stimulant (see page 82)

Continual anger and rage
Dieting (starving)
Eating a low-fat diet
Eating too many carbs (sugar/starch)
Excessive or unnecessary thyroid hormone replacement
Sleep deprivation
Smoking
Stress
Drugs (prescription, OTC, recreational)
Using steroids

When you do any of the things listed above, you will either put too much sugar into your system by eating it, or your behaviors will cause your adrenals to secrete stress hormones that will break down internal stores of sugar. Either way, if too much sugar is released into your bloodstream, insulin will be secreted to store that sugar away into cells. Your cells have locked receptors, and insulin opens those receptors and shoves the sugar safely inside, where it fuels the cells. But if you continue to flood your bloodstream with sugar, after a period of time your cells will be filled to capacity with sugar, and they will lock their receptors. As a result, your cells are now insulin resistant. When insulin resistance occurs, the pancreas secretes even more insulin, which hammers at the cellular receptors in an attempt to cram more sugar in. In addition to already being too full of sugar, cells also resist this assault by shutting down their receptors because they no longer have enough mitochondrial energy factories to process incoming sugar.

Regardless of whether your cells have closed because of filling up with sugar, or if they've closed because they don't have the mitochondrial energy factories to process any more sugar, your body will produce less energy and your metabolism will be less efficient.

Meanwhile your pancreas will react to the alarming situation of insulin resistance by pumping out more insulin, resulting in too much sugar and too much insulin in your bloodstream. Your body will have no recourse but to turn all that extra sugar into fat. That fat is stowed around your waist first—don't ask me why, as it falls under the heading of "Horrifying but True Bodily Mysteries." Eventually even your fat cells will be stuffed, and you will have both high sugar and high insulin floating around in your bloodstream which is defined as type 2 diabetes.

During my recovery, I wanted to heal from insulin resistance, so I continued to eat a balanced diet, including protein and fats.

Inflammation

Neurosurgeon Russell L. Blaylock, M.D., C.N.N., who wrote the Foreword to this book, is another major influence on my health philosophy. I use the term "enlightened doctors" to refer to doctors who continue learning after medical school, and who are versed in nutrition. Dr. Blaylock is one such doctor. A keen observer and researcher who never stopped learning, Dr. Blaylock has spent decades plumbing scientific research, connecting dots, writing books and newsletters, teaching, and speaking. Consequently, Dr. Blaylock has emerged as a leading alternative doctor who is legitimizing alternative medicine and educating both medical practitioners and laypeople on nutrition.

Dr. Blaylock has identified "smoldering inflammation" as the cause of most disease (aging). Smoldering inflammation certainly conjures up an image of something you intuitively want to avoid, doesn't it? Inflammation radically accelerates metabolism thereby producing an overabundance of damaging free radicals in your system. You age faster, you get sick, and you die—and not in the peaceful way that I wish for myself and for everyone.

Some Factors That Create Inflammation

Aspartame, MSG, and other excitotoxins
Burns (including sunburn)
Caffeine
Exposure to toxins
Factory-produced food
Factory-raised meat and dairy products
Food dyes
Fried food
Infection
Lack of dental hygiene
Menopause and andropause (or any other hormonal imbalance)
Pesticides/herbicides/insecticides

Processed vegetable oils (corn, canola, soy, safflower, sunflower, peanut, cottonseed)

Sedentary lifestyle

Soy

Stress

Sugar

Transfats (partially hydrogenated fats)

Traumatic injury

White flour products or other refined grains

Aging in a Nutshell

If you're overweight and unhealthy like I was back then, you have free radicals generating in your system, damaging mitochondria and DNA; your body and brain are breaking down on a cellular level more than they are rebuilding; you're suffering from insulin resistance, which means that you're hormonally imbalanced as one hormone imbalance (in this case insulin) leads to other hormone imbalances; you have inflammation smoldering in your tissues (especially in your brain); and you're exhausted because your mitochondria are generating less energy. As a result, your brain, GI tract, and adrenals are wasted. Your sex drive probably has nosedived too. Who wants to have sex when it's so difficult simply to get through the day?

If you want to lose weight, reverse accelerated aging, and get your groove back, then it makes sense to increase the efficiency of your metabolism by reversing insulin resistance, restoring mitochondrial (to the degree possible) and DNA function, and reducing inflammation. The *Healthy, Sexy, Happy* program is designed to prevent the aging process and to rejuvenate. Before you begin, it would be good to determine your current state of health (and keep this information and compare where you are in six months).

Look over the following lists and check all that apply to you:

Food

☐ You skip meals, diet, eat low-fat/high carb, low-carb/high protein, or low-calorie.

- ☐ You eat way too many carbs for your activity level and most are refined white flour, corn, sugar, and high fructose corn syrup.
- ☐ You consume heat and chemically processed, oxidized, transfat, and/or partially hydrogenated vegetable fats (corn, soy, canola, cottonseed, peanut, safflower, sunflower).
- ☐ You live on caffeine.
- ☐ You guzzle soft drinks.
- ☐ You use saccharine, aspartame, and/or sucralose (Splenda).
- ☐ You drink too much alcohol.

Drugs

- ☐ You pop handfuls of over-the-counter drugs.
- ☐ You're on a daily cocktail of prescription drugs (this is not intended to disparage or discourage people who are HIV positive or anyone else who must manage their health issues with drugs).
- ☐ You use natural stimulants like ginseng and ma huang to stay alert or to try to lose weight.
- ☐ You use recreational stimulants (amphetamines, cocaine, heroin, other street drugs).
- ☐ You use steroids.
- ☐ You use diet pills.

Lifestyle

- ☐ You smoke tobacco.
- ☐ You rarely, if ever, exercise.
- ☐ You're overworked, with no balance in your life.
- ☐ You rarely, if ever, indulge in mind-clearing activities.
- ☐ You're totally stressed out.

Health

- [ ] You're overweight, with a fat roll around your waist.
- [ ] You're skinny with no muscle tone.
- [ ] You have the outward manifestations of rapid aging (flab, cellulite, wrinkles, bags under your eyes, dry, thinning hair, brittle nails, tooth loss, broken facial capillaries, veined legs, swollen ankles).
- [ ] You have symptoms of hypoglycemia (nausea, shakiness, clamminess, sweating, lightheadedness, irritability, racing heart, anxiety).
- [ ] You have high blood pressure.
- [ ] You're chronically tired.
- [ ] You crave stimulants (carbs, caffeine, alcohol, tobacco).
- [ ] Your sleep is terrible.
- [ ] You're depressed, obsessive, and suffer from mood swings.
- [ ] You're the queen of PMS.
- [ ] You're in perimenopause or menopause or andropause.
- [ ] You have acne, allergies, asthma, chronic pain, chronic yeast, headaches, infertility, gastrointestinal problems, joint pains.
- [ ] You've been diagnosed with osteoarthritis, cancer, cholesterol abnormalities, coronary artery disease, high blood pressure, osteoporosis, stroke, type 2 diabetes, an autoimmune condition.
- [ ] Your sex drive has tanked.

No need for a rating system. You know the status of your health by all the check marks you made, by how you feel, and by your reflection in the mirror. If you are in your twenties, you may notice health and appearance changes that you don't like. If you are in your thirties, you may feel you are really going downhill. If you are in your forties, fifties, or beyond, you may feel as if you're falling apart at the seams. If something is going wrong, it should be a significant wake-up call. As I said earlier, how you act on the state of your health now will define the rest of your life.

Our culture worships youth and beauty and is obsessed with sexuality, yet many people are entangled in disease, aging rapidly, wasting their lives in depression and misery, and can't remember the last time they had (or wanted to have) sex. The tailspin begins as early as childhood these days, a slow turn that increases in the twenties, crashes and burns by the time people are in their thirties, and deteriorates into total disaster in the forties, fifties, and beyond. There is hope, though, and it starts by not eating factory-produced food products.

three

Ultimate You Skill No. 2: Stop Eating All Factory-produced Food

Prior to 150 years ago, people died of infectious diseases. Now we have refrigeration, sanitation, and an understanding of the germ theory of disease, so people aren't dying routinely of infectious diseases. Today we suffer obesity, disease, and ugly death to a great degree because the majority of what passes for food in our culture is not recognized as nutrition by the human body. These food products are manufactured in a factory (including factory-raised animal products) and are nutritionally dead. In effect, they are poison.

Eating Factory-produced Food Kills Your Sex Drive

Eating factory food poisons the human body in many ways, including killing your sex drive. If you're eating factory food, you're likely malnourished, even if you're overweight. The Minnesota Semi Starvation Study in the early 1940s beautifully demonstrated how malnutrition affects sex drive. Researchers wanted to better understand how to deal with starvation victims after WWII. They recruited twenty-three to thirty-three-year-old men who were conscientious objectors but wanted to help the war effort. After six months of semi-starvation, this virile age group of men had zero interest in sex.[3] Their lack of sex drive makes a lot of sense, because if you're malnourished, your brain is going to say, "Uh-oh, we can't have babies now when there's inadequate food in the environment. I'll tamp down the libido and take care of this problem." And if you're past childbearing age, malnourishment reduces sex drive, as it results in adrenal fatigue and sex hormone decline, which we'll talk about later.

Regardless of your age, to your body, factory food products are not recognized by the body as food. You may be chewing, tasting, and swallowing, but once onboard these substances lack nutrition, are mostly toxic, and leave you malnourished.

Factory food products are made, for the most part, from real food that is broken down in laboratories and factories, using heat and chemical solvents, into basic components. The components are then mixed with colored dyes, preservatives, synthetic vitamins, and hundreds of other substances, including thousands of dangerous chemicals and drugs that migrate into your subcutaneous fat, delivering these toxins into your system causing mitochondrial decay, DNA oxidation, inflammation, and ultimately disease. Nevertheless, chemists and "food flavorists" manipulate the chemical composition of recipes so that the resulting products titillate tastebuds, have appealing "bite characteristics" and "mouth feel," and maintain a maximum shelf life. Likewise, industrialized animal products (meat, dairy, fish, chicken, and eggs) that are produced in Concentrated Animal Feeding Operations (CAFOs) are tainted by the hormones, antibiotics, and hundreds of drugs the animals are given. The FDA has either formally approved or turned a blind eye to most of the toxins in our food supply. Please see page 233 for an appendix reviewing a sampling of toxins in manufacturing processes in factory food products.

Here I'll devote some space to aspartame, MSG, and soy because they are so huge in the factory food supply, and so dangerous.

Aspartame

Madison Avenue is ingenious. They could sell us Agent Orange in a little packet and tell us with a smiley face that it will make us younger, healthier, and slimmer, and we would open our wallets and spill billions of dollars into their coffers. It's basically what happened with aspartame and now Splenda. When I see the ads on TV for Splenda—and I worked on TV commercials for ten years—I marvel at the production values (casting, hair, makeup, wardrobe, sets, and locations), the gorgeous cinematography, but most of all the brilliant presentation of lies.

At a Peace Summit in Vancouver in 2009, the Dalai Lama stunned the audience by proclaiming, "The world will be saved by the Western woman." Of course

I loved that he said that, and he's right, because Western women are warriors. They are fighting many just causes right now, and one of the most righteous wars they have taken on for the sake of their own health and the health of their families is the battle against factory food. The problem is that there is a lot of confusion about what is healthy and what's not healthy. There's a lot of misinformation coming from all directions, including Madison Avenue, which is intent on getting us to consume products like aspartame and Splenda because these products are huge moneymakers, and they are "FDA approved." Let's look at the facts about artificial sweeteners. Consider these fighting words. Because what you are about to read will cause you to draw your sword.

Aspartame is a genetically modified sugar substitute made from three components: phenylalanine, an amino acid; aspartic acid, an excitotoxic amino acid; and methanol, a toxic alcohol. All three are poisonous to the nervous system and cells. Aspartame metabolizes into formaldehyde (which is used to preserve corpses), which is known to be a powerful cancer-causing agent and can lead to neurodegenerative diseases. Studies show that aspartame dramatically increases the risk of leukemia and lymphomas. Aspartame is thought to be behind the dramatic increase in breast, pancreatic, prostate, thyroid, liver, lung, uterine, and ovarian tumors. Another metabolic breakdown product is diketopiperazine, another carcinogen, which may account for the 4,700 percent increase in brain tumors in the last decade. [4]

A Link Between Aspartame and Multiple Sclerosis

We live in a culture where many people subsist on Diet Coke, which contains aspartame (associated with the nerve disease multiple sclerosis).[5] At the same time, many Diet Coke drinkers avoid cholesterol, which is used by the body to form insulation around the nerves to keep electrical impulses moving. Without this insulation there's an increase in the potential for diseases of the nervous system, like multiple sclerosis. Doesn't that freak you out? It does me.

Aspartame is an amino acid excitotoxin. Excitotoxins damage and kill cells by overactivation. Aspartame crosses into the brain and facilitates a cascade of chemical reactions that end with the rapid and uncontrollable firing of synapses, resulting in the death of brain cells and the generation of free radicals. Remember, free radicals damage mitochondria, the energy factories in your cells. As they are damaged and shut down, your metabolism becomes less efficient, resulting in weight gain.

In addition to free radical damage of mitochondria, the body responds to aspartame exactly as it does to sugar, resulting in a drop in blood sugar and the accompanying cravings for foods high in calories and carbs. That's one reason why aspartame is linked to obesity and the metabolic syndrome. The other reason is that aspartame metabolizes into formaldehyde, which degrades cellular structures. People who drink a lot of diet drinks containing aspartame are flabby with a lot of cellulite.

Although I'm going to talk about "picking your poisons" (harmful ingredients and activities that you feel you can't live without), aspartame is not one that anyone should choose. Splenda (sucralose) is not an alternative, as it is a chlorinated molecule and chlorine is definitively linked to cancer.[6] Before cancer sets in, you'll have a lot of mitochondrial damage (and a less efficient metabolism). Artificial sweeteners belong on the same shelf as drain cleaner, insecticides, and rat bait.

Monosodium Glutamate (MSG)

MSG is another excitotoxin that causes nerve damage, allergic reactions, neurological disorders, and the "metabolic syndrome" insulin resistance/obesity/type 2 diabetes, hypertension, and abnormal blood lipids. MSG is proven to store fat and cause obesity even if you eat normal amounts of food.[7] The FDA allows factory-food makers to put MSG in their products in amounts less than 100 percent without including "MSG" on the label (an ingredient within an ingredient).

Additives That Always Contain MSG

Autolyzed yeast
Calcium caseinate
Hydrolyzed oat flour
Hydrolyzed plant protein
Hydrolyzed protein

Hydrolyzed vegetable protein
Plant protein extract
Sodium caseinate
Textured protein
Yeast extract

Additives That Frequently Contain MSG

Bouillon
Broth
Flavoring
Malt extract
Malt flavoring

Natural flavoring
Natural beef or chicken flavoring
Seasoning and spices
Stock

Additives That May Contain MSG or Naturally Occurring Glutamate

Carrageenan
Enzymes
Soy protein concentrate

Soy protein isolate
Whey protein concentrate[8]

Soy

I never eat soy, except a dash of naturally fermented shoyu (soy sauce), very occasionally. I first became interested in finding out about soy when I was researching my book *Death by Supermarket*. The media hype that would have us believe that the reason Asians are (supposedly) healthier than we are is because they eat mountains of soy. I lived in Japan for two and a half years (1966–68) and during that time I ate in countless restaurants. I never once saw a Japanese person eat soy, except teensie weensie pieces of tofu in miso soup. Thinking back on those experiences was my first clue that what the media was telling us about soy consumption was not exactly accurate. And where there is smoke there is generally fire.

As it turned out, I unearthed hundreds of clinical studies that link the consumption of soy to cancer, gastrointestinal problems, thyroid problems, early cognitive decline, reproductive problems (infertility, for example), birth defects, immune system problems, heart disease, and malnutrition. Ninety percent of all soy worldwide is GMO Monsanto Round-Up Ready.[9] (Monsanto is a dominant agri-corporation.) Even "natural" soy is dangerous, as it contains high levels of manganese, fluoride, and glutamate (which is an excitotoxin like aspartame), all of which result in neurological problems. What's more, fluoride damages the thyroid, resulting in obesity and other problems associated with hypothyroidism. Soy blocks calcium and can cause vitamin D deficiencies. Processed soy foods contain MSG. Infants on soy formula are vulnerable to developing autoimmune thyroid disease when exposed to high amounts of isoflavones (plant estrogen) over time. These isoflavones have been found to have serious health effects, including infertility, thyroid disease, and liver disease in a number of mammals. Long-term feeding with soy formulas can raise the risk of thyroid cancer.

The must-read book for anyone with entrenched beliefs in the health benefits of soy is *The Whole Soy Story: The Dark Side of America's Favorite Health Food*, by clinical nutritionist Kaayla T. Daniel, Ph.D. For now, let's just review a few of the major problems with soy.

Phytoestrogens

Phytoestrogen is an estrogen-like chemical found in plants. The major phytoestrogen groups are isoflavones, (soy), coumestans (beans and peas), and lignans (flaxseed). The highest concentrations of phytoestrogen are found in soy and flaxseed. Phytoestrogen disrupts endocrine function and is an antithyroid agent. Phytoestrogen is present in vast quantities in soy. A hundred grams of soy protein provides the estrogenic equivalent of the pill. Phytoestrogen in soy is linked to infertility, breast cancer, hypothyroidism, thyroid cancer, earlier cognitive decline, cancer, and reproductive problems in men and women.

The soy industry has funded zillions of studies to convince us that phytoestrogens are good for us. The fact is that plenty of studies not funded by the soy industry, as well as heartbreaking stories of people who have been harmed by eating soy, indicate that you do not want to consume plant estrogen. Hormonal balance is delicate. We already have way too much fake estrogen in our food and environment from xenohormones, which are foreign, man-made estrogen mimickers. Xenohormones are released from plastic, and are abundant when plastic is heated (water bottles getting hot in your car/microwaving in plastic). They are also created by exposure to toxic chemicals and bovine growth hormone. Both plant estrogen and xenoestrogen are estrogen mimicking, endocrine disruptors that cause cancer, autoimmune disorders, and other serious illnesses. Estrogen replacement, if necessary, should be prescribed by a doctor in a clinical setting, not concocted in your kitchen. Estrogen dominance is a major contributing factor to the rise in hypothyroidism, breast cancer, endometriosis, uterine fibroids, infertility, and low libido. Men and boys should never eat soy for obvious reasons. In fact, in ancient times monks were fed soy to maintain impotence.

Goitrogens

Goitrogens block thyroid function. Having survived a thyroid crash and living with low thyroid function, I can attest to how difficult it is to lose body fat and regain optimal health. Many people with a low-functioning thyroid never recover and remain overweight and obese. See page 145 for hypothyroidism.

Phytates

Phytates are natural plant toxins that ward off total destruction by predators. For humans, they are enzyme-inhibitors that block minerals such as zinc from being absorbed in the gut. Long-term affects include early cognitive decline (dementia). In ancient times (actually, until just recently) Asians prepared soy by naturally fermenting it, which rid it of most of the phytates. That's not the case with modern food processing.

Protease Inhibitors

Protease is an enzyme necessary to digest protein. Soy contains protein, but it also contains protease inhibitors so you don't get the full benefit of the protein. And because the protein is rendered indigestible, you may experience stomach cramps, diarrhea, pancreatitis, and even internal bleeding.

Manganese, Fluoride, and Glutamate

Manganese, fluoride, and glutamate (which is an excitotoxin like aspartame), are natural substances that unfortunately can cause neurological problems. Manganese toxicity is a serious threat to babies under six months of age who are fed soy milk, because it can affect their developing brains and result in neurological problems such as hyperactivity and ADD. Fluoride assists in damaging the thyroid, resulting in obesity and other problems associated with hypothyroidism. And glutamates are excitotoxins that excite brain cells to death.

Allergy Trigger

Even soy advocates don't dispute that soy is highly allergenic, which is the reason it is listed among other highly allergenic foods like peanuts on packaging disclaimers.

Soy Allergic Reactions

- Acne and other skin conditions, such as eczema
- Anaphylaxis
- Asthma
- Canker sores or fever blisters
- Colitis and other GI problems, including diarrhea
- Conjunctivitis, or pink eye
- Fever, fatigue, weakness, and nausea
- Hay fever
- Hives
- Itching
- Low blood pressure
- Nasal congestion
- Shortness of breath
- Swelling

Aspartame, MSG, and soy are staples in many people's lives. The reason is that Madison Avenue has been clever in selling these substances under the banner of beauty (thinness), satisfaction, and health. It's not only that food corporations don't have our best interests in mind. Governmental policies and standard-of-care medical practices support the use of toxic substances like aspartame, MSG, and soy as safe and healthy. A person's ability to survive in our modern world is determined to a great degree on becoming educated, recognizing, and acting with clarity and determination.

If you want to get an idea of what your diet really looks like, write down every single thing you eat and drink over a three-day period. Be honest!

Give Your Taste Buds Time to Reboot

We all know the power of psychological conditioning. Deciding not to eat factory food products takes determination. You have to abstain long enough to allow your taste buds to reboot so that you can taste real food again—or maybe for the first time in your life.

Your tongue is the home of ten thousand taste buds with receptors that react to different tastes: sour, bitter, salty, savory, sweet, astringent, and umami, a taste identified by the Japanese to define the flavor of amino acids in meat, shellfish, mushrooms, potatoes, and seaweed. Taste buds become desensitized to taste by a prolonged exposure to extreme tastes of factory food products that are adulterated with more than three thousand food additives, preservatives, colored dyes, mineral-stripped salt, aspartame (which is two hundred times sweeter than sugar), heat- and chemical-processed vegetable oils, and the two most deadly: MSG and flavorings. MSG is a flavor enhancer, and flavorings are the weird science product of multibillion dollar chemical research that produces artificial, highly addictive, taste bud–blasting flavors that keep people hooked.

The best way to purge your life of factory food products is to literally throw products away in your kitchen pantry and refrigerator, and start fresh. Purging your life of poisonous garbage and learning how to shop for and prepare real, living food is a process that simply takes dedication and discipline.

Never Diet Again

If you eat factory food you will also diet, because factory food is fattening. Again, I don't believe in dieting. I'm not going to review all diets in this book because I did so thoroughly in *Death by Supermarket*, but before I tell you what *does* work, I'll briefly mention extreme calorie restriction and low fat dieting.

Extreme Calorie Restriction

I'm sure you've heard about the studies on extreme calorie restriction that have demonstrated increased longevity in lab animals. This increased lifespan and its accompanying health benefits are supposedly due to the slowing of the metabolism. You may have a slow metabolism and the only "benefit" you've gotten from it is a fat roll around your waist and many other signs and symptoms of accelerated aging. So how is it that lab animals experience health benefits from having a slower metabolism?

The reason lab animals live longer is because they're fed semistarvation diets, which means that with little energy food (sugar) coming in, less than average amounts of energy are produced in their cells. With less oxygen and sugar entering the cells, fewer free radicals are generated and fewer mitochondria and DNA are damaged. Equally significant is that the animals' insulin levels are kept low. All of this equates to lowered inflammation. These three factors account for all the health benefits. What researchers zeroed in on however was the "slowed metabolism." Because food is so scarce, the little mouse or monkey brains perceive this as a time of famine and slow down their thyroids (i.e., slowing metabolism).

However we're not lab animals in cages. We live in a very real world of over-the-top stress and toxic exposure. Lowering your nutrition intake in extreme calorie restriction would be dangerous and life threatening, as it would leave your body defenseless to these ongoing assaults.

The Low-Fat Diet Will Never Die (but It Will Kill You)

I'm regularly asked if I've read this or that book based on "studies" that almost always lead back to the low-fat diet, a diet that apparently will never die. Speaking of dying, it kills me how this concept is so entrenched in the conventional health wisdom that to foist it on us, history is rewritten and truths twisted. Let's take the Mediterranean diet as an example. We keep hearing about how healthy this way of eating is. I spent two weeks in Corfu as a hippie hitchhiker in 1968. The following is an excerpt adapted from my upcoming memoir *Hippie Chick* in which I remember so clearly the Mediterranean diet:

> *In Corfu, my Swiss German boyfriend continued my education in real food. In the morning we ordered eggs so that he could keep his sexual stamina status quo. They came over-easy with deep orange yokes cradling bloody embryos and swimming in puddles of green olive oil. The butter was dark yellow, and we slathered it on heavy bread from wood-burning ovens, and then poured on honey the color of burnt caramel from the hundreds of beehives that dotted the island. His coffee was as dense as motor oil before he laced it with thick cream. We ate bowls of rice pudding or goat yogurt that had congealed leathery skins on top that we pierced with spoons and chewed like cud. Lunches and dinners were mutton with potatoes, or sardines served with plates of red, ripe tomatoes with crumbled sheep's milk cheese, salty olives dripping with olive oil, balsamic vinegar, and sea salt. Past the lips that had previously nibbled on fish sticks from "your grocer's freezer" slithered squid from plates that were floating seas of inky olive oil. I had*

not yet learned how to drink wine, but all around me people were pouring glasses of retsina from jute wrapped jugs.

Contrary to my direct personal experience in the Mediterranean before the American corporate invasion, if you visit the Mayo Clinic website you'll see that they downplay the amount of meat the Mediterraneans really eat. The Mayo Clinic advises against salt, though the Mediterraneans season their food with plenty of sea salt. The site doesn't mention eggs. And worse, they recommend canola oil, which is deadly and furthermore wasn't even available until just recently.

Except for the jugs of red wine, Mediterraneans ate the way Dr. Price's "savages" ate—and the way I eat today. But to make this diet palatable to conventional medical wisdom, the Mayo Clinic and others have to twist the truth and rewrite history to lessen the amount of meat, fats, and cholesterol really consumed. Why? I guess they have to continue to justify a diet that was a mistake to begin with and that has launched millions of people on a road to doom.

By the time I ate that meal in the Hollywood restaurant, I understood that the low fat diet my girlfriends were on was suicidal, as fat and cholesterol are necessary for the ongoing regeneration process. (More about that shortly.) I ordered steak and lathered my veggies in butter because I wanted to heal my metabolism so that it would be more efficient. This is something that's not fully appreciated by the medical community, which would have people avoid fat at all costs. I was fat and had suffered a blow to my health and that's why I continued eating. I also wanted to find balance in my life, and was ultimately rewarded with optimal health . . . including a healthier, happier brain. But neither happened overnight.

Celebrity weight-loss books proliferate every year because millions of readers are unwilling to accept the fact that weight loss can't be purchased by any quick-fix means. People tell me that they've lost weight on these extreme dietary approaches. And when they gain it back, they spend a lot of time musing in a resigned way about going back on the very same program. I sincerely hope you'll toss those celebrity books in the recycling bins rather than giving them to the Salvation Army for someone else to pick up for 25 cents.

The Ten Reasons People Are Fat

1. Factory-food products aren't recognized as nutrition by your brain and body. Dieting is a time of famine. As you're breaking down on a cellular level, your brain reacts to the lack of quality rebuilding supplies (famine) by resetting your insulin response to food. When you break your diet, your body will store more of the food you eat in preparation for the next famine. Thus you will gain even more fat every time you break a diet.

2. Heavy use of caffeine and other stimulants contribute to this time of famine, which is explained on page 82.

3. Chronic prescription and OTCs create free radicals in your body, which damage mitochondria (your cellular energy factories) leaving you with a less efficient metabolism.

4. Factory-food products and drinks contain aspartame and MSG, which are proven to contribute to fat storage.

5. Factory-food products contain toxins, and because many toxins are fat soluble, the body must hang on to fat if your toxic load is high so that toxins have somewhere to go.

6. Dieting results in irresistible cravings and bingeing. This was demonstrated in the Minnesota semi-starvation studies done before the end of WWII. This study and the ramifications of starvation are discussed at length in *Death by Supermarket*. In short, this study on twenty-two to thirty-three-year-old men proved that starvation causes the brain to go crazy demanding sustenance. So if you deprive your body of nutrition, your brain will work against you and you will crave, binge, and get fatter.

7. Estrogen mimickers in soy (phytoestrogen) and the environment (xenoestrogen) have damaged people's thyroids, leaving them with sluggish thermostats (think of a sputtering fire in a coal-burning locomotive).

8. All the factors of imbalanced eating and lifestyle create accelerated aging, which translates to hormonal imbalance. All hormones are interconnected, so when one hormone is knocked out of balance, the rest are dragged over the cliff. Accelerated aging wreaks havoc on insulin, cortisol, thyroid, and sex hormones, among others. And when hormones are imbalanced all metabolic processes are slowed. A less efficient metabolism needs less energy, yet ...

9. Many people eat way too many refined carbs (energy foods) for their activity levels. What's worse, the eating of refined carbs perpetuates the eating of refined carbs (craving and bingeing).

10. Okay, stay with me now, because this last point is the *coup de grâce* to any weight loss beliefs you may be holding onto (like losing weight with some packaged meal "system" for example): All toxic influences, such as eating a diet of factory food, including toxic fats and soy, drinking city water, ingesting stimulants, OTC and prescription drugs, as well as exposure to medical and environment toxins create an overload of toxins in your body. Researchers are beginning to understand that fat cells (filled with sugar and toxins) secrete hormones that create a very bad situation in your body. These are not normal hormones, but are referred to as obesogens. These chemical compounds/hormones are endocrine disruptors that ultimately contribute to obesity.[10] Obesogens are thought to muck up normal fat metabolism, triggering abnormal fat storage. Obesogens change your metabolic set point, alter energy production, and confuse satiety (so you feel ravenous all the time).[11]

Understanding basic physiology helped me regain my health and achieve my optimal body weight. The *Healthy, Sexy, Happy* nutritional approach—which allows your body to heal malnutrition and your brain to calm down—is based on the way that people historically ate: balanced meals, rich in protein and fat.

The way to lose weight and stop aging so fast is to achieve optimal balance in all things, including eating. The word "balance" has been used to death in the media, so it's lost its edge. I'd like to refresh the word. Once you learn to live a balanced life, you'll get what I meant in the Preface when I said it's such a fun ride. Every aspect of this program is designed to achieve optimal metabolic function, balance hormones, regenerate mitochondria and DNA, reverse insulin resistance, and lower inflammation.

Optimal health equates to optimal body weight, automatically. You're not going to see results in one week, two, three, or even the famous "eight" weeks that we've seen on so many book covers. If you're overweight and sick, it took you a long time to get that way. Cellular regeneration doesn't happen overnight. That's why I say that I'm not the "Quick-fix Girl," rather I'm the "Permanent-fix Girl." What the *Healthy, Sexy, Happy* program offers is a chance to change your life forever. But it's going to take patience.

My position is not to eat less factory food, my position is to not eat any at all, except for in dire emergencies when you have no other choice. To be healthy, sexy, and happy requires quality building materials: real, living food.

four

Ultimate You Skill No. 3: Eat a Balanced Diet of Real, Whole, Living Food

In radio interviews I'm often asked, "What is real food?" At first that question stumped me, and I thought, *You're kidding, right?* But then I realized that some people really don't know. Real food is alive so it rots, unlike food products that have indefinite shelf lives. Real, whole, living foods are foods that were consumed 150 years ago before factory products were invented and introduced.

Eat Foods You Could Pick, Gather, Milk, Hunt, or Fish

Dairy (butter, cream, whole milk, and cheese)
Dietary oils (such as butter, cod liver oil, olive oil, coconut oil)
Eggs
Fish and shellfish
Fruit
Grains
Legumes

Meat

Nuts and seeds

Nonstarchy vegetables, including seaweed algae "sea veggies"

Poultry

Ten Basic Principles of a Real, Living Food Diet

1. Eat a balanced diet of real, whole, living food.
2. Eat free-range, humanely raised, or wild caught animal/fish food (protein).
3. Eat healthy, healing fats and cholesterol.
4. Eat fresh, organic, nonstarchy vegetables.
5. Eat the amount of carbs appropriate for your health and set point.
6. Add enzymatic foods to your diet.
7. Eat locally grown, organic food if possible.
8. Eat raw and cooked foods.
9. Become a modern hunter-gatherer.
10. Do your best and don't worry about the rest.

Eat a Balanced Diet of Real, Whole, Living Food

To maintain the rebuilding process within your body and brain you need to eat protein, fat, nonstarchy veggies, and carbs. They should be consumed together in balanced meals to keep the body's systems working harmoniously—especially your endocrine (hormone) system.

Your brain demands a continuous drip of blood sugar at all times. However, because sugar is a catalyst for free radical oxidation that damages cellular structures, when you eat a meal, the liver prevents any excess sugar from reaching the brain. If no sugar is incoming through food, the liver releases sugar from its storage to supply your brain with the necessary constant drip of sugar.

Food is digested and assimilated in your intestinal tract. When you eat a balanced meal, over a four-hour period, small amounts of digested nutrition will enter the portal vein, which is located between the small intestine and the liver.

From there it will pass through to your liver, which is a staging area. Your liver holds up the nutrients in order to regulate how much of the sugar in what you just ate should pass into your bloodstream. This system works continually to supply your brain and body with sufficient and tightly regulated amounts of blood sugar. So eating balanced meals keeps your body continually supplied with building materials and nutrients for repair and regeneration.

Eat Free-range, Humanely Raised, or Wild-caught Animal/Fish Food

Protein is our primary food group, both crucial to survive and to heal from the malnutrition that is keeping us fat, dumb, depressed, and sick (with no sex drive!). In addition to making structures like bones, nails, and hair, proteins (amino acids) are necessary for the formation of all the chemicals necessary for survival, such as hormones, enzymes, neurotransmitters (chemical messengers that transmit information from one cell to another), immune function, and every metabolic process in your body.

Herbivores produce an enzyme that can turn plants into essential amino acids, but humans don't have this enzyme and therefore must eat foods that contain complete proteins to obtain all the essential amino acids for the constant rebuilding that goes on within the body. Without complete proteins, metabolic processes break down, but there are not adequate building supplies to rebuild. The body ceases to regenerate, and hormone production declines and/or becomes imbalanced. Another contributing factor to insulin resistance is the lack of muscle mass, as muscle is another storage place for sugar. Diets low in complete amino acids and fat result in low muscle mass.

There are twenty amino acids that are important for human metabolism. Ten of these can be produced within the body and are called nonessential. Two are conditionally essential, which basically means that age, stress, geography, and any number of factors can determine whether or not your body can make these, or make them in the correct proportions. Eight essential amino acids are required for life but not made in the body. Failure to obtain enough of even one of these eight essential amino acids results in cannibalization of lean body mass (muscle and bone) to obtain the one amino acid needed. The body doesn't store excess amino acids for later use, so amino acids must be included in your diet every day.

The Ten Amino Acids That We Can Produce in Our Bodies

Alanine	Glutamine
Asparagine	Glycine
Aspartic acid	Proline
Cysteine	Serine
Glutamic acid	Tyrosine

Conditionally Essential Amino Acids

Arginine	Histidine

Essential Amino Acids We Get from Food

Isoleucine	Phenylalanine
Leucine	Threonine
Lysine	Tryptophan
Methionine	Valine

Although I encourage the consumption of historically eaten animal foods, I discourage eating factory-produced animal products. Factory animals are tortured in concentration camps called concentrated animal feeding operations (CAFOs) from birth until gruesome slaughter. Whether you eat a fast-food burger or a steak from a five-star restaurant, you are eating a tortured animal. Nature is exacting its revenge on us now with the hibernation of bovine spongiform encephalopathy (BSE), the bovine brain-wasting disease more commonly known as "mad cow disease." More urgent is the epidemic of obesity and disease from eating animal products that are contaminated with estrogen, rBHG (growth hormone), pesticides, herbicides, fungicides, chemical fertilizers, antibiotics, and literally thousands of dangerous chemicals and drugs that are administered to or fed to CAFO animals.

Eating factory animals is inhumane, and we're better than that. As Ghandi said, "The greatness of a nation and its moral progress can be judged by the way its animals are treated."

Eat Free-range, Grass-fed, or Wild-caught Animal Foods

Beef	Lamb
Buffalo	Pheasant
Chicken	Quail
Duck	Shellfish
Eggs	Squab
Fish	Turkey
Game	

NOTE: *Beef and lamb cooked rare are good sources of enzymes (see page 68). Salmonella, Listeria monocytogenes, and E. coli O157:H7 breed in confinement, but do not proliferate in pasture-raised animals and wild caught fish. Never eat rare pork or chicken.*

Eat Healthy, Healing Fats, and Cholesterol

In the nineties I read a fluffy but convincing book about weight loss that claimed that it was fat, not sugar, that makes people fat. Like most Americans, I bought into the lie that dietary fat was unhealthy and fattening. But when I ate a low-fat diet for a couple of years, I developed cellulite for the first time in my life. Outward signs of aging are merely indications of what's going on inside—and my body was imploding from not having this crucial building material. Like protein, fat makes structures like bones, nails, and hair, and it is necessary to make hormones, enzymes, and what I call "happy" neurotransmitters. If you remain on a low-fat diet for a prolonged period of time, your energy will begin to flag; your brain will fog up; you'll blimp out around the middle, even if the rest of your body remains prison camp thin; you'll have more cellulite on your hips, butt, and thighs; you'll feel depressed and down; and worst of all, you'll begin to suffer from serious illnesses because the body needs fat to survive and thrive.

Even though serious doubts about the low-fat diet have surfaced in the last few years, many people just can't make the leap to eating healthy fat because the low-fat mentality and fear of cholesterol is entrenched like cement. It all started after World War II with the lipid hypothesis, the belief that saturated fat and cholesterol caused coronary heart disease. I hope you'll read *Death by Supermarket* for the entire story, as it's fascinating, but way too long for this book. Over the years this theory was disproven by both numerous studies and empirical evidence (Americans didn't suffer fewer heart attacks on a low-fat/low-cholesterol diet).[12]

Although most medical doctors support eating low fat, it's really been food industry advertising that's perpetuated the theory. This industry has firmly established a foothold in our food chain by supplying the highly refined carbohydrate products that Americans turned to as an alternative to the real, whole, living food diet that they had eaten previously. Ironically, many of these factory food products contain toxic oils, which are not at all "low fat," but make the food products tasty and addicting. These oils also provide a long shelf-life, which makes them lucrative for food makers.

Dr. Weston A. Price, who is my ultimate food guru, found that his healthy, thriving, happy, fertile native people with gorgeous teeth were all consuming a certain fat-soluble nutrient. He called it "Activator X," as it was an "activator" or catalyst for mineral and fat-soluble-vitamin absorption. He analyzed all the foods the healthy native people ate and found that Activator X (which was later identified as containing vitamin K, A, and D_3) was in fish liver oils, fish, eggs, organ meats, sea animal blubber, and the butterfat from grazing animals. We may not have access to edible blubber, but we can always eat good, old-fashioned butter, which is rich in vitamins A and D_3.

Getting Simple About Food Fat

Another of my major influences was Mary Enig, Ph.D., an internationally recognized biochemist in the field of fats and oils and an authority on trans fats. Dr. Enig took on the FDA and fought for decades to educate the medical community not just about the dangers of trans fats (like margarine) but also to dispute the lipid hypothesis that has wrought so much damage on our health with the misguided low-fat/low-cholesterol diet. Basically everything I know about fats and cholesterol I learned from Dr. Enig. I feel lucky to have stumbled upon her writings years ago.

Fatty acid (lipid) biochemistry is impenetrable for the average person and has made my own head spin around like Linda Blair's in the *Exorcist*. Because of the complexity of lipid biochemistry, we're just going to look at the very basics. Fats (lipids) are organic substances that are not soluble in water. Mary Enig writes, "Fatty acids are chains of carbon atoms with hydrogen atoms filling the available bonds."[13] That doesn't mean a lot to most of us who aren't chemists. All we really need to know about are polyunsaturated, monounsaturated, or saturated fatty acids, which are defined depending on the level of "saturation" of the carbon bonds by hydrogen atoms. Still not getting it? Well, I have trouble with it too! To simplify further, these different "saturations" result in polyunsaturated oils being fragile and easily oxidized (referred to as "rancid") when exposed to heat, light, and oxygen. Oxidized fats contribute to arterial plaquing. Monounsaturated fats are slightly more resistant to oxidation; and saturated fats are not easily oxidized and thus are optimal for cooking and unlikely to end up in your arteries. If this is too generalized for you and you have a grasp of biochemistry, I suggest Mary Enig's comprehensive book *Know Your Fats: The Complete Primer for Understanding the Nutrition of Fats, Oils, and Cholesterol*.

The oxidation/rancidity process caused by heat/chemical processing and exposure to oxygen creates free radicals (which damage mitochondria), hindering metabolism and resulting in obesity, disease, smoldering brain inflammation (leading to neurological problems), and all the outward signs of accelerated aging. The gleaming bottles of oils lined up in your supermarket are the very same oils that are used in all restaurants, from five-star to drive-throughs. Oxidized/rancid fats are also used in factory-produced foods—everything from powdered dairy creamer to microwave popcorn to the so-called "healthy" omega-3 imitation butter spread. In part, because of the high consumption of rancid/oxidized polyunsaturated veggie fat, we've seen rates of cancer, heart disease, autoimmune conditions, and other problems skyrocket over the past fifty years.[14]

Polyunsaturated Oils Not to Eat

Corn
Cottonseed
Safflower
Soy
Sunflower

To make matters worse, these oils are then partially hydrogenated (turned from liquid to semisolid) to be used as margarine and shortening in factory food products, including to fry fast foods like french fries. Due to the heroic and truly tenacious efforts of Dr. Mary Enig, most everyone understands that partially hydrogenated oils are trans fats that cause disease.

Because of the heat/chemical/oxygen processing of oils, two other oils, canola and peanut, which are mostly monounsaturated fatty acids, should also be avoided. Basically any time you see oil in a clear glass bottle you know that it's toxic, including olive oil, which is a healthy oil but must be processed with care and stored in dark glass. This warning extends to anything made with these oils. A few other miscellaneous fats not to eat are any kind of fake buttery spread, margarine, bottled salad dressing (even the health food store brands), shortening, movie popcorn oil, mayo, and any other highly processed fat/oil.

Polyunsaturated Fats

Just because the food industry has processed the wrong types of polyunsaturated fats in very unhealthy ways, doesn't mean that you should give up on all polyunsaturated oils, because naturally occurring polyunsaturated fats are health giving and will heal you.

Omega-3s

The two polyunsaturated fatty acids that are the most important for you to understand are linolenic acid (omega-3) and linoleic acid (omega-6). Omega-3 and -6 are referred to as "essentially fatty acids," or EFAs or vitamin F because they are required by the body but can only be obtained through eating the right foods. Omega-3s have received mainstream attention in the past decade of burgeoning awareness. However, when I was in the third grade I must have read about omega-3s in one of my grandma's kooky health books because I devised a science experiment for school using our hamsters Chubsy Wubsy and Speedy Gonzales. Speedy got cod liver oil (omega-3) for thirty days; Chubsy did not. At the end of the trial, I evaluated their fur and weight and so forth and charted my evaluations for the exhibition. Speedy got stellar grades on all counts (according to my extensive expertise on the subject). All that to say that the alternative medical world has known for a very long time about the value of omega-3 EFAs.

Omega-3 promotes lean body mass (i.e., it will help you burn fat and build muscle). Omega-3 fats are essential to cellular health and to reduce inflammation. A diet low in omega-3 results in dry skin, premature wrinkles, thin, brittle hair and nails, depression and other neurotransmitter imbalances, chronic constipation, and a malfunctioning immune system, which leads to muscle and joint pain and arthritis.

EFAs can metabolize into docosahexaenoic acid (DHA) and eicosapentaenoic acid (EPA), but it's best to get them readymade by eating food rich in omega-3s. DHA is essential for the proper functioning of our brains as adults, the development of the nervous system, and visual abilities during the first six months of life. EPA reduces inflammation and the risk for heart disease by keeping your arteries supple. Our bodies naturally produce small amounts of DHA, but we must get adequate amounts from our diet.

Examples of Healthy Omega-3 Polyunsaturated Fats and Oils

Cold-water fish such as cod, herring, mackerel, salmon, sardines, and their oils

Flax seeds (small amounts, once in a while)

Krill oil

Marine plankton

Walnuts

Flaxseed oil has become extremely popular and people are swigging it like crazy and thinking they are doing the right thing. Flaxseed is high in lignans, which are phytoestrogens. Too much phytoestrogen can pose a problem for people whose thyroids are on the cusp of crashing. This is really a huge part of our population these days given the thrashing our thyroids go through in our modern world. A small amount of flaxseed from time to time would be healthy. However, flaxseed oil goes rancid/oxidizes very quickly, so you only have a couple of weeks from the date of purchase to consume it.

Cod liver oil is the preferable EFA (over fish oil extracted by pulverizing other types of fish and flax) as cod liver oil contains omega-3 as well as EPA and DHA (explained above). The best brands of cod liver oil also contain both vitamin A and D_3, and it's always best to consume synergistic vitamins together the way nature packages them, as there is less likelihood of having a problem overdoing either A or D_3. Because flax is so popular, food makers have rushed into manufacturing all sorts of products with flax, including bread, cereal, and crackers, thus creating toxic foods riddled with free radicals. If you want to consume flax, buy it in an opaque bottle, refrigerate it, take a few sips over a two-week period, and then throw it away. Keep seeds refrigerated, grind them fresh each time, and consume them in small quantities.

Omega-6

The ideal and traditional ratio of omega-3:6 polyunsaturated fatty acids is about 1:1–2. Today we consume a 1:20–50 ratio. Too much omega-6 promotes inflammation, and this high ratio of omega-3:6 has been shown to be a major contributing factor in the development of cancer and other degenerative diseases. Omega-6 is found in meat—but unfortunately factory-raised animals are fed an unnatural diet that has distorted the ratio. Like humans, animals are what they eat, so when we eat them, we're eating too many omega-6s. Because we still need some omega-6 (and saturated animal fat), it's important to eat free-range, grass-fed animal foods.

Omega-6 is the precursor of gamma-linolenic acid (GLA) in your body. GLA reduces inflammation, and other inflammation related issues. Some people are not able to convert omega-6 to GLA, so you can get GLA in supplement form.

GLA Supplemental Oils

Black currant
Borage
Evening primrose

The balanced diet of real, whole, historically eaten foods that I advocate provides a perfect 1:1–2 balance of omega-3:6. In addition, you can supplement your diet to ensure you're getting adequate EFAs. Unfortunately, with the mainstream awareness of the skewed omega-3:6 ratio, some people have started glutting on omega-3 oils. This isn't balance and can lead to a lot of other problems such as way too thin blood that doesn't clot appropriately, allergies, acid reflux, diarrhea, and dangerously low blood pressure if you're taking beta-blockers. A tablespoon or two, depending on your size, of cod liver oil every day is plenty.

Monounsaturated Fats

Monosaturated fats lower LDL-cholesterol in the blood, are necessary for healthy skin, maintain the structural integrity of neural membranes, and are high in the antioxidant vitamin E, which boosts immunity and provides protection against certain cancers such as breast and colon cancer. Monounsaturated fats are more prone to creating oxidizing free radicals than saturated oils when they are cooked, so it's best to eat monounsaturated foods and oils at room temperature (the exception of olive oil, which can be used for cooking).

Examples of Healthy Monounsaturated Fats

Almonds	Lard
Avocados	Olives and olive oil
Cashews and cashew butter	Peanuts and peanut butter
Fowl fat	Pork (including bacon)
Hazelnuts	

Saturated Fat

Saturated fat comes not only from animal foods and tropical oils, but your body also makes it. Saturated fat is a historically eaten, life-giving fat, imperative for healing. Following are ten reasons to eat saturated fat as a therapeutic food:

1. Saturated fats are healthy building materials to make cells and hormones.
2. Fifty percent of every single one of the hundred trillion cells in your body is made up of saturated fat. That means that the cells of your big dumb pet—your brain—are made in part with saturated fat.
3. If you're worried about osteoporosis, saturated fat is necessary for calcium to be incorporated into the skeletal structure. So stop drinking 2% milk for your calcium and switch to whole, organic (preferably raw) milk.[15]
4. Saturated fat protects the liver from toxins like Tylenol and alcohol.[16]
5. If you're taking EFAs without saturated fat, you're not going to have optimal absorption of the EFAs.[17]
6. The fat content of the lining of your lungs is made up of saturated fatty acids.
7. Saturated fats support your endocrine system (the hormones that are your body's communication system).

8. Saturated fat lowers Lp(a), a genetic variation of LDL cholesterol that makes some people prone to heart disease.[18]
9. Saturated fat strengthens the immune system.[19]
10. Saturated fats are satisfying, so you feel full longer.

For all of these reasons, Dr. Weston A. Price found all of his "savages" to be healthy, fertile, and beautiful. Plus they had nice teeth. And all from a diet of grass-fed saturated fat.

Examples of Healthy, Grass-fed/Organic Saturated Fat

Activator X (X Factor)	Crème fraîche
Beef	Egg
Butter	Lamb
Cheese	Red palm oil
Cocoa butter	Sour cream
Coconut	Whole coconut milk
Coconut butter and oil	Whole milk
Cream	

Coconut Oil

You may be surprised to see coconut, palm kernel, and palm oils listed under healthy saturated fats because you've heard that tropical oils cause heart disease. These oils have been vilified as "artery clogging," but saturated fat doesn't easily oxidize, so it doesn't collect in the arteries. And when the deposits in arteries have been analyzed, only 26 percent of the stuff was saturated; the lion's share was polyunsaturated.[20]

I write about coconut oil and the Pacific islanders in *Death by Supermarket*, and again I encourage you to read that book to have a better understanding of the erroneous low fat/low cholesterol debacle. In short, the Pacific Islanders who still get 30 to 60 percent of their total caloric intake from saturated coconut oil have non-existent rates of cardiovascular disease.[21] I'm going to talk more about artery clogging shortly.

Coconut oil is particularly healthy for numerous reasons. For one, it raises HDL (good) cholesterol. It also contains antiviral and antimicrobial properties that have been found to be effective in destroying or combating viruses that cause influenza, measles, herpes, mononucleosis, hepatitis C, and AIDS; the fungi and yeast that result in ringworm, candida, and thrush; parasites that cause intestinal infections such as giardiasis; as well as bacteria that cause stomach ulcers, throat infections, pneumonia, sinusitis, rheumatic fever, food-borne illnesses, urinary tract infections, meningitis, gonorrhea, and toxic shock syndrome. It's one fat that I eat in spoonfuls from the container.

Therapeutic Coconut

- Effective in the treatment of kidney and urethral stones
- Fights viruses that cause the flu, herpes, and AIDS
- Helps control diabetes
- Helps correct eczema
- Helps eliminate candida yeast infections
- Helps eliminate pinworms
- Helps in gallbladder disease
- Helps keep skin soft and smooth
- Helps kill the Giardia lamblia parasite
- Heals mouth ulcers
- Helps prevent osteoporosis
- Improves digestion and helps regulate peristalsis
- Kills intestinal worms
- Maintains body temperature
- Maintains the human body's natural fluid levels
- Promotes healthy thyroid function
- Provides quick energy
- Relieves stress on pancreas and enzyme systems of the body

Cholesterol

I've eaten eggs every morning for years. I eat a pound of butter a week. I glut on lobster and fish all summer long. I attribute my recovery and survival in this toxic wasteland to eating copious amounts of cholesterol. The reason I eat so much cholesterol is that it's both protective and healing. Dr. Enig writes, "Our blood vessels can become damaged in a number of ways—through irritations caused by free radicals or viruses, or because they are structurally weak—and when this happens, the body's natural healing substance steps in to repair the damage. That substance is cholesterol."[22] When I was recovering from my thyroid crash, it was of utmost importance to me to do everything I could to achieve normal functioning of my endocrine and immune systems. So there was no way that I was going to deprive my body of cholesterol. Following are ten of the many reasons to eat cholesterol as a therapeutic food:

1. Cholesterol acts as a precursor to the adrenal hormones DHEA and cortisol, which help us deal with stress. (Cortisol got a bad reputation from that silly diet pill CortiSlim but cortisol really is a good hormone.)

2. Every single one of the hundred trillion cells in your body are made up, in part, of cholesterol.

3. Cholesterol is an essential component of cell membranes and keeps those membranes permeable.

4. It is essential to build a solid brain that functions well.

5. Cholesterol is the precursor to pregnenolone, the mother of all hormones. Without fat in your diet, your body is going to falter in making sex hormones such as progesterone, testosterone, and estradiol (referred to as steroid hormones). So if you're on a low-fat diet, your sex drive is likely bottoming out. Re-introducing cholesterol to your diet will help return your sex drive to normal.

6. It insulates nerves and keeps electrical impulses moving.

7. Cholesterol is necessary for the production of serotonin, the happy neurotransmitter, which explains why low cholesterol levels are linked to aggression, violence, depression, and suicidal tendencies.

8. Maintains a healthy immune system and protects the body against heart disease and cancer.

9. Cholesterol is necessary to convert sunlight to vitamin D_3, which is imperative for a healthy nervous system and bones, proper growth, mineral metabolism, muscle tone, insulin production, reproduction, and immune system function.

10. Cholesterol maintains gut health, and low cholesterol can result in leaky gut syndrome and other GI problems.

Some Things That Can Go Wrong if You Don't Eat Cholesterol

- Accelerated aging
- Brittle nails
- Cancer
- Cognitive problems
- Constipation
- Cravings for carbs and stimulants
- Dry, limp, thinning hair
- Dumbing down
- GI problems, including leaky gut
- Infertility
- Insomnia
- Lose muscle and gain a fat roll
- Memory problems
- Mood disorders
- Osteoporosis
- Scaly, itchy skin

Earlier we talked about how your liver acts as a staging area for incoming nutrition. The liver releases just enough blood sugar for your body and brain to operate. However, if you don't eat balanced meals, it's a different story. Say you eat pasta with marinara sauce, and a glass of red wine (all sugar). After you chew and swallow, the meal is broken down into sugar in the small intestine. Sugar then leaves the small intestine and enters the portal vein, triggering a fire hose release of insulin, which then communicates to the liver that a load of sugar has entered your system.

The liver goes into action. Since the liver won't allow that much sugar to pass to the brain, the liver must convert some sugar into other forms of energy. There are a few options. The excess sugar can be used immediately as energy (say, if you're going on a twenty-five-mile bike ride), or it can be stored for later use in the form of glycogen. If your body doesn't need the energy and the liver is already full of glycogen, the liver will either convert the sugar into cholesterol—which is utilized as building material for hormones, membranes, and other structures—or it will convert the sugar into triglycerides, which are fatty acids that are used for energy or stored as fat. This emergency strategy results in a tightly regulated amount of sugar being sent to the brain. (If you have high triglycerides, your doctor will tell you that you've been eating too much fat, but in reality triglycerides are made in the liver from eating too much sugar and refined carbs, which can't be used up as energy.)

It's normal and healthy for the liver to change *some* sugar into cholesterol and triglycerides. However, this normal process will go on tilt when you deprive your body of cholesterol and instead overeat carbs. When you don't eat cholesterol, you create an artificial state of famine. During this famine, your liver will overproduce cholesterol from the carbs you eat. This is why people on low-fat, low-cholesterol, high-carb diets eventually end up with abnormal cholesterol numbers, blocked arteries, and bypass surgery, not to mention fat rolls.

On the contrary, dietary cholesterol doesn't result in overproducing cholesterol in the liver. In fact, the best low-cholesterol diet you can go on is a diet rich in cholesterol because eating cholesterol tells your brain that the famine has ended.

Eating cholesterol-laden food will not lead to arterial plaquing. Free radical production caused by all the factors listed on pages 13 and 14 causes arterial plaquing by oxidizing and "caramelizing" the LDL cholesterol (too much sugar in the bloodstream causes LDLs to become gooey and sticky). Arterial plaque is hardened by oxidized and caramelized LDL cholesterol, but you can prevent the oxidation and caramelizing of LDL cholesterol by bombarding your body with antioxidants and by avoiding sugar and refined carbs. Only 20 percent of strokes and 50 percent of heart attacks are accompanied by elevated cholesterol.[23] If the LDL cholesterol floating around in your bloodstream, where it is performing various tasks essential to life, is not oxidized or caramelized, then your cholesterol number doesn't matter. A balanced diet of real, living food will provide your body with antioxidants to protect your "working" cholesterol from being oxidized or caramelized, and in turn your body can benefit from cholesterol doing its job. (More about carbs shortly.)

Besides your brain and body being made up of fat and cholesterol, fat also fuels biochemical processes that protect your immune and endocrine systems. Without dietary fat, the body takes fat from a diet too high in carbs and from muscle wasting. Even if a person remains very thin by eating very little, but all she eats is carbs, the constant influx of insulin—which is implicated in every degenerative disease—will be extremely damaging to her health. A low-fat, high-carb diet also depletes hormones, as hormones are made out of fats. Since the brain is 60 percent fat, the body uses whatever fat is onboard to build brain cells. All the toxic fats in our food supply account for the dumbing down of our population and the epidemic of depression, anxiety, paranoia, and other mental health issues.

It makes sense that all of your body's mechanisms would function more efficiently if you provided your body and brain with the quality building materials necessary to make cells, and if butter is reclaimed Southern pine heartwood then *I Can't Believe It's Not Butter* and *Smart Balance Omega-3 Spread* are linoleum!

Real, Whole, Organic, Cholesterol-Laden Foods

Beef	Lamb
Butter	Liver
Cheese	Lobster
Chicken	Pork
Crab	Roe
Crayfish	Shrimp
Eggs	Whole milk
Fish	

Miscellaneous Healthy Fats

When it comes to fats—as with any part of your diet—it's important to eat a variety. One fat simply can't do what a broad spectrum of fats can do. The body functions optimally when it has a varied array of foods/fats as building materials. It's especially important to consume only organic fat, because fat stores toxins, and if you eat fat containing toxins they will concentrate over time.

Healthy Specialty Fats

Almond oil	Rice bran oil (good for cooking)
Avocado oil	
Grapeseed oil	Sesame (good for cooking)
Hazelnut oil	*Walnut oil*
Hempseed oil	*Wheat germ oil*

NOTE: *Italicized fats should be consumed quickly and be protected from heat, light, and oxygen.*

Since specialty oils will become rancid before you can use them up, it's best to eat whole foods containing oils such as almonds, avocados, hazelnuts, walnuts, and wheat germ.

Vegetarians/Vegans and Fats

Vegetarians should consume whole raw milk, free range eggs, a variety of beans, and properly soaked nuts (see page 297), as well as therapeutic oils (cod liver oil, coconut and red palm, primrose or another GLA, and Activator X also known as X Factor, explained on page 41). During pregnancy and nursing, vegans should consider these same additions for their health and the health of their baby.

Sardine Vegans

It's not my goal to pick a fight with vegans. I'm on your side, really. My mission is to help everyone achieve optimal health. I respect and honor any vegan's decision not to consume animal foods. That said, a decision made from the heart doesn't change human physiology. The human body must have complete proteins and essential fatty acids every single day, both of which are required for life. So I've coined the term "sardine vegan." You can still be a vegan and respect animal life, but protect yourself from an imploding immune system and metabolic breakdown by consuming a tin of sardines (including the oil) every day. You'll get complete protein and essential fatty acids. Sardines are very small fish, with tiny brains. They are low on the food chain and contain very little mercury. You can chelate any mercury out of your system by drinking parsley and cilantro juice. I hope I can convince at least some vegans to become sardine vegans.

Eat Fresh, Organic, Nonstarchy Vegetables

In addition to lowering insulin levels, nonstarchy vegetables are useful sources of vitamins, minerals, and fiber. Personally I'm a huge fan of juicing green veggies—more on page 138—but any way you get them I can't say enough about the miraculous nature of nonstarchy vegetables! They contain micronutrients—vitamins, minerals, trace minerals, and enzymes—that work synergistically with macronutrients—proteins and fats—to rebuild and repair your body on a cellular level. These micronutrients stave off cancer and other diseases by keeping your body naturally detoxified. Non-starchy vegetables also keep blood sugar levels balanced by slowing down the absorption of carbs.

But even though veggies (and herbs) are marvelously rich in micronutrients, we're not herbivores and we don't have the enzyme that converts plants into protein, so veggies need to be eaten along with protein for a balanced diet.

Examples of Nonstarchy Vegetables

- Arugula
- Asparagus
- Bamboo shoots
- Bean sprouts
- Bell peppers
- Broad beans
- Broccoli
- Brussels sprouts
- Cabbage
- Carrots (raw)
- Cauliflower
- Celery
- Chicory greens
- Chives
- Collard greens
- Coriander
- Cucumber
- Dandelion greens
- Eggplant
- Endive
- Fennel
- Gardencress
- Garlic
- Ginger root
- Green beans
- Hearts of palm
- Jicama
- Jalapeño and other chili peppers
- Kale
- Lettuce
- Mushrooms
- Mustard greens
- Onions
- Parsley
- Radishes
- Radicchio
- Scallop squash
- Snap beans
- Snow peas
- Shallots
- Spinach
- Spaghetti squash
- Spirulina and chlorella (green algae)
- Summer squash
- Swiss chard
- Turnip greens
- Watercress

Examples of Fresh Herbs

Anise	Lovage
Artemisia	Marjoram
Basil	Nasturtium
Bee balm	Oregano
Borage	Parsley
Burnet	Peppermint
Calendula	Perilla
Caraway	Rosemary
Catnip	Rue
Chamomile	Sage
Chervil	Santolina
Chives	Sorrel
Clary Sage	Southernwood
Coriander	Spearmint
Costmary	Summer savory
Dill	Sweet marjoram
Fennel	Sweet woodruff
Feverfew	Sweet rocket
Geranium	Tansy
Germander	Tarragon
Horehound	Thyme
Hyssop	Valerian
Lavender	Winter savory
Lemon balm	Wormwood
Lemon verbena	Yarrow

NOTE: *Spices, though not listed, also contain antioxidants. Make sure to buy non-GMO and non-irradiated spices.*

Salt

Current research has demonstrated that only 10 percent of the population suffering from hypertension needs to restrict salt intake. Our bodies contain fluids (such as blood plasma and lymphatic fluids) that closely resemble the electrical balance and chemical composition of ocean water. We need a little salt to replace the salt that is lost through daily sweating and urinating. Our adrenal glands need sodium to function properly. If you have very low blood pressure, it could be an indication of adrenal fatigue, and a little more salt could benefit you. But there's a difference between out of control cravings and cravings for something your body needs.

Sea salt, on the other hand, contains all of the minerals your body's systems require. Sea salt naturally contains trace minerals, sodium, and potassium salts. There are many types of salt on the market today, and it's really neat to explore them for various recipes.

Sea Salt Varieties

Black salt: From Kala Namak, India, is a blend of minerals characterized by a strong sulfur odor.

Fleur de Sel de Guérande: Organic gray/lavender-colored sea salt from the coastal area of Guérande, Brittany, France.

Hawaiian sea salt: Pink salt from Hawaiian water. A natural mineral called alaea (a red clay from Kauai rich in iron oxide) is added to the salt to add beneficial trace elements.

Kosher salt: While not sea salt, it's often called for in recipes as it's an additive-free coarse-grained salt that disperses more readily than some other salts.

NOTE: *If you have been put on a low-sodium diet, consult with your doctor before making any adjustments in your sodium intake.*

Eat the Amount of Carbs Appropriate for Your Health and Set Point

Most people understand by this point that any carb, whether it's an apple or a candy bar, turns into energy (sugar) in your body, acting as fuel. For that reason, carbs can be fattening and are associated with weight gain.

I believe in eating a balanced diet of real, whole food. But if you've got fat on your body that you want to get rid of, the only way to empty fat cells without creating an artificial state of famine is to decrease your carbs *slightly* below your metabolic needs and eat more fats, proteins, and nonstarchy veggies. Your brain, which needs a constant drip of sugar, will still get its sugar, but your body will be forced to empty stored sugar and fats from cells to use for metabolic needs. It's a win-win move.

There's a saying in the arts that when an artist or performer has a success, the public expects him or her to do it again, "the same, only different" (thus the dreaded movie sequels). But it's a good description of the human being: the same, but different. The diet industry would like you to believe that everyone is basically the same and produce one-size-fits-all pills, products, exercise programs, diet programs, and other "systems" to address our sameness. Yes, we all have the same physiologies. For example, we all need the hormone insulin to get nutrients and sugar into cells or we'll die. Type 1 diabetics do not make any insulin at all and must inject it to live. The rest of us make our own insulin. Some of us have pancreases that over-secrete, some have normal secretions, and some have subnormal secretions of insulin in response to incoming food. So in that sense we are the same, but different. Other factors that make us different are different genetics, different lifestyles, and different dietary histories.

So within the parameters of our same-but-different physiologies, everyone can attain maximum metabolic potential by adjusting carbs/energy food intake according to his or her own metabolic needs. Eating in this balanced way balances your endocrine system (hormones). A set amount of carbs can't be applied to every single person on the planet. How absolutely absurd! Again, it's primarily what we do to our bodies and what we put into our bodies over the extended period of our lifetime that differentiates us. The amount of carbs we need to eat relates directly to our individual current metabolic health and activity levels—and these can change daily.

If you're sick and overweight and are reading the newspaper in bed, you need far fewer carbs than someone in the third stage of an Iron Man competition, but you still need to eat to fuel ongoing metabolic processes and to provide building supplies for internal repair. But if you are that same overweight, sedentary, unhealthy person and you happen to be moving, and you work like a common laborer for weeks, then you need to add more carbs in your diet. Carbs are fuel. If your body needs more fuel on a given day, then put more fuel into it. By the same token, if you are an extreme athlete but you are lying in bed sick—even with your fantastic metabolism—you don't need as much fuel as you would need if you spent the day surfing.

Basic physiology dictates that weight management is determined in part by how much energy you put into your system versus how much energy you expend.

Eating a balanced diet means that you must *continually* adjust your carb intake as your health (and metabolic rate) fluctuates. I want to make sure that you really get this, because your mitochondrial energy factories use the carbs you eat to make the energy for all metabolic processes. If you don't eat enough carbs for your level of activity and health, your energy is going to plummet and your body is going to fundamentally malfunction.

Fat Doesn't Turn into Fat on Your Body

Fat doesn't turn into fat on your body so long as you don't eat it with too many carbs. Fat and carbs are both energy sources. However, fat can't be stored unless insulin is secreted. This is why my grandma could glug olive oil from the bottle and not gain any weight. My grandma, even as an old lady, did not have much of a fat roll around her waist.

The Perfect Ratio of Carbs to Protein

Few Americans can do anything in moderation. We enjoy the take-no-prisoners approach, which combined with the fact that we've been indoctrinated to believe that losing weight can only be achieved through deprivation, makes for a bad recipe of overkill. The goal is to achieve equanimity, and that's impossible through extremes.

Read the descriptions and identify your metabolic set point and begin to follow the guidelines for carb consumption.

If you experience insomnia at any of these set points and are hormonally imbalanced, you'll either need bioidentical hormone replacement (BHRT) or more carbs in your meals. If you're pre- or postmenopausal, you may be more sensitive to carbs and may have to go back to the previous level. If you're hormonally imbalanced and you gain weight on a balanced diet of real, living food and it's not muscle, then you'll need to adjust your carbs accordingly.

If you eat too many carbs for your set point, you'll gain weight, have more inflammation, feel fatigued and bloated, and experience cravings. Your triglycerides will go up (above 100). Again, you don't want triglycerides to be high because it indicates blood sugar, and can caramelize your working LDL cholesterol. If you don't eat enough carbs for your set point, on the other hand you won't feel full/satisfied. You'll have difficulty sleeping, experience hunger in the middle of the night, and crave stimulants.

It's physiologically impossible to burn off more than one to two pounds of fat in a week without doing damage to your metabolism. If you cut your carbs too low and lose pounds quickly, you will lose some fat but most of the loss will be muscle mass because your body has broken down muscle to convert it to sugar. Muscle mass uses more energy than the rest of the tissues. The more muscle mass you have, the more efficient your metabolism, and the less muscle mass the less efficient your metabolism, so your body will break down more than it builds back up—and that is exactly what you *don't* want.

Six Small Meals a Day or Three?

I support the way people historically ate: three balanced meals of real, whole, living food every day, and no snacking. Snacking was never part of human behavior until after WWII when food manufacturers introduced the concept. Now that snacking has fallen out of favor, there's this whole new concept of eating six small meals a day. Don't you find that interesting? I really do. I know that the current conventional argument is that eating six small meals a day balances blood sugar levels. But eating six times a day is obsessive and keeps people constantly thinking about food and eating. Snacking places undo burden on your system, especially your liver, which has to process all that incoming food. More importantly, because your digestive system needs a four-hour window to allow food to pass from the stomach to the portal vein to the liver, if you eat all the time then you bog this system down. When you eat a balanced meal of real whole food, the food is slowly digested over four hours and assimilated, providing your body and brain with a nice even supply of blood sugar. When the food is fully processed, you start to feel hungry again. Then you eat another meal. It's the way we were designed. Just make sure to eat enough at every meal. If you eat three substantial, well-balanced meals a day, you're not likely to need a snack, unless you're hypoglycemic or suffer from type 2 diabetes, chronic fatigue syndrome, or another serious illness, or if you're exercising a lot, say on an all-day hike.

Sometimes you have to have a snack. At these times it's optimal to always eat a carb with a protein. However there are foods, like apples, that are low on the glycemic index (the measure of how fast blood sugar levels rise as a response to incoming food) and can be eaten in small amounts alone. Again these snacks are

15 grams of carb. If you can eat more, then please do. Any leftovers you had for meals can be eaten as a snack.

Snacks Containing Carbohydrates and Proteins

8 tablespoons almond butter on celery stalks

1 small apple, sliced and sprinkled with cinnamon

Chicken breast with a small bunch of grapes

Steamed mixed veggies, including ¼ potato or yam topped with Parmesan cheese

Cut up carrots, bell peppers, and cucumbers and a scoop of hummus

2 medium apricots, string cheese

6 to 8 Brazil nuts

18 cashews

20 filberts or hazelnuts

12 macadamia nuts

½ avocado with a scoop of tuna salad or sardines

Cut up red, yellow, or orange bell pepper and a scoop of chicken salad with ½ cup walnuts

¼ cup blackberries or blueberries with ½ cup cottage cheese

½ cup boysenberries with ½ cup cottage cheese

3 tablespoons cashew butter on celery stalks

1½ cups strawberries with whipped cream and a pinch of Stevia

2 medium dates, 1 medium dried fig, or 2 medium fresh figs with string cheese

½ large grapefruit

small bunch of grapes

1 cup raw whole milk (see realmilk.com, or buy organic if you can't obtain raw milk)

4 tablespoons peanut butter on celery stalks

22 almonds

28 peanuts or 2 tablespoons peanut butter

20 halves pecans

47 pistachio nuts

Ultimate You Skill No. 3: Eat a Balanced Diet of Real, Whole, Living Food

- 3 tablespoons pine nuts
- ¼ cup pumpkin or squash seeds
- 14 walnut halves
- 1 medium nectarine
- 1 medium orange
- 1 cup organic plain yogurt
- ½ cup papaya
- 1 medium peach
- ½ large pear
- 2 medium plums
- 3 cups air-popped popcorn seasoned with melted butter and sea salt
- 3 prunes with your choice of cheese
- ½ cup raspberries with ½ cup cottage cheese or whole plain yogurt
- ½ cup sunflower seeds
- 2 tablespoons peanut or almond butter on half an apple
- 2 small tangerines

NOTE: *Some foods, such as nuts and cottage cheese, naturally contain protein, fat, and carbs.*

Progressing from Unhealthy to Optimal Metabolism

By eating the right amount of energy (carbs) you can progress through the stages of set points from one point to the next. On pages 62 through 68 are carb amounts for each metabolic set point. They're not calculated for weight loss per se, rather for you to live with balanced insulin levels, which will ultimately translate to optimal health/body weight. Below each category is an example of what a day's meals would look like so you can get an idea of how much carb (in italics) is optimal for you at each meal and snack. Protein and fat measurements aren't provided because proteins and fats don't need to be restricted. Proteins and fats make things (hormones, cells, tissues, and so on), but carbs are strictly energy so you need to monitor how much energy you're taking in. Don't worry if you don't like the foods chosen for your set point, as these are only examples and you can create your own meal plans according to your preferences using the Carbohydrate Counter beginning on page 294.

You may look at these and think, "I don't know how to cook," or "I don't have time." Well, there are tricks, like making bigger portions and having some the next day, buying prepared foods, majorly simplifying these suggestions and substituting green juice for cooking veggies or making salads. Like my grandma said, "Do your best and don't worry about the rest." "Carbs at current set point" are the carbs you would eat on a normal day. "Carbs if you're very active" are the carbs you should eat if your activity level increases.

Too Thin

I'm not a medical professional, so if you're sick you should check with your doctor before making any dietary changes. Being too thin is an indication that your body isn't getting the nutrition it needs to keep up metabolic processes. At this set point, you should snack.

Carbs at Current Set Point

Meals 40 grams

Snack 15 grams

Carbs if You're Very Active

Meals 50 grams

Snack 15 grams

Example of meals for your set point if you're not active (add more carb if you're more active):

Breakfast: ¾ cup cooked steel cut *oatmeal* with ¼ cup coconut milk, butter, ¾ cup *blackberries*, soft-boiled eggs; 12 ounces green veggie juice (40 grams carb)

Snack: 1 medium *orange* (15 grams)

Lunch: Chicken salad made with shredded chicken, 15 *grapes*, ¼ cup *peanuts*, ½ *avocado* and a dressing of mayo, lemon, mustard, and olive oil, served on a green salad (tossed with sprouts) and olive oil, mustard, and balsamic vinegar dressing; 8 ounces organic, preferably whole raw *milk* (40 grams)

Snack: Bell pepper strips with ¼ cup *hummus*, scant ¼ cup *sunflower seeds* (15 grams)

Dinner: 2 cups *tomato soup*; poached salmon with herbed lime butter;

asparagus roasted with grated, raw Romano cheese; mixed greens salad with homemade *Green Goddess dressing*, made with mayo, *sour cream*, heavy cream, tarragon wine vinegar, lemon juice, garlic, parsley, scallions, chives, and tarragon leaves; 2 cups *cherries* for dessert (40 grams)

Snack: 1 *date*, ½ cup whole *cottage cheese* (15 grams)

Overweight/Obese, Sedentary, Unhealthy

Again, I'm not a medical professional, so if you're diabetic or unhealthy you should check with your doctor before making any dietary changes. That said, I hope you'll find an enlightened doctor, because it's very well documented that insulin resistance and type 2 diabetes can be completely reversed with a balanced diet of real, whole, living food.

If you're overweight by twenty-five pounds or more, unhealthy, and sedentary, you still need some carbs for the biochemical processes that go on inside your body. The goal is to keep your carbs appropriate to your activity level and metabolic level. Fifteen grams of carb is the lowest anyone should ever go per meal and you should not have to stay there very long. As you lose body fat and become more active, you'll quickly need more carbs per meal. Snacking is important at this set point, because the carb requirement is so low.

Carbs at Current Set Point **Carbs if You're Very Active**

    Meals 15 grams   Meals 30 to 45 grams

    Snack 10 grams   Snack 15 grams

Examples of meals for your set point if you're not active (add more carbs if you're more active):

Breakfast: Omelet made with eggs, ham, cheese, spinach, mushrooms, and bell peppers; ½ cup cooked *amaranth* with whole cream, butter; 12 ounces green veggie juice (15 grams)

Snack: ½ cup *boysenberries* with ¼ cup whole *cottage cheese* (10 grams)

Lunch: Veggie soup made with a medley of nonstarchy veggies such as celery, broccoli, onions, green cabbage, garlic, parsley, seasoned with thyme, basil. Add ⅓ cup *black beans*, and top with grated, raw Parmesan cheese and slices of roasted turkey (15 grams)

Snack: scant ¼ cup *cashews* (10 grams)

Dinner: Roast beef with wasabi sauce, made with cream, garlic, and wasabi, ½ medium *baked potato* with butter, a spoonful of sour cream and chives; roasted Brussels sprouts with butter; mixed greens salad with homemade Thousand Island dressing: mayo, chili sauce, sour cream, organic *pickle relish*, hardboiled egg, scallions (15 grams)

Snack: 6 ounces organic, preferably whole raw *milk* (10 grams)

Plump but Active

You're overweight by fewer than twenty-five pounds. Say you have a busy, active career. Or maybe you're chasing kids up and down flights of stairs. Or you have added a daily exercise program to your routine. Snacking is not necessary at this set point, unless you are, say, out on a marathon hike or doing something else major like all-day garage cleaning and you really feel done in.

Carbs at Current Set Point   **Carbs if You're Very Active**

Meals 30 grams   Meals 45 to 60 grams
Snack 15 grams   Snack 15 grams

Example of meals for your set point if you're not active (add more carbs if you're more active):

Breakfast: Bacon and eggs scrambled in the bacon grease or in coconut oil; ½ *mango* with ½ cup whole plain *yogurt*, 12 ounces green veggie juice (30 grams)

Snack: 4 tablespoons *peanut butter* on celery sticks (15 grams)

Lunch: *Watermelon* and shrimp salad made with green salad with chopped mint and sliced red onions, raw feta cheese, tossed with oil, white balsamic vinegar, and mustard dressing, topped with garlic-grilled shrimp, and 1 ¼ cup *watermelon*; 12 *macadamia nuts* for dessert (30 grams)

Snack: 2 medium fresh *figs* with string cheese (15 grams)

Dinner: New York style rib-eye steak on a bed of sautéed watercress; ½ cup steamed beets; ½ cup garlic mashed *potatoes* lathered in butter; Asian greens with quartered *tomatoes* tossed with homemade French dressing made with olive oil, red wine vinegar, garlic, oregano, basil, tarragon, and Dijon mustard (30 grams)

Snack: 1 ½ cups *strawberries* with whipped cream made with a pinch of Stevia (15 grams)

Ideal Body Except for Fat Around Your Middle (and/or over 50)

You've always been active—shooting baskets, beach walking, golfing. But you can't seem to get rid of all the fat that has accumulated around your waist, hips, and thighs. This is the typical set point for pre- and postmenopausal women as well as men older than 50. Snacking isn't necessary at this set point, unless you end up doing something really over and above your energy level, like your car breaks down and you have to walk five miles because you forgot your cell phone. Otherwise eat well at meals, and skip the snacks.

Carbs at Current Set Point

Meal 35 grams
Snack 15 grams

Carbs if You're Very Active

Meal 30 to 60 grams
Snack 15 grams

Example of meals for your set point if you're not active (add more carbs if you're more active):

Breakfast: Chorizo with scrambled eggs, sour cream, and salsa; ½ *grapefruit* topped with 1 cup *blackberries*; 12 ounces green veggie juice (35 grams)

Snack: 1 medium *nectarine* (15 grams)

Lunch: Turkey patties with 1 cup *cottage cheese* and sliced *tomatoes*; large mixed greens salad with any types of nonstarchy veggies, with olive oil, mustard, lemon juice dressing; ¾ cup *papaya* (35 grams)

Snack: ½ cup *peanuts* (15 grams)

Dinner: Crab cakes (cooked in coconut oil) made with crab, eggs, *bread crumbs*, parsley, cilantro, scallions, bell pepper, mayo, on a bed of ½ cup fresh *corn* topped with caper sauce made with mayo, lemon juice, and capers; with a salad of mixed greens with olive oil, mustard, lemon juice dressing (35 grams)

Fit and Healthy

You're in your twenties, or you're older but very fit. Maybe your job is physically challenging and/or extracurricular exercise is a priority. If you are really honest about your carb consumption, you'll see how easy it is to eat too many carbs at one sitting. But if you are fit and healthy, your body needs more energy foods. Pay attention to how you feel. If you need to eat more carbs to feel energetic and to sleep soundly, gradually add more in per meal. Even if you're ultra-active, you don't need to snack unless something truly demanding famishes you, like summiting a mountain.

Carbs at Current Set Point   **Carbs if You're Very Active**

Meal 45 grams   Meal 45 to 75 grams
Snack 20 grams   Snack 20 grams

Example of meals for your set point if you're not active (add more carbs if you're more active):

Breakfast: Huevos Rancheros made with eggs, red onions, jalapeño peppers, *tomatoes*, garlic, cilantro, raw Gruyère cheese, ½ *avocado*, sour cream, and salsa, with ½ cup cooked *corn grits*; 1 cup *honeydew melon*; 12 ounces green veggie juice (45 grams)

Snack: 2 large *plums* (20 grams)

Lunch: *Lentil*, arugula, and feta salad, made with sautéed red onions, bell peppers, 2/3 cup *lentils*, raw feta cheese, and arugula; 2 *tangerines* (45 grams)

Snack: 1 cup *kefir* with a few *raisins* (20 grams)

Dinner: 2 cups chicken coconut soup made with chicken broth, unsweetened *coconut milk*, fresh lemongrass, diced chicken breast, *lime juice*, *Thai fish sauce*, chili paste, and cilantro; Ginger beef with bok choy and 1 cup *brown rice*; jicama, red onion, ½ *orange* in a dressing of *lime juice*, white wine vinegar, olive oil (45 grams)

Snack: 2 tablespoons *cashew butter* on ½ small *apple* (20 grams)

Extreme Athlete

If you are in the upper one percentile of the population who spend several hours a day doing extreme sports like long distance running, biking, ashtanga yoga, rock climbing, iron man competitions, competitive swimming, and/or body-building, you need a lot more energy than the average person. But it's not necessary to eat more than 80 grams of carbs per meal even if you are competing the following day. (See page 214 regarding carbo-loading.) You should snack, especially if you're cycling the Pyrénées.

Carbs at Current Set Point   Carbs if You're Very Active

Meals 60 grams   Breakfast 60 to 80 grams
Midmorning snack 20 grams   Snack 20 grams

Example of meals for your set point if you're not active (add more carbs if you're more active):

Breakfast: Crustless quiche made with eggs, raw Gruyère cheese, whole cream, sun-dried *tomatoes*, and Jalapeño peppers, 1 cup whole plain *yogurt*, topped with 1 sliced *pear*, 1 sliced *peach*, sprinkled with 2 tablespoons *wheat germ* and 2 tablespoon *currants*; 12 ounces green veggie juice (60 grams)

Snack: Trail mix of ¼ cup *coconut meat*, 2 tablespoons *sunflower seeds*, ¼ cup *almonds*, 2 tablespoons *pistachio nuts* (20 grams)

Lunch: Tuna salad made with tuna, mayo, mustard, red onions, celery, organic *pickle relish*, 10 *red grapes*, scooped onto a bed of 1 *avocado* and sliced tomatoes; 1 cup *pineapple* (60 grams)

Snack: 4 cups air-popped *popcorn* with butter and sea salt (20 grams)

Dinner: Pulled pork with sauerkraut and mixed roasted veggies: ⅔ cups *parsnips*, eggplant, ½ cup *turnips*, and 1 cup *carrots*; ½ cup unsweetened *banana and kiwi sorbet* (60 grams)

Snack: ½ cup *cottage cheese* with two slices of *papaya* (20 grams)

You can reset your body's set point weight by eating the amount of energy foods that are appropriate for your current set point, eating adequate protein, and exercising. As you age and your activity level declines, you'll notice you need less carb (energy) foods and that you will have to find a more appropriate set point.

Add Enzymatic Foods to Your Diet

Factory-produced foods are dead. Not only are they stripped of nutrition, and harbor toxins, but the living enzymes have been killed. Losing enzymes from our food chain is a major contributing factor to the epidemic of disease. Enzymes are essential to life, because they are biochemical catalysts of cellular function both inside and outside of cells. Without enzymes, no biochemical activity would take place. In effect, vitamins, minerals, and hormones cannot perform in the body without enzymes. There are five thousand identified enzymes, divided into three categories: (1) Metabolic enzymes enable all bodily processes and functions, including maintaining immune function. (2) Digestive enzymes are manufactured in the pancreas to break down food. (3) Food enzymes jumpstart digestive processes when you eat.

Eating enzymatic food reduces the pancreas's need to produce digestive enzymes. If your pancreas is overtaxed during your lifetime because you don't eat enzymatic foods, its function will decline and you will age, become diseased, and die much faster than if you eat *live* enzyme-rich food. That's why food enzymes are one key to staving off degenerative disease, slowing accelerated aging, and promoting longevity.[24]

Throughout history, people fermented food to preserve it, which serendipitously created beneficial microorganisms. Fermented foods facilitate digestion, and their enzymes increase the absorption of nutrients. Fermented foods boost your immune system and provide your gut with friendly intestinal flora—billions of live organisms that prevent the growth of unfriendly bacteria, yeast, mold, and fungi.

Examples of Enzyme-Rich Foods

Fermented foods [sauerkraut, veggie-kraut, kefir, kim-chee, kombucha tea, yogurt, rejuvelac (sprouted grain beverage), shoyu (naturally fermented soy sauce), raw apple cider vinegar, and pickles]

Raw beer	Raw milk and cream
Raw eggs	Raw veggies (especially juiced)
Raw cheese	
Raw fruit	Spirulina and chlorella
	Sprouted seeds

Eat Locally Grown, Organic Food if Possible

We've all heard about the benefits of eating locally, and it is respectful of the planet. I would be remiss if I didn't suggest eating locally as an option. However, I recently spent three winters in Boston. Eating locally would have meant that I couldn't drink my green juice all winter. I would not have had a salad or a piece of fruit for six months or more. I care about people, animals, and the planet. That said, you know when you're on an airplane and the flight attendant instructs you in case cabin pressure drops to put on your mask first before assisting others? In our toxic world, where we direly need sustenance, it would be reckless, I believe, to go for six months without a green vegetable. Eating locally is great in the summer months. In the winter, if you live in regions that can't grow veggies, I recommend consuming the organic vegetables that are shipped in, and finding other ways to reduce your carbon footprint.

I'm pretty dogmatic about eating only organic. When I eat in restaurants I realize that I'm most likely not eating organic, and I'm probably eating chemicals like MSG and molecularly damaged vegetable oils. Eating out falls under the heading of "pick your poisons" (see page 129). When I buy groceries, however, I buy organic. Today for the first time in the history of humankind, we have at our disposal an array of foods that humans have never had. Historically, even monarchies and the aristocrats could not eat the vast variety of foods available to us contemporary commoners. Because we live in an extremely toxic world, eating non-GMO, non-irradiated organic foods that could be picked, gathered, milked, hunted, or fished—that were historically eaten (that is 150 plus years ago)—is the only way to decrease your risk of developing cancer, heart disease, autoimmune conditions, and other terrible illnesses. Eating organic will also increase your chances of living a good life (with a healthy, happy brain) and dying a peaceful death.

Eat Raw and Cooked Foods

The call for enzymatic foods doesn't mean that all foods should be consumed raw or fermented. Cooking has its place, and historically many foods were consumed cooked, including grains, legumes, and veggies. Cooking some foods can neutralize the natural toxins and break down fiber in foods that would otherwise be indigestible like in yams, potatoes, and eggplants. Cooking makes minerals available and proteins more digestible. The ideal is to eat a balanced diet of real, whole food, including some raw enzymatic foods, some fermented foods, and some cooked foods.

Become a Modern Hunter-gatherer

I advocate going back to hunter-gatherer ways. In primitive times people didn't just put anything in their mouths. They learned that there were substances in nature, like certain mushrooms, that would kill them. Today it's the same, only the lethal substances are made by corporations. We have to be smart and outwit these entities that are operating with ruthless disregard for our health.

Modern Hunter-gatherer Strategies

When grocery shopping, stay on the periphery of the store and avoid the inner isles where the poisons lurk.
More and more supermarket managers have realized that shoppers are avoiding the inner isles these days and are moving the poisonous stuff to places where consumers can see and reach for them, for instance, near produce. The point is to scope out your shopping resources, understand where the food is, and avoid the areas where you either can't breathe because of all the toxic detergents and so forth, or where all the fake food products are shelved.

If you can afford it, shop in markets that specialize in organic, real, living food.
It's true that food is expensive, but today we are spending a fraction of our budgets on food compared to thirty years ago. Having a healthy, happy, sexy body is

so much more desirable in the long run than having a designer bag or sunglasses. Revamp your priorities so that you are taking care of what's important: You.

Order grass-fed meat and dairy online.
Demand drives supply and there are a lot of small organic farmers and ranchers who as a result of this demand now ship humanely raised animal foods to people in cities. On *eatwild.com*, for example, you can find sources for grass-fed animal foods from all over the country.

Buy as much of your food as possible at local farmer's markets.
Not only will you get the best prices at farmer's markets, but you will be supporting local farmers and ranchers. I always find it a lively, cathartic experience to be in the world of real, living food. An alternative is to join a garden share, where you commit to either picking up or having delivered a fixed amount of produce from a local farmer.

Plant your own garden if you can, compost, buy worms, and use fish oils and other organic fertilizers.
This is a book on its own, and I'm not versed enough in worms and bats to offer tips. All I can say is that it's worth noting that anyone can do it, and that people who garden are like people in love, so there must be something addicting about it. After the economic crash of September 2008, a lot of people started their own gardens. It cuts down food bills, but is also a guaranteed way of knowing how your food is grown.

Plan ahead.
A primitive tribe didn't just up and leave a secure setting without making sure they were supplied with food for their journey. Today you would not want to, say, go to a movie, sporting event, drive across country, or, God forbid, check into a hospital without taking a supply of real food. Coolers in various sizes come in handy for the car, and storage bags are great for airplanes. Learn to plan. Because primitive humans didn't have drive-throughs, they didn't dare leave a camp without food. Today we are much more cavalier. But if you're going out of the house, just remember, you can eat that factory poison, suck it up and starve all day, or prepare your own food ahead of time. I prefer to take food with me. I also make a point of becoming familiar with my surroundings. I know where I can go to get something non-poisonous to eat.

Do your best and don't worry about the rest.

My goal is not to create a cult following of zealots who never eat sugar and are the food police (I know I don't like being thought of that way). When it comes to sugar, desserts are a fun, enjoyable part of life. During the early years of my recovery, I went a little crazy with a no-sugar rule. I never ate it, even at my own birthday dinner parties. I would serve cake but abstain. Then on September 10, 2001, I was scheduled to fly from Boston to LAX on American. I'd had a long day and was fed up and was debating on whether or not to change my flight to the following morning. Luckily I didn't, as I wouldn't be writing this now. After that awakening, I realized I could have died without ever having had another piece of birthday cake. Now I eat small portions of real desserts from time to time. Like my grandma used to say, "I do my best, and I don't worry about the rest."

If real food is all that you can afford while progressing through the *Healthy, Sexy, Happy* program, you'll be light years ahead. Even though you may be all excited about eating real food, craving and bingeing patterns may seem entrenched in your brain. You may feel that your brain isn't really supporting this new plan. If that's the case, it's because you haven't taken care of your brain, which is now running the show. Like Cesar Millan with his dogs, you can gain control over your big dumb pet—your brain.

five

Ultimate You Skill No. 4: Properly Care for and Feed Your Big Dumb Pet—Your Brain

In the fourteen years that I researched and wrote health books, one glaring detail kept jumping out at me: the epidemic of brain disorders. All of a sudden it seemed like nearly everyone was medicated for something brain related.

Common Brain-Related Problems We See Today

Babies and Kids: Impaired IQ, depression, learning disabilities, developmental delays, poor concentration, anxiety, violent behavior, headaches, sleep problems, brain tumors, ADD, ADHD, autism

Adults: Impaired IQ, OCD, ADD, ADHD, craving, bingeing, sexual and other obsessions and compulsions, depression, poor concentration, anxiety, violent behavior, headaches, brain fog, problems with memory, phobias, dementia, insomnia, brain tumors, MS, ALS

Seniors: Impaired IQ, depression, poor concentration, anxiety, violent behavior, headaches, brain fog, problems with memory, insomnia, brain tumors, dementia, Alzheimer's, Parkinson's

It didn't take me long to conclude that the reason we're having so many brain problems is because people haven't been taught how to take care of their brains. Instead we've had this very strange notion that the brain is somehow independent and self-sufficient. But the fact is, our brains are dumb, reactive, and helpless. Due to a lack of vigilance, our toxic food supply, and our poisonous environment, the typical brain has been "modified" into a zombie-ish, hyperreactive yet oddly sluggish command central run amuck that dictates weird quirks; runs people into the ground with depression; compels people to binge on food, alcohol, prescription, OTC, and recreational drugs; and ultimately collapses with neurological disease.

I don't think I'm the only one who's noticed that people are getting dumber in a really bizarre way. Consider the proliferation of inane TV shows (Jerry Springer, Are You Smarter Than a 5th Grader? "reality"TV, etc.), moronic commercials that peddle obvious poisons that the public happily buys, nearly every one of the eight hundred movies on cable at any given time, and obsessive fascinations with glossy/blingy celebrities who display virtually no redeeming social qualities.

Along with the disturbing evidence of our dumbing down is the even more alarming explosion of pharmaceuticals to "treat" brain disorders in patients from infancy to old age. Brain issues—from quirks and disease to lowered IQ, to behavioral problems to mood disorders—are a result of accelerated aging, but it doesn't have to be that way. Brain health is paramount to good overall health because as your brain goes, so goes your body.

And so goes your sex drive. Brain health is crucial to sex drive and sexual pleasure. Malnourishment leaves you with an unhealthy brain. As I said, most people think that the brain is independent and autonomous and will take care of itself. In reality, the brain is a big dumb pet that is led around by primal instincts, the most prevalent of course is survival. The habituated brain craves and demands unhealthy stimulants (see list on page 82). If you're eating a factory food diet, or using stimulants, your brain will eventually knee jerk react to every stressful event (hunger, emotional pain, insecurity, exhaustion) by demanding factory food (refined carbs) and stimulants. Now you're in a craving/bingeing pattern, and you're most likely depressed too. When you're depressed and lack self-esteem, which goes hand in hand with being hormonally depleted, overweight, out of shape, and locked in a lifestyle that revolves around craving and bingeing, you're not going to feel very sexy. Rebuilding your brain with healthy cells is absolutely essential to being healthy, sexy, and happy.

The Seven Basic Principles of a Healthy, Happy Brain

1. Eat real, living food (especially healthy fats) to build a healthy brain.
2. Supplement your diet with brain nutrition.
3. Protect your brain from inflammation.
4. Protect your brain from stimulants (see Chapter 6).
5. Protect your brain from toxins (see Chapter 8).
6. Allow yourself to sleep so that your brain can repair (see Chapter 11).
7. Practice self-compassion meditation to calm your brain (see Chapter 12).

Eat Real, Living Food (Especially Healthy Fats) to Build a Healthy Brain

As I developed the *Healthy, Sexy, Happy* program for myself, I paid special attention to building a strong new brain, cell by cell, and flooding it with happy neurotransmitters.

I don't suffer from cravings. I can eat a forkful of dessert—a tiny scoop of ice cream, a bite of a cookie, a fragment of a brownie, or a chunk of chocolate—because that's all I want, just a taste of something sweet. I'm satisfied and don't tear down the street looking for the nearest bakery for two reasons: I keep my blood sugar levels balanced by eating a balanced diet of real, whole food. And the most important reason, I've made a point of properly taking care of and feeding my big dumb pet, my brain.

Because of our crummy diet of poisonous pretend food, most people are being led around by their brains. That's because the brain is not very smart, and like any dumb animal it's extremely reactive. Right now if you're craving a doughnut, for example, it's because your dumb pet is reacting to the fact that you've starved it. In this depleted state, your brain is doing the only thing it can do: Struggle to keep you going by forcing you to reach for something that will give you enough of a liftoff so that you can put one foot in front of the other. As long as your body keeps moving, there's a chance of survival.

Real, living food is the alternative to this failed strategy. I use the word "failed" because we already know what it's like to live with depression, anxiety, insomnia, cravings, bingeing, ADD, ADHD, OCD, increased risk of developing neurological problems like Parkinson's disease, Alzheimer's, and all the other unpleasant outcomes of having unhealthy, highly reactive brains. The human brain is a model of structure and design, infinitely mysterious and marvelous. But what's happened to the modern brain is akin to rebuilding the Egyptian pyramids with Play-Doh. The brain is made up of 60 percent fat. The remaining 40 percent of the brain is made up of amino acids (from protein). In the ongoing breaking down and rebuilding process, the body does not reject fats, but uses some of whatever fat is onboard to replace brain cells. If you eat molecularly damaged veggie fats, your body is going to appropriate those fats to rebuild your brain.

Processed vegetable oils (corn, cottonseed, safflower, sunflower, soy, canola) are extremely dangerous fats; unfortunately they make up the majority of brains today. Using these factory-produced fats and proteins to rebuild your brain could be compared to scavenging junkyards for asbestos insulation, bent nails, and sheets of oily plywood with which to remodel your house.

The modern brain is not only built of shoddy materials, but it also receives a steady supply of deadly toxins. Without the materials to rebuild and to replenish happy neurotransmitters, and with a steady supply of toxic insults, it's no wonder we've seen a billion dollar boom in the antidepressant drug trade.

Neurotransmitters

Your endocrine system generates hormones, which comprise the chemical communication system that controls every function in your body. Your nervous system is actually an endocrine gland that generates impulses (chemical messages) and conveys these messages by jumping from neuron to neuron. Synapses are gaps between neurons, which are jumped by the chemical messengers called neurotransmitters. This jumping of the gaps is known as the "firing" of a synapse, a process through which your brain choreographs the complex orchestra of speech, hearing, sight, emotions, and the trillions of metabolic functions that comprise human physiology. A healthy brain will have a healthy supply of what I call "happy neurotransmitters," which are inhibitory transmitters that calm the body, mind, and, indirectly, the spirit. Following are a few of the more than fifty neurotransmitters scientists have identified:

- Dopamine: Acts as a stimulant (you feel energized)

- Endorphins: Our brain's painkiller and pleasure chemical (pains of life are diminished and you instead feel a sense of joy)
- Serotonin: Responsible for a sense of well-being (you feel high on life)
- Gamma amino butyric acid (GABA): Promotes a sense of calm (you feel calmly in control).

Vitamin B-6, magnesium, and essential fatty acids play an important role in neurotransmitter production. Ideally, your brain will get these nutrients through your new diet of real, living food.

Supplement Your Diet with Brain Nutrition

Because I eat real, living food, 40 percent of my brain is made of amino acids from organic meat, fish, poultry, and dairy. The other 60 percent of my brain is made up of fats from cod liver oil, Activator X, fish, seeds, coconut oil, and butterfat from whole milk and cream. I also supply my brain with enough vitamin B-6, magnesium, and essential fatty acids (EFAs) from food and supplements for it to make happy neurotransmitters.

Sources of Essential Fatty Acids

Omega-3	Omega-6	Gamma-Linolenic Acid
Cod liver oil	Chicken	
Flaxseed oil (see pages 27 and 44)	Egg	Black currant oil
Krill oil	*Flaxseed oil* (see pages 27 and 44)	*Blue green algae (chlorella and spirulina)*
Mackerel	*Grape seed oil*	Borage oil
Marine plankton	Meat	Evening primrose oil
Salmon	Turkey	
Sardines	*Wheat germ oil*	
Tuna		
Walnut oil		

NOTE: *Polyunsaturated oils are extremely fragile (become easily rancid/oxidized by heat, oxygen, and light). You never want to heat the italicized EFAs listed.*

Amino Acids for Happy Neurotransmitter Production

Gamma Aminobutyric Acid (GABA)

Glutamine

Glycine

L-Tryptophan and 5-Hydroxy Tryptophan (5-HTP)

Tyrosine

NOTE: *Don't take L-tryptophan or 5-HTP if you are taking serotonin-reuptake inhibitors such as Prozac or Zoloft. Both are contraindicated in interstitial cystitis. Don't take tyrosine if you are taking MAO inhibitors.*

Foods to Build a Healthy Brain

Magnesium	Vitamin B-6	Tryptophan
Almonds	Brown rice	Almonds
Apples	Chicken	Cottage cheese
Avocados	Corn	Peanut butter
Brewer's yeast	Eggs	Peanuts
Brown rice	Green leafy vegetables	Shellfish
Cod	Legumes	Tuna
Flounder	Meat	Turkey
Green leafy vegetables	Nuts	
Halibut	Peas	
Salmon	Poultry	
Sesame seeds	Salmon	
Shrimp	Shrimp	
	Spinach	
	Sunflower seeds	
	Tuna	

Protect Your Brain from Inflammation

In addition to building a solid brain and flooding it with happy neurotransmitters, we need to do everything we can to reduce brain inflammation, which has been identified as the single most significant marker for depression and disease. Dr. Blaylock writes, "There is overwhelming evidence that chronic brain inflammation is the major cause of most neurodegenerative diseases."[25]

It's not inevitable that your brain is going to melt down into senility and neurological disease, even though that is most people's fear these days. In a healthy brain, most problems are repaired through the normal process of rebuilding cells. Brain plasticity means that your brain is constantly building new connections (synapses) and neural fibers (dendrites). Synapses and dendrites, however, are the most vulnerable cells of your brain when it comes to free-radical damage. The brain also has one of the highest oxygen concentrations of any organ, consuming 20 percent of all the blood's oxygen. It has one of the highest metabolic rates of any organ, and it never rests, even when you're sound asleep. For all of these reasons, the brain is exquisitely vulnerable to free radical oxidation.

DNA is most vulnerable to free radicals during cell division. Many brain cells don't divide after the age of twenty, so the brain is somewhat protected. This also means that the brain depends on DNA-repair enzymes to fix any damage that might occur. Fluoride, mercury, MSG, aspartame, pesticides, vaccines, and any other free radical generators can damage DNA-repair enzymes.

Inflammation generates free radicals and other chemicals that encourage arterial plaquing and wreak havoc in the body, leading to accelerated aging. So even if you're in your twenties, you want to think about doing something about inflammation, especially brain inflammation, which disrupts happy neurotransmitters and contributes to depression.

Factors That Reduce Brain (and Body) Inflammation

- Eating a balanced diet of real, living food
- A high-veggie diet that includes a modest amount of fruit
- Addressing your stress (sleep, fun, meditation)
- Avoiding all factory food, including factory-animal products and factory fats
- Drinking green veggie juice

Supplements That Decrease Brain Inflammation
(See appendix on page 238)

- Acetyl-L-carnitine
- Aged garlic
- Alpha-lipoic acid
- Antioxidants, including vitamin B (oral and injectable)
- Curcumin
- Ginkgo biloba
- Magnesium citromate
- Marine phytoplankton
- N-acetyl-cysteine (NAC)
- Omega-3 oils
- Probiotics
- Quercetin
- Selenium
- Silymarin
- Spirulina and chlorella
- Vitamin C
- Vitamin E

I'm not a zealot. Zealotry ultimately leads to unhappiness due to self-hate and condemnation of others. What I discuss in the next chapter, "Quit Addictions," is only meant to be helpful to those who have a hard time finding balance.

six

Ultimate You Skill No. 5: Quit Addictions

People reach for different substances to give them the lift they crave to get through their days. You may not be a full-blown alcoholic or a burned-out stoner, but you might have a two-to-four glasses a day wine habit, or you're smoking pot every night. An occasional glass of wine or puff of pot is a wonderful thing, but a grinding wine habit or pot dependency are symptoms of low happy neurotransmitters. My mantra is "get educated" about food, diets, and drugs, so that you can better understand your challenges and define your defense strategy. Becoming educated about how food and lifestyle contribute to addictions can provide you the incentive and tools to quit.

Protect Your Brain from Stimulants

An addiction is being abnormally tolerant to and dependent on something that is psychologically or physically habit forming. All addictions are stimulants.

Examples of Addictive Stimulants

Alcohol

Amphetamines, cocaine, heroin, and other recreational drugs

Aspartame

Caffeine

Chocolate

Dexadrine, Ritalin, diet pills, including ginseng and ephedra (ma huang)

Dieting

Extreme exercise

OTCs and prescription drugs

Oxocontin, Percocet, Vicodin, and other pain medications

Refined carbs and sugar

Tobacco

Vomiting (purging)

An addicted brain is not a happy brain, and what addict wants to stay enslaved? Very few, I would venture to say. Addictions also mess with your happy neurotransmitters. That's a major concern if you want to be healthy, maintain optimal body composition, regain a sex life, and enjoy all the benefits of a healthy, happy brain. Here are four pretty good reasons to quit addictions:

1. Stimulants mess with your brain chemistry and cause brain inflammation, which leads to depression and disease.
2. Stimulants create free radicals in your body that lead to disease and early, ugly death.
3. Stimulants result in prolonged high insulin levels, which also lead to early, ugly death.
4. Stimulants result in belly fat.

Stimulants Trigger the Stress Response

Stimulants generate free radicals and damage mitochondria, but another bad thing they do is cause a flood of the hormone insulin. Earlier we reviewed what happens when you overeat sugar (carbs), and how insulin is called upon to store excess blood sugar. Stimulants cause the same sequence of events to occur within your body. Let's say you skip breakfast except for a few cups of coffee. Coffee and all stimulants—including sugar—stimulate the adrenals, which your brain registers as, "A stressful event is occurring!" In response, the stress hormone cortisol is secreted. One of cortisol's functions is to keep you alive by making sure there is enough sugar to fuel brain and metabolic functions during stressful times. Cortisol breaks down your lean body mass (muscle and bones) to provide that sugar. The corresponding secretion of insulin stimulates an excessive "rush" of stored neurotransmitters in the brain.[26] The sensation of this rush is delicious and addicting.

While you're loving the high, inside your body it's panic time, because now there's too much sugar in your bloodstream. Insulin is secreted to stow that sugar away, and you're back to the cycle described earlier that leads to the "Horrifying but True Bodily Mystery": belly fat. While your belly is growing bigger, so is your addiction to the high you get from stimulants.

Now you may be picturing people you know—alcoholics, drug addicts, or smokers—who are prison camp thin. The reason is that once a person gets to a point of poisonous saturation, the body must use every single shred of incoming nutrition as well as cannibalizing lean body mass just to keep that person alive. But if you are just a "normal" addict (you know what I mean), then the explanation above is the reason why addictions ultimately result in the accumulation of belly fat. The goal is to build a healthy brain by providing your body with quality building materials, which are the very same materials that create a flush supply of happy neurotransmitters. This process is going to be muddied if you continue your addictions. Very few people can remain addicted and also maintain healthy eating habits.

We can't review every single addiction to stimulants, but let's look at a few, especially cigarettes, caffeine, and extreme exercise, all of which I feel qualified to give my two cents on.

Smoking

By now even the French have admitted that smoking causes a major health problem: early, ugly death. Smoking may look sexy, but it robs people of their beauty and sexuality. Deaths from lung cancer are now up to 140,000 each year. And cigarettes cause other cancers, too, as free radicals know no bounds. The hydrocarbons in tobacco damage cells. Nicotine stimulates the release of insulin and increases blood pressure and heart rate. Smokers have an increased risk of developing type 2 diabetes, lung cancer, osteoporosis, emphysema, and heart disease. Tobacco is an oxidant that damages cholesterol, as well as brain and body cells. Of the 4,000 chemicals in cigarettes, 250 are known to be harmful, and 60 are known to cause cancer.

Some of the Known Carcinogens in Cigarettes
(See appendix on page 261.)

Arsenic	Ethylene oxide
Benzene	Nickel
Beryllium	Polonium–210
Cadmium	Vinyl chloride
Chromium	

This knowledge was in my distant future when as a rebellious teenager I started smoking at the age of fourteen in 1964. I started on Kents because the girl who I emulated smoked that brand. They came in a clean white package that looked sanitary and modern. My family moved to Japan when I was fifteen, and I began smoking Marlboros that I bought in the commissary vending machine on base for fifteen cents a pack, thanks to the U.S. government. The popular Japanese brand was Hi-Lite, which when inhaled, felt like radioactive fingernails scraping the inside of my lungs.

After Japan I went to India, where I first smoked Four Square, which came in a classy flat box, and later when trying to scrimp on money, bidis, the cigarette of untouchables, hand-rolled, green tobacco leaves, laced with cloves and very hard on the lungs. I also spent a few years in Europe, where I smoked Parisian Supers, another harsh cigarette, and an occasional Gauloise, the notoriously hardcore French brand that came in a patriotic white and blue package with the winged helmet of the ancient French Gauls. I suppose that there is no greater love-generation memory than sitting in an Amsterdam movie theater watching *Easy Rider* while passing around the proverbial dove-tailed joint (made with tobacco and hashish).

But my teens slipped into my twenties and smoking was definitely not a joke. Back in the States, I was desperate to quit my pack-a-day Marlboro habit. In the midseventies there were no support groups, and smoking was entirely socially acceptable. You could smoke on airplanes, and there weren't even smoking sections. In movie theaters cigarette smoke spiraled into the funnel of light created by the 35-millimeter projector beam. Parents (like mine) packed their kids into the family car, windows rolled up and cigarettes blazing. You could smoke just about anywhere, including hospitals—on your deathbed.

And so it wasn't like people were tripping over themselves to help me quit. Without resources, I did the only thing I could think of. I sat down by myself and reviewed the many clever arguments that devilish voice would offer the minute I put out my last cigarette. Anyone who has attempted to quit an addiction is familiar with this voice. Like a brilliant and charismatic attorney arguing a case, this voice provides a litany of convincing arguments as to why you should indulge. I already knew the voice was going to tell me: "Such and such movie star smokes, and she's so gorgeous! And so does that model, and she's amazing! And look at that actor who just won an Academy Award—he's so cool. You can cut down instead of quitting. It would feel so good just to have one puff. One little cigarette is not going to hurt you!" And when you are in withdrawals these simplistic arguments sound very, very credible. Having experienced the voice throughout numerous prior attempts at quitting, I carefully reviewed all the arguments in preparation for what I hoped would be my final and successful attempt.

Fortified with my strategy, I embarked on quitting. When I heard that siren voice I reminded myself of the list of arguments I'd made when I was not out of my head with withdrawals. It took six months to reach the magic moment when I realized that I was not thinking obsessively about lighting up and that the voice was barely audible. To this day I remember how arduous those months were. I still consider quitting smoking one of the biggest accomplishments of my life, and, of course, I have never for a second regretted it.

Today we understand that my heart-to-heart with myself is called "psyching up," and that it's a very powerful tool to help solidify one's intentions. People also receive so much more support for quitting smoking than we did back then. For one, smoking is no longer socially acceptable, and in many parts of the country, smokers are scorned as social pariahs. There are also self-help groups and support telephone lines.

The American Cancer Society (ACS) offers numerous tips for quitting smoking, including taking the antidepressant bupropion (also known as Wellbutrin and Zyban), which is thought to mimic nicotine's effects on the brain by boosting levels of the chemical messengers dopamine and norepinephrine, stimulants that make you feel energized. However, you can raise neurotransmitter levels naturally. After all, if you are trying to quit one chemical, why put another chemical into your brain?

The ACS suggests numerous other drugs, such as varenicline (Chantix), that introduces a host of lovely side effects: headaches, nausea, vomiting, insomnia, unusual dreams, flatulence, and changes in taste. It also endorses nicotine replacement patches, gum, or lozenges, which have put billions of dollars into the coffers of pharmaceutical companies from "ex" nicotine addicts who have switched from one nicotine delivery device (cigarettes) to another (patches, gum, lozenges).

The ACS website goes on to disparage acupuncture, hypnosis, and other natural methods of reducing cravings. In *Death by Supermarket*, Samuel Epstein, M.D., who is one of the world's leading experts in cancer prevention and causes says, "The American Cancer Society is more interested in accumulating wealth than saving lives. Their CEOs have high salaries. They have a billion dollars of cash assets in reserves. They have major internal conflicts of interests." He goes on to elaborate on the fact that the ACS depends on large donations from pharmaceutical companies and that the ACS supports research on drugs that will keep cancer patients alive for a couple of added months rather than concentrating on preventing cancer in the first place. So let's get real about how you can quit smoking without taking drugs. (If you really can't quit an addiction without drugs, see "Pick Your Poisons" page 129.)

Research that is not paid for by drug companies demonstrates that quitting smoking cold turkey with willpower is the single most successful approach.[27] When you quit smoking, the physical addiction can be broken in three days, but the psychological addiction—cravings—can last for months, even years. That's because most people attempt to function in life with funky brains that are made out of molecularly damaged fats, and they also are hobbled by an extremely low supply of happy brain neurotransmitters. When I quit smoking at age twenty-four, I started drinking coffee for the first time in my life. That's because my big dumb pet, my brain, went on full tilt. I also had irresistible cravings for French toast drenched in maple syrup. Because I didn't know what I now know about building a healthy, happy brain, I was compelled by my reactive brain to unwittingly reach for other stimulants. It would be twenty years before I quit my addiction to coffee.

Caffeine

Caffeine, a bitter, white crystalline alkaloid, is a psychoactive stimulant drug that depletes happy neurotransmitters. Psychotropics cross the blood-brain barrier and act on the central nervous system to create changes in perception, mood, consciousness, cognition, and behavior. Grocery store decaf is stripped of caffeine either with methylene chloride, otherwise known as dry cleaning fluid. The FDA has approved methylene chloride for use in decaffeination. Many companies use methylene chloride because consumers tend to prefer the taste compared to the safer Swiss Water decaf, which tastes blander.

Caffeine is such a powerful addiction that we even have health experts plaintively touting its benefits. From time to time announcements appear in the press that researchers have concluded that coffee provides hydration or some such nonsense. The truth is that caffeine is a legal psychotropic drug with no redeemable health or medical benefits. Following are ten good reasons not to use caffeine:

1. Overstimulates the adrenal glands/central nervous system, leading to increased risk of heart attacks, irritability, insomnia, and rapid and irregular heart rate
2. Elevates blood pressure (hypertension)
3. Hardens your arteries
4. Elevates blood sugar
5. Results in heartburn and other GI problems, like sour stomach, that cause horrendous breath
6. Causes fibrocystic breast disease
7. Causes diuresis (excessive urination), which can lead to dehydration
8. Increases the risk of birth defects if used during pregnancy
9. Contains tars, phenols, and other carcinogens, as well as traces of pesticides and toxic chemicals used in the growing and extraction processes
10. Stains your teeth brown

Caffeine directly affects your adrenal glands, so you need a slightly different approach to quitting (in addition to the program outlined below). Regular caffeine use depletes your adrenal reserve. If you stop drinking coffee abruptly the demand on your exhausted adrenals stops suddenly. Since it takes time for your adrenals to recover enough to begin to respond again, you may feel weak, headachy, fatigued, nauseated, and experience cravings, which may discourage quitting.

Although you can do everything outlined below, instead of going cold turkey like with cigarettes, you should cut down slowly to allow the craving for caffeine to gradually diminish. Your adrenals will repair and begin to respond again. Weaning off coffee slowly will allow you to feel better along the way, instead of suffering from withdrawal symptoms. Give up one half of a cup of coffee every few days. If you drink three cups of coffee a day then you can quit in two to three weeks. If you drink ten cups it may take you up to two months to quit entirely. But you have to schedule your quitting plan onto your calendar so you don't unwittingly start ramping up the coffee or caffeinated soft drinks again.

If you really can't quit, then see "Pick Your Poisons" (page 129), and make a point of drinking no more than one cup of coffee a day. Sodas, especially diet sodas, are not an optional poison.

Stress

Acute stress floods your body with adrenaline, which is a stimulant. Workaholics are addicted to the adrenaline rush. The adrenal toll that emotional stress (even the fun adrenaline rush type of stress) takes on you eventually depletes happy neurotransmitters. Whether you're pushing yourself intentionally or experiencing a life crisis, if you're trying to quit an addiction it's crucial to continue to eat a balanced diet of real, living food and to follow the rest of the *Healthy, Sexy, Happy* program. One single emotional trauma can lead to sinking depression and cravings for stimulants, putting you right back where you started.

Emotional stress brought on by a crisis is out of our control for the most part, but workaholism is within our control. If you're addicted to stress and love the adrenal rush of pressure, it's understandable. Happy neurotransmitters flood your brain. But it can't last forever. And being addicted to the adrenaline rush is every bit as destructive as being addicted to a drug. It's up to you to decide if you want to ride the wave of your current high or if you want to consider the larger picture of your life.

Extreme Dieting and Vomiting

Millions are addicted to the high they get from starving. Starving and purging panic your brain, as they are indicators of famine. Without nutrition onboard, the stress hormone cortisol breaks down your lean body mass to convert it to sugar for survival. Insulin rushes in to stow that sugar away, which releases a flood of happy neurotransmitters that hit your brain. You feel happy temporarily, but meanwhile, your body is breaking down. Given this cycle, if you are starving to be thin, prepare for a future fat roll. Others are addicted to the rush they get from vomiting, as vomiting causes microscopic tissue injury and, as with any other injury, your brain reacts with a flood of opiate neurotransmitters.

But artificial states of bliss don't last forever, because neurotransmitters are made from food, and if you don't eat and/or you purge, your body won't have the food it needs to make neurotransmitters. This depletion accounts for the other addictions that creep into dieters' and purgers' lives (like caffeine, alcohol, diet pills, aspartame, and cigarettes), which force a flood of happy neurotransmitters. Eventually, when a person is depleted, starving, vomiting, smoking, popping diet pills, drinking Diet Coke, and walking around like a depressed zombie, they will end up asking their doctor for a prescription for SSRIs (selective serotonin reuptake inhibitors), which inhibit the disposal of serotonin from the brain. SSRIs supposedly lead to longer lasting normal levels of serotonin (see page 91 for more on antidepressants). If you have a deep emotional problem, please seek professional help, but don't forget to continue to work on building a healthy, happy brain.

Extreme Exercise

Overexercising results in the same flood of cortisol and insulin as any other stimulant. Over-exercising has been one of my addictions, and I understand how hard it is for people to give up. Extreme exercise is injurious, which results in a flood of endorphins—natural opiates—from the brain. Thus the addictive nature of exercise.

Because extreme exercise increases metabolism, there is also an increase of free radicals. (Sugar and oxygen entering the cell to create energy for locomotion produces free radicals. The more energy you produce, the more free radicals are created.) I'm not going to discourage extreme exercise, as it's one of the most profoundly enjoyable experiences of life. All I want to do is emphasize that extreme athletes must diligently provide their bodies with a constant flood of antioxidants. You can do that by juicing green veggies and taking quality supplements. However, if you're an extreme exerciser who runs a marathon and then eats a banana, you're going to break down much faster than you rebuild. Notice the faces of world-class marathon runners. They're gaunt, drawn, pinched, with significant nasal labial folds. They're not faces of people whose bodies are rebuilding. So think about that if you're an extreme exerciser who doesn't eat enough food. (More about extreme exercise on page 227.)

Regardless of your stimulant addiction, I recommend that you do everything you can to create a healthy, balanced brain before you try to quit the addiction. It wouldn't be unreasonable for you to embark on your brain-building project *months* before you attempt to quit.

Alcoholism and Drug Addiction

I've never kicked a drug habit, nor have I ever been an alcoholic. These are serious brain issues. Although I have enormous respect for Alcoholics Anonymous and Narcotics Anonymous, I have to wonder about the cigarettes, coffee, and cake at their meetings. The way to kick a habit is by creating healthy brains that are flooded with happy neurotransmitters. Cigarettes, coffee, and cake do not lend to that plan. I would never trivialize drug or alcohol addictions in a million years. What I am trying to convey is not to underestimate the power of a healthy, happy brain made and fueled with happy neurotransmitters by eating real, living food.

I researched heroin addiction for my novel, *Karma*, a psychological thriller about an American woman doctor who is abducted in Istanbul and taken to Mumbai to work as the doctor for sex traffickers. As part of her seasoning, my character, Meredith Fitzgerald, is hooked on heroin.

I wanted to understand why cold-turkey withdrawal from heroin was so excruciatingly painful. What I learned is that our nerve endings are so sensitive that we would be in agony just walking around or typing on our keyboards if it weren't for the steady supply of opiates in our brain that kill pain. Using heroin shuts down the production of opiates in the brain. So if someone goes cold turkey, it may take up to two weeks of agonizing withdrawals before the brain is able to ramp up production again. I find it obnoxious when people give unsolicited advice about a topic they know absolutely nothing about—so I can't say more about this subject—except that if you have an alcohol, street, prescription, or OTC drug addiction, seek professional help. But please don't forget that caffeine, cigarettes, and cake further deplete the brain of happy neurotransmitters. Also, do everything listed in the "Create a New, Healthy, Happy Brain" sidebar (including and especially eating a diet of real, living food) to build a healthy brain before going cold turkey.

Antidepressants

One thing that really bothers me is the way the food and diet industries have totally wrecked modern brains and how the drug industry has exploited these unhappy brains to the tune of billions and billions of dollars. It's really such a travesty.

In 2009, *Newsweek* featured a cover story, "The Depressing News About Antidepressants" with the heading "Studies suggest that the popular drugs are no more effective than a placebo.[28] In fact, they may be worse." I waved that magazine around and exclaimed, "I'm vindicated!"

The article chronicled the twenty-plus years of research on antidepressants, concluding that although antidepressants can lift depression in most patients, the benefits are hardly more significant than what patients experienced when they unknowingly took a placebo. The article went on to state, "As more and more scientists who study depression and the drugs that treat it are concluding, that suggests that antidepressants are basically expensive Tic Tacs."

I'm not suggesting anyone throw away his or her antidepressants. All I'm saying is that if you are depressed, it may be situational or because you have not taken care of your big dumb pet—your brain. And maybe you'll see your depression resolve if you build a solid brain and flood it with happy neurotransmitters, which will enable you to change your situation.

Create a New, Healthy, Happy Brain

Follow the detox lifestyle (page 125).

Stop eating all factory-food products, especially white flour and sugar (cake!).

Eat a balanced diet of real, living, organic food.

Incorporate healing fats into your diet (any of the fats listed in chapter 4), especially Activator X, and butter for vitamins A and D_3.

Take supplemental cod liver oil every day for EFA, and vitamins D_3 and A (capsules or the flavored oil to keep you from gagging), and eat small oily fish like sardines.

Exercise every day to boost natural opiate levels in your brain.

Twenty minutes of exposing your arms and legs to full afternoon sunlight without sunblock will synthesize 20,000 IUs of vitamin D_3 (this is not feasible for extremely fair-skinned people).

Take N-acetyl cysteine (NAC), an amino acid that helps decrease withdrawal symptoms. It has antimucolytic (antimucous) properties and has been shown to increase mucocilary transport in smokers [how mucus is transported in the membranes—cilia (like little sea weeds) weaves and moves the mucus along].

Take quality multivitamins and added antioxidants.

Use bioidentical hormone replacement, if you need it.

Learn to practice self-compassion meditation to alter your physical brain and to foster feelings of calm control.

Drink organic green tea, which has half the caffeine of coffee and contains health-giving properties.

Have acupuncture treatments to help calm your brain.

Use hypnosis and neurofeedback therapy to continue to calm your brain.

Supplements to Use for Brains Depleted of Neurotransmitters

Alpha lipoic acid	Melatonin
Cod liver oil	Tyrosine
CoQ_{10}	Vitamins B_3 and B_6
L-Tryptophan or 5-HTP	

Neurofeedback Therapy

Neurofeedback therapy is based on a very simple premise that retraining brainwave patterns will correct many neurological problems. (EEG is short for electroencephalograph, which is a computer that uses electrodes placed on the scalp to monitor and record the electrical activity of various areas of the brain.)

The brain generates wave patterns beta, alpha, theta, and delta (measured in "hertz" or cycles per second) that reflect and determine your level of awareness. When you are awake and functioning, beta waves (above 13 hertz) generate highly alert, focused concentration. The next level of awareness results from alpha brainwaves (8 to 13 hertz). In an alpha state you are more relaxed and contemplative. Between a waking state and a sleep state, your brain generates very relaxed theta waves (4 to 8 hertz). Theta ushers you into delta, or sleep state, which are the slowest brainwaves (.5 to 3.5 hertz).

Brainwaves fluctuate so that your body can either function or rest optimally. Dysfunction occurs when brain waves are either overactive or underactive. Neurofeedback retrains the brain to restore appropriate brainwave patterns.

Neurofeedback has been around since the late 1960s. Since that time neurofeedback has been used to treat ADD, ADHD, addictions, anxiety, autism, brain injury, cerebral palsy, cognitive decline, coma, depression, epilepsy, headaches, insomnia, OCD, PTSD, Parkinson's schizophrenia, stroke, tinnitus, and Tourette's, as well as conditions not normally associated with the brain such as autoimmune disorders, chronic fatigue, fibromyalgia, and hypertension.

Neurofeedback therapy is an effective, safe, and enjoyable therapy to assist you in quitting an addiction.[30]

Acupuncture for Addictions and Pain

When I was working as a stylist in the film industry, I began to regularly suffer from a stiff neck. If I were in a room with air conditioning, my neck would seize up. The last episode of neck seizing left me immobilized in bed. A friend told me she'd had the same problem and had found relief with acupuncture. I looked up "acupuncture" in the Yellow Pages and found myself in a Santa Monica clinic, sitting opposite an enormous man with diamond rings on every finger and a big, fat gold watch on his wrist. After he finished my "intake," he ushered me into an exam room and told me to lie down on a table. A few minutes later, a tiny Vietnamese man in black pajamas floated ethereally into the room. He proceeded to dart acupuncture needles all over my back. A deep calm settled over my being. I left the clinic thirty minutes later 80 percent cured of my stiff neck. By the next day it was completely fine, and I have never suffered from that problem again. (Clearly the big dude was exploiting the gifted acupuncturist who could barely speak English, but that's another story.)

Acupuncture is a Chinese medical technique that was developed and refined for more than three thousand years. Acupuncture consists of inserting a number of very fine steel needles into the skin at specific meridian points. The majority of acupuncture points lie on the body surface along the fourteen major meridians.

These meridians branch out to smaller meridian channels. This branching continues until the channels eventually become as miniscule as capillaries. This is how meridians connect every part of the human body. In fact, meridians and the *Qi*, the energy flow that travels inside of them, are the foundation for the wholeness of your body. The fourteen major meridians and all the connecting channels have acupuncture points, close to the body surface, for a total of 365 acupuncture points. An ailment on one part of the body often requires needling in a distant site, which suggests the "wholeness" of the body.

Acupuncture points are energy junctures close to the surface of your skin that are access points to your internal energy system. Think of these points as tiny valves where *Qi* is drawn in and out of your body's energy flow. All acupuncture points are points on your body surface where there is lowered electrical resistance and higher concentration of sensory and tiny nerve structures underneath the skin. These areas are more sensitive or more responsive to physical stimulation. Acupuncture needles are inserted into these specific channels to influence your body's *Qi*, allowing your body to balance and heal itself. Think of acupuncture needles as antennas through which we can strengthen deficient *Qi* or disperse stagnant *Qi*.

Because acupuncture is used to reestablish harmony within your energy systems, it can be used to treat a vast range of illnesses and pain disorders and to provide effective anesthesia during certain surgical procedures. I met my lifelong friend Jitka Gunaratna in the jungle of Sri Lanka when I was a hippie hitchhiker in 1968–69. Jitka was fishing with a piece of coconut on a safety pin. She caught a fish and made a curry, and we have been friends ever since. Jitka subsequently studied acupuncture for twenty-five years with Lord Pandit Raja-Guru Professor Doctor Sir Anton Jayasuriya. Dr. Jayasuriya (apparently an ugly man who was also a lady killer) was Jitka's anesthesiologist, using acupuncture when Jitka delivered her son by C-section.

It's really neat that acupuncture can be so powerful when performed by an experienced practitioner. It can be used to treat chronic pain because it stimulates the release of endorphins, your body's natural pain relievers; to counteract the side effects of chemotherapy; and to help reduce cravings when going through cigarette, alcohol, or drug withdrawals.

Addictions suck. They rob you of your liberty and age, before ultimately killing you. Quitting addictions initially takes the desire to quit. Remember that voice in my head that tried to talk me into smoking because the movie stars were smoking? When I see some movie stars around my age, I don't doubt that they've aged as badly as they have because they continued smoking. Today's twenty-four-year-olds may some day bid an early adieu to the current stable of glamorous smokers, or at the very least cringe at how hideously they have aged. I hope in that distant day all you ex-smokers will say, "It was a challenge to quit smoking, but it was a lot easier than it could have been because I took the necessary steps to build a happy, healthy brain." The same is true for drug users, diet-drink addicts, alcoholics, and others.

There are uncountable problems—from minor glitches to organ failure—that can go wrong with the human body. However, the degeneration caused by eating a dead/toxic diet of factory-food products, taking pharmaceutical and OTC drugs, and other exposure to toxins is pretty systematic.

seven

Ultimate You Skill No. 6: Supplement Your Diet

First you notice small annoyances like constipation, tummy aches, and sniffles. You get a lot of yeast and fungal infections. And if you keep eating factory-food products, using drugs, and exposing yourself to toxins, more glaring health problems will crop up. Ultimately your immune system can flip out, manifesting in allergies and sensitivities. If you persist, the breakdown can escalate to extreme environmental sensitivities, severe immune reactions and adrenal burnout, culminating in autoimmune conditions, neurological disorders, cancer, and that cold impersonal hospital death. (This is not to say that people who eat and live in a very pristine way cannot also get sick, as we live in an extremely toxic world.)

Providing your body with real food and then supplementing your diet can halt and even reverse this accelerated aging process to some extent and protect you from further harm. Let's go through one example of the progression of disease to see how it works and what strategies may reverse it.

Stopping the Progression of Disease

The GI tract, the passage from the mouth all the way to the exit, is the barometer of our overall health. As much as you want to build your brain, you need to give equal attention to your GI tract. It's imperative to have a healthy intestinal tract because that is where nutrition is introduced and assimilated into your body. GI problems are your body's way of saying, "I don't like what you're putting into me. Please stop!"

Watch Out for These GI Symptoms

- Bad taste in the mouth and foul breath
- Bloating
- Constipation or diarrhea
- Cramping
- Heartburn/GERD
- Gas
- Gurgling stomach
- Lactose intolerance
- Tummy aches
- Yeast infections

Constipation

Constipation is the primary cause of many of the above listed symptoms. It's always blown my mind how cavalier the medical profession is about drugs that can cause constipation. Constipation isn't just an annoyance with a good trade-off of risk versus benefit; it's a serious assault on your body and your overall health. Constipation is the paralysis of your GI tract, which leaves you with undigested food caught midway, causing tummy aches, bloating, cramping, and gas and resulting in poor nutrition assimilation and increased toxicity. This leads to inflammation, serious GI problems, compromised immune function, and all kinds of illnesses.

When your GI tract is paralyzed, the inflammatory cascade of heat, pain, and swelling leads to bad things. Two thirds of your immune system is in your gut. You need a healthy GI tract to eliminate viruses and bacteria in your food, absorb vital nutrients, and eliminate toxins.

The pH of Your Gut

The proper functioning of all the body's systems, including all biochemical processes within these systems, depends on a precise system of checks and balances that adjusts your body's pH accordingly. For example, the digestive system goes from a pH of 1 to 3.5, which is acid, all the way to a pH of 7 to 8, which is alkaline, by the time food is fully processed and eliminated. In every one to two feet of your twenty-eight feet of intestines the pH is monitored and regulated by an interactive feedback system between your brain and digestive system.

Normally, peristalsis, the organized rhythm-like muscular contraction of the digestive track that moves food from the mouth to elimination, systematically regulates the movement of food through the digestive system. When fully operational, peristalsis advances food along the way, breaking it down and assimilating nutrients. When each stage is complete, peristalsis pushes the food along to the next process. Digestion begins in your mouth with chewing and salivary enzymes, which start to break down the food you're eating. Next, stomach acids begin dissolving food and activating protein-digesting enzymes. When food goes from the stomach to the entry of the small intestine, the pancreas releases alkaline fluids and enzymes, which are used to neutralize stomach acid. The partially digested food then progresses through your small intestines where, now that the acid has been buffered, enzymes can assimilate nutrients without being destroyed.

This system works beautifully, unless peristalsis is interfered with. There are many contributing factors to impaired peristalsis. Toxic factory food (including toxic oils), sugar, lack of fiber in your diet, food intolerances, excessive coffee or alcohol consumption, and many prescription drugs assault your digestive tract and will paralyze your GI tract, directly or indirectly, through inflammatory responses. While the food sits in your stomach and/or small intestine, it may belch back up, which is called gastroesophageal reflux disease (GERD), better known as heartburn. Likewise, if the food is held up anywhere along the digestive process, you may experience other types of problems such as a tummy ache, bloating, cramping, and gas.

If you have garden-variety GI problems and you choose to ignore the causes, you could face worse problems in the future. The longer your GI problems continue, the longer your body is going to go without optimal nutrition.

Early GI-related Problems

Aches and pains	Runny nose
Chronic colds and flu	Sneezing/wheezing
Fatigue	Yeast (candida)
Headaches	Waking at night/tossing and turning
Overreaction to bug bites	

If you stop eating all factory-food products and start eating a balanced diet of real, living food and avoiding drugs and toxins, you will likely regain full health, including GI health. Unfortunately, TV commercials hawk shrink-wrapped miracles for people to pop for every malady under the sun. Popping pills at this point only escalates the breaking-down process. The next stage is much worse.

When You Ignore Your GI Problems Too Long

Ballistic allergy symptoms

Crippling fatigue

Debilitating joint and muscle pain

Migraines

Severe GI problems from constipation, diarrhea, irritable bowel syndrome

Vulvodynia (pain in the vulva and urinary tract)

Yeast, yeast, and more yeast

Food Sensitivities

People begin complaining about food sensitivities when their GI tract has been so abused that it can't really process a lot of the stuff that's coming in. Allergic reactions run the gamut from life threatening to relatively mild. The most severe involve immediate, violent reactions, such as to shellfish or peanuts, and chances are that you'll have to avoid those foods for the rest of your life. But 80 percent of all allergies are milder reactions, and the onset of symptoms is often delayed from two hours to two days.

Systematic Desensitization from Food Allergies

The logical approach to dealing with food allergies is to avoid the allergen. However, when some people begin to avoid some foods, then others, and then others, their body becomes increasingly sensitive. Eventually their diets become hyper restrictive, and who wants that? You can have a blood test to determine, to some extent, what you're allergic to and your level of intolerance, but none of these tests are completely reliable. The best way is to listen to your body.

If your allergic reactions are mild to moderate, the antibodies to the foods that you're allergic to will usually subside if you completely avoid those foods for three to six months. At the end of this period of abstinence, introduce a small amount of one food. Three months later, introduce a larger amount of that food, gradually increasing the amount of that type of food you can eat until you feel that you have reached your allergic threshold. Rotate the food in this process and eat it no more than once every three days. Repeat this process with all the foods on your allergy list. Use a wall calendar to keep track. I know it's a pain, but it will be worth it in the long run. (NOTE: *I'm talking about real, living food here, not factory food products.*)

Yeast (Candida)

When I lived on a rural ranch, the rats and mice were ubiquitous, which was no surprise since we were usurping their territory. I read a book called *Rats*, and learned that the surefire method for getting rid of them has not changed since the beginning of humankind: get rid of the source of food. The same holds true for yeast. If you're suffering from yeast problems, stop feeding the yeast sugar (carbs). This includes all factory food as well as factory-produced milk products and alcohol. Take probiotics every day. Follow the *Healthy, Sexy, Happy* program. (NOTE: *Even if you don't suffer from yeast, if you must take antibiotics, take probiotics—billions of live organisms that benefit the GI tract.*)

Leaky Gut

"Leaky gut" is a lovely term, isn't it? You can call it "increased intestinal permeability," but it won't make it any nicer. Leaky gut is caused by microscopic damage to the intestinal lining that results after GI problems and food sensitivities have gone on too long. Bacteria and toxins, incompletely digested food, and waste can leak out through the microscopic tears into the bloodstream, triggering a virulent immune reaction that escalates over time to an over-revving immune system. At that point your immune system will always be on.

A major cause of leaky gut is a factory-food diet, which, instead of providing nutrition for the human body, introduces way too many poisons. Other causes are damage from taking nonsteroidal anti-inflammatory drugs (NSAIDS) and other drugs, antibiotics, radiation, too much alcohol, or compromised immunity.

Some Symptoms of Leaky Gut

- Acute sensitivities to noise, sound, foods, odors, and chemicals
- Alcohol intolerance
- Allergies
- Anxiety
- Brain fog
- Chills and night sweats
- Chronic athlete's foot
- Chronic headaches/migraines
- Chronic sinus problems
- Chronic yeast infections
- Crippling fatigue
- Dandruff
- Depression and mood swings
- Eczema
- Extreme tightness in the shoulders and neck
- Gluten and/or casein intolerance
- Hyper-acidity/acid reflux
- Insomnia and un-refreshing sleep
- Irritability
- Jock and rectal itching
- Low sex drive
- Muscle twitching and muscle weakness
- Poor concentration and short-term memory
- Rashes and dry, flaking skin
- Recurrent yeast and fungal infections (Candida)
- Tinnitus

Leaky gut syndrome is thought to trigger or worsen certain disorders like Crohn's disease, celiac disease, rheumatoid arthritis, fibromyalgia, and asthma.

Gluten Intolerance

Gluten intolerance causes very uncomfortable allergic, gastrointestinal, and immunological reactions when you eat gluten, which is a large complex protein in grains, such as wheat, barley, rye, and oats. You may be genetically predisposed to gluten sensitivity, but the current epidemic of gluten sensitivity is likely due to eating way too many refined grains in factory-food products. I found it telling when researching this subject that one of the big moans and groans come from gluten sensitive people who couldn't find any "foods" to eat: pizza, bread, crackers, cereal, cakes, and cookies. Reality Check: Pizza isn't food. There are plenty of real foods to eat if you've developed gluten sensitivity.

Some Symptoms of Gluten Intolerance
(varies by person)

Alternating diarrhea with constipation

Brain fog

Chronic fatigue or weakness

Diarrhea

Gas, bloating, abdominal cramps, and pain

Headaches

Irritability

Malnutrition and anemia

Mouth ulcers

Muscular aches and pains

Skin problems (like eczema)

Because you can't be medically tested for gluten sensitivity, it's kind of a guessing game—but if you're sensitive, you probably know it by now. If unaddressed, gluten sensitivity can progress to a much more serious autoimmune condition, celiac disease. You can be tested for celiac disease, which is when the immune system actually attacks the small intestine. This leads to severe malnourishment and the risk of developing other autoimmune illnesses.

Some Symptoms of Celiac Disease
(varies by person)

Abdominal pain

Bloating, gas, indigestion

Constipation

Decreased appetite

Diarrhea, chronic or occasional

Lactose intolerance

Nausea and vomiting

Smelly stools that float, are bloody, look fatty

Unexplained weight loss (although you can be over, or at normal weight)

Irritable Bowel Syndrome

Irritable bowel is a disorder wherein peristalsis doesn't function properly. The most common symptoms are severe tummy aches defined as cramping, bloating, gas, diarrhea (sometimes very severe), and constipation. You'll notice white mucous in your stool, have a bloated tummy, and you'll feel like you're not quite finished eliminating even if you just went. People who have been diagnosed with IBS are told to stop eating french fries, milk, chocolate, caffeine, sodas, and sugar (duh). They are also told that their condition is incurable. I personally don't believe that anything is "incurable." Irritable bowel may be incurable with drugs and surgery, but what about pampering your GI tract, nourishing your body, avoiding all toxins, and building your immune system with real, living food? It's worth a try.

Autoimmune Conditions

One of the last stops in the progression of disease from toxic food or other toxic exposure is autoimmune conditions. These conditions occur when your immune system no longer distinguishes between healthy organisms and dangerous foreign invaders, and either attacks healthy cells, or abnormally stimulates receptors on cells. There are about a hundred autoimmune conditions. Autoimmune conditions are among the most poorly understood illnesses. There are a number of theories about how and why autoimmune conditions develop, but essentially all theories point to toxins. Autoimmune conditions are something you want to avoid. Modern medicine has very few treatment options for autoimmune conditions, and those options—drugs—are like throwing gasoline on a fire.

If you have an autoimmune condition, it can improve dramatically by following the *Healthy, Sexy, Happy* program, which revolves around eliminating toxins and supporting metabolic processes with real, living food.

Fixing GI problems

In a perfect world, doctors would automatically take an interest in healing our GI tracts, because to ignore our GI problems spells inevitable deleterious effects on our health. The perfect-world doctors would approach healing our GI tracts with nutrition (food) first, and then with supplements, nutraceuticals, homeopathy, enzymes, and Chinese and Ayurvedic herbs, and other healing modalities. The sad reality is that if you are suffering from GI problems, your doctor is likely pushing drugs and disregarding nutrition, especially supplementation.

If you're on your own because your doctor isn't versed in nutrition, the first reasonable course of therapeutic action is to stop eating and drinking all factory-food products and start eating only real, living food. Follow the elimination diet, if applicable. Stop eating all white flour products and sugar. Quit coffee. It has no redeeming qualities and it's going to stand in the way of your optimal health plan. Nothing fuels accelerated aging like coffee. You also need to eat fats to heal your gut and flood your system with building supplies. In addition to saturated fat and meat from grass-fed animals, lots of butter, whole yogurt, and whole raw milk, you need supplemental fats. My current healing fats are Activator X, cod liver oil, primrose oil, coconut, and red palm oil. Basic supplements are next. And by the way, supplementation is crucial to healing and absolutely code-red necessary if you're compelled to take drugs or undergo toxic medical treatments.

Get Real About Supplements

The general public has a vague idea that vitamin and mineral supplementation is beneficial. Thus we have manufacturer's Big Box mentality which supplies the most useless, and scarily toxic supplements, like those hard little, unabsorbable, once-daily bullets that you can buy, super cheap, in oversized containers. Saving money on supplements is one way of salting money away so that you can afford a more expensive funeral. But if you really want bang for your buck, you need to get educated about what you're popping, and, moreover, who is supplying it. Is it the same corporation that fills up plastic water bottles with fluoridated, chlorinated city water and then adds toxic "smart" flavorings, questionable herbs, and fake electrolytes? Hmmm, could be. The following is a primer on supplements that will help you pick out good-quality, bioavailable multivitamins and minerals, which your body can actually absorb and use and that contain no toxins, allergens, aspartame coating, or fillers.

The Basic Multi

Vitamins and minerals are the catalysts of biochemical processes, and without them your metabolic function would decline due to mitochondrial and DNA destruction, leading to accelerated aging and disease. Historically, people ate vitamins and minerals in food. Today our farmlands are depleted, and even shipping organic foods to market can deplete them of some nutrients. I remember when I first read a book by Adelle Davis when I was eighteen and learned about this, and how freaked out I was rushing home from the market with a head of lettuce so I could make a salad before all the vitamins vanished. I've since calmed down, but I know a lot more about nutrition and supplements now too.

The best argument for taking supplements is that we are experiencing a toxic assault unlike any experienced by humankind. The only sensible thing to do is to use a therapeutic intake of supplements like smart bombs to attack and destroy enemy combatants within our bodies and brains, as well as to build the best possible defense against foreign invaders. But keep in mind that supplements are only effective when used to augment a diet of whole, real, living food. Supplements cannot take the place of food.

I personally haven't even bothered checking what the FDA Recommended Daily Intake (RDI) is for various supplements. In short, what do they know? The FDA has repeatedly demonstrated its ineptitude. In addition, the RDI is unrealistic when it comes to a living, breathing human being.

To find out what I need, I've done my own research and consulted with numerous health practitioners over the years. My personal supplement regimen changes regularly to ensure that my bloodstream is rich in nutrients bathing my cells with the nutrition necessary to neutralize free radicals, to repair mitochondria and DNA, to cool inflammation, and to supply nutrients for the ongoing metabolic regeneration processes.

Because vitamins and minerals work synergistically in the metabolic and enzymatic systems in our bodies, we should take vitamins and minerals in certain combinations. The proper combination can be found in high-quality multiple vitamin/mineral supplements that are formulated by nutrition experts. Although we can use a particular vitamin or mineral therapeutically in response to a symptomatic need, by doing so we often create an increased need for other vitamins and minerals. That's why I take the proper combinations in a multi first. If a condition persists that indicates specific nutrient deficiencies, my defense strategy is to research what therapeutic amounts to use of individual vitamins and minerals, nutraceuticals, enzymes, and Chinese and Ayurvedic herbs to facilitate repair. And I don't have any fantasies that repair is going to happen overnight.

Shopping for a quality supplement isn't easy; even the clinical nutritionists I've spoken with are often confused. There are quality-control issues; problems with fillers and magnesium stearate, a hydrogenated fat used to grease the machinery. Vitamins and minerals are available in a variety of forms. Some people think high-dose supplements have a better chance of doing the job, others believe in using low levels of highly absorbable forms. Some products offer a.m. and p.m. doses. Again, even the experts have problems figuring it all out. What's optimal and necessary for one person isn't necessarily best for another. That's why testing is really the best way to go, but it's just not feasible financially for everyone. With all of this in mind, here are some basic guidelines to help you choose a supplement line. I'll continue to research quality supplements and provide updates on my website.

Vitamins (Micronutrients)

Vitamins are called micronutrients because we need less of them than macronutrients—fats, carbs, and proteins. Vitamins assist and initiate biochemical processes that sustain life (the breaking down and building up we talked about earlier). Vitamins are either fat soluble or water soluble. Fat-soluble vitamins—A, D, E, and K—dissolve in fat and can be stored in your body. Fat-soluble vitamins cannot be absorbed without adequate fat in your diet. If you don't eat enough fat, the vitamins simply travel though your digestive tract, which is another reason the low-fat diet is contributing to poor health. Water-soluble vitamins—C and B-complex vitamins such as vitamins B_6, B_{12}, niacin, riboflavin, and folate—dissolve in water so they aren't stored in your body. Whatever isn't used passes out of your system, so you have to consume them every day.

Consider Antioxidants

The goal every day in every way is to balance the generation of free radicals—from the metabolizing of food, exercising, and pollution and other toxins—with enough antioxidant intake to neutralize those free radicals. The first course of action, of course, is to eat a balanced diet of real, whole foods. I also advocate drinking green veggie juice (and stirring in a teaspoon each of spirulina and chlorella) to fortify your defense. I also take antioxidants in supplements.

Antioxidants stop oxidation by neutralizing free radicals by either providing the extra electron that is missing, or by breaking down the free radical molecule so that it's neutralized. Antioxidants stop the chain reaction of free radical formation. A good multi will contain antioxidants, but you might want to add extra to your regimen. NOTE: *For a description of all supplements see the appendix on page 238.*

Antioxidants to Look for in a Multi

- Alpha-carotene
- Beta-carotene and other carotenoids
- Calcium ascorbate
- Chromium picolinate
- CoQ_{10}
- Cryptoxanthin
- Lutein
- Magnesium
- Selenium
- Vitamin C (ascorbic acid)
- Vitamin E (as mixed tocopherols)
- Zeaxanthin
- Zinc

Other Vitamins You Might Find in Quality Supplements

- Choline
- Citrus bioflavonoid complex (not ascorbic acid alone)
- Inositol
- Para-aminobenzoic acid (PABA)
- Vitamin A (retinol)
- Vitamin D_3 (not vegetarian D_2)
- Vitamin K_2 (not K_1)

B-Complex Vitamins

B vitamins are important for optimal health. All B vitamins help the body to convert carbs into fuel (glucose), which is burned to produce energy. Often referred to as B-complex vitamins, they also help the body metabolize fats and protein. B-complex vitamins are necessary for healthy skin, hair, eyes, and liver. They also help the nervous system function properly and are useful in nearly every aspect of energy and repair systems, including the production and the effect of hormones, antibiotics, and neurotransmitters.

B-Complex Vitamins

B_1 (thiamin)

B_2 (riboflavin)

B_3 (niacin)

B_5 (pantothenic acid)

B_6 (pyridoxine)

B_7 (biotin AKA vitamin H)

B_{12} (as methylcobalamin)

Folic or folate acid

Minerals (Micronutrients)

Minerals are also micronutrients, and we would not survive without them. While vitamins are organic substances made by plants or animals, minerals are inorganic elements originating in soil and water. We need larger amounts of some minerals than others and still less of trace minerals—but both are necessary every day for metabolic processes to operate smoothly.

Minerals You Might Find in a Quality Supplement

Calcium

Chromium

Copper and zinc

Iodine

Iron

Magnesium

Manganese

Potassium

Selenium

Vanadium (vanadyl sulfate)

Zinc

Healing Your Body

Once you're set with a multi, you can then start exploring supplements to help you heal from whatever condition you're suffering from (and most people have something). There is only space to cover a few of the most prevalent conditions. But just remember that whatever condition you are addressing, allover health is the path to healing.

Healing Your Gut

A healthy GI tract is imperative to healing any condition from acne to cancer. One of the most common GI problems is heartburn—the burning sensation of stomach acid rising up into the esophagus. Heartburn can be the result of stuffing your stomach too full, drinking too much fluid with your meal, drinking too much coffee, or consuming noxious factory drinks or food products. You could also need more healthy flora in your gut (i.e., probiotics). You could at least consider stopping what you're doing that may be causing the problem. Or if you're eating a low-fat or nonfat diet, this diet may be causing your heartburn. Your body assumes it will receive protein when you eat, so your stomach produces hydrochloric acid, which activates enzymes to digest proteins. On a low-fat, low-protein diet, your carb meals flush right through your stomach so quickly that the outpouring of acid has nowhere to go but up. To complicate the issue, carbs stimulate insulin which further increases acid production by activating other hormone systems. So for goodness sake, add some animal protein and healing fats (like butter, olive oil, coconut oil) to your diet.

GI Supplements

- Boswellia
- Cod liver oil
- Deglycyrrhizinated licorice root
- Green veggie juice
- Marshmallow root
- Probiotics
- Stabilized rice bran

Digestive Supplements

- A high-quality digestive enzyme containing carbohydrase, amylase, protease, lipase, and cellulase
- Betaine hydrochloric acid (HCL)
- Bromelain
- Pancreatin
- Papain
- Pepsin
- Phytase, Hemicellulase, and Xylanase

Mitochondrial Restoration

Now that your GI problems are solved, let's delve into the nitty-gritty of aging. Mitochondrial decay, the free radical oxidation of energy factories in your cells, is a major contributor to aging and the associated degenerative diseases of aging. Inadequate intake of vitamins and minerals from a poor diet can lead to mitochondrial decay and DNA damage. Certain nutrients can help to arrest accelerated aging, restore some mitochondria function, and stave off aging.

Nutrients That Help Restore Mitochondria

Alpha-lipoic acid
B-complex vitamins including riboflavin (B_2)
CoQ_{10}
Creatine
L-carnitine
Selenium

Deeper into the Land of Anti-aging

If you want to protect your mitochondria and DNA, it doesn't make a bit of sense to start taking osteoporosis drugs, statins, or any of the other highly commercialized pharmaceuticals as soon as you reach a certain age. The *Healthy, Sexy, Happy* approach keeps your body healthy, which is a much more effective strategy than waiting until your bones are brittle and your arteries are clogged and then adding more poisons, in the form of drugs, to your already limping system. If you want to build bone and tamp down the inflammation that contributes to arterial plaquing, it's as simple as eating a balanced diet of real, whole, living food, and adding the appropriate supplements.

Anti-aging Supplements/Hormones

Acetyl L-carnitine arginate
Alpha-lipoic acid
Apple cider vinegar
B-complex vitamins
Blackstrap molasses
Calcium
Cholesterol (see page 48)
CoQ_{10}
Cortef
DHEA
Estrogen

Garlic
Green tea extract
Human growth hormone
Magnesium
Melatonin
Omega-3 oils

Progesterone
Pregnenolone
Proanthocyanidins (flavonoids) and vitamin C
Resveratrol
Testosterone
Vitamin D_3

Adrenal Fatigue

Adrenal fatigue is the unhappy companion to anything else you're suffering from. It's so important that I dedicated chapter 12 to it. Caring for your adrenals is a huge part of being healthy. In addition to sleep, meditation, mind clearing, and all the other modalities that rest and rejuvenate your adrenals, you can take herbs and supplements to baby and care for them.

Supplements and Herbs to Treat Adrenal Burnout

Aloe leaf extract
Ashwaganda
Boswellia
Colostrum
Cordyceps
Garcinia cambogia
Glandulars
Glutamine
Holy basil

Medical marijuana (cannabis)
Royal maca
Siberian ginseng
Silymarin (milk thistle seed), buplerum, dandelion root, beet leaves, burdock, and goldenseal
St. John's wort

Heart Health

If you are suffering from or worried about heart disease, the best course of healing and prevention is the overall mind, body, spirit approach health presented in this book. Heart disease is caused primarily by inflammation, so it's important to get off the accelerated aging path by never eating damaged fats (see page 42) and always eating a balanced diet of real food that includes cholesterol. You will keep your working LDL cholesterol from caramelizing by finding your metabolic set point on page 62 and revising your diet accordingly. Maintain high HDLs by consuming essential fatty acids and fish. High levels of the amino acid homocysteine are associated with heart disease. You can lower your levels by taking B-complex vitamins and, of course, avoiding damage from free radicals.

Heart Supplements/Hormones

Antioxidants (dietary and supplements)
B-complex vitamins
CoQ_{10}
Essential fatty acids
Estrogen (women)
Grape seed extract
L-carnitine
Magnesium citramate

Multi-vitamin/mineral without iron (unless you are deficient)
Niacin
Quercetin
Selenium
Testosterone (men)
Vitamin C
Vitamin D_3
Vitamin E
Vitamin K_2

Antiviral Supplements

We can't just pop supplements and expect to be immune from disease. But there are some very good supplements to assist our immune systems in fighting off viruses.

With all the flu scares we've had in recent years, way too many people have gotten unnecessary and dangerous vaccines. The very best defense against flu is to strengthen your immune system. Herpes is most active when your immunity is lowered. The following supplements can assist your immune system to fight viruses.

Viral Suppressers

Coconut oil
Lysine

Vitamin D_3
Zinc

NOTE: *For strategies to prevent herpes see page 227.*

Allergy Blasters

Allergies are another ginormous moneymaking arena for pharmaceutical companies. There are many nutritional formulas today that contain a cocktail of antihistamine nutrients. The best course of action if you suffer from allergies is to address GI tract health, and to focus on building a strong immune system. You can also add specific nutrients.

Allergy Blasters

Bioflavonoids	Quercetin
Carotenoids	Vitamin A (retinol)
N-acetyl-cysteine (NAC)	Vitamin C
Omega-3 oils	

Cancer

The *Healthy, Sexy, Happy* program is designed to do everything possible to avoid cancer. As I've said before, even if you are devoted to healthy eating and living, because our environment is so toxic—and because we all have strikes against us (I was raised on factory-food products and smoked for ten years), no one is exempt. All we can do is, like my grandma said, our best.

Anticancer Supplements

Alpha-lipoic acid	Multivitamin/mineral
Beta carotene	Selenium
Bioflavonoids	Vitamin A (retinol)
CoQ_{10}	Vitamin B_6 and B_{12}
Curcumin	Vitamin D_3
Essiac tea	Vitamin E
Green tea extract	Vitamin K_3
Magnesium	Zinc

Medicinal Herbs

Pharmaceutical drugs were developed directly from herbology. Before the early ninth century, doctors and pharmacists were one and the same. The herbalist both prescribed and prepared medical compounds. Medicines were once just a step removed from their plant sources. It's only been since the late eighteenth century that advances in chemistry and biology enabled pharmaceutical drugs to be standardized. Pharmacology recognized that a natural substance contains many ingredients, not all of which are responsible for its medicinal effect.

Researchers first isolated the ingredient from a plant source that was thought to have the primary healing property for a given condition. Active ingredients are the constituents within the natural substance responsible for a particular biological effect. Isolating the specific active ingredient(s) responsible for a therapeutic effect has been the focus of pharmaceutical advancements in medicine.

The next step was to determine or standardize how much of the ingredient to prescribe. In the early nineteenth century, chemists began to make exciting progress in isolating active ingredients—aspirin (from the bark of willow trees), morphine (from the seeds of poppy flowers), strychnine (from the poisonous Nux Vomica tree), quinine (from the bark of the cinchona tree), penicillin (from molds on grains), and many others—from their crude plant sources. In the twentieth century, and particularly since WWII, pharmacological researchers developed drugs like there was no tomorrow. Also, since then more drugs have been made by chemical synthesis—many of which are chemical imitations of plant medicines.

Thousands of years ago ancient herbalists from many different cultures became aware of active ingredients and actually isolated them from plant sources. However, they quickly noted the problem of side effects and decided to stay with the use of whole natural substances, which contain ingredients that are meant to interact synergistically and to counteract potential side effects. We're used to medicine that comes in sanitary, often hermetically sealed packages with enclosures only the scientifically trained can read and understand. Pharmaceutical drugs are sugar-coated, perfectly formed pills and capsules in childproof and tamperproof containers. Sterile drugs are administered via tubes directly into a vein or given as an injection. In comparison, herbal medicine, especially Chinese and Ayurvedic herbs, can appear earthy and primitive.

Chinese and Ayurvedic Medicines

So far we've talked about weight loss, preventing illness, and healing with nutrition and supplements. But there are health problems, including some we reviewed in this chapter, that require medicine. If you're done with treating illnesses with drugs then you might be interested in Chinese and Ayurvedic medicines. At the very least, an understanding of these ancient medicines is beneficial to understanding the healing integration of mind, body, and spirit. Chinese and Ayurvedic medicines are both energy/life-force-based medicines. In Chinese medicine, energy is referred to as *Qi*, in Ayurvedic medicine *prana*. Both Chinese and Ayurvedic medicines developed methods of diagnosis via external means such as observing, touching, and listening to the patient. In other words, they are focused on symptoms.

We are way overdue in the West for a change in attitudes about the role of energy in healing, and how symptoms are factored into the healing strategy. Talking about energy healing is about as out there as you can get for many Western-minded doctors, even though science clearly tells us that we are made up of energy! And for way too long symptoms—what a person feels and experiences in his or her own body—have been shunted to the back burner while doctors study lab reports and other diagnostic tests. If we are to heal and really be healthy, medical practitioners need to acknowledge that paying attention to the body's energy systems is a major factor in healing. Listening to our symptoms will tell them what needs to be healed. I'm encouraged about the number of enlightened doctors I know and continue to meet. These enlightened doctors have at least some knowledge of Chinese and Ayurvedic medicines, and they are interested in symptoms!

Chinese Medicine

If you have had no exposure to Chinese medicine, it may seem strange. When I was little, my grandma would take my sister and me on errands with her into Detroit. On those excursions I first saw the bizarre-looking storefronts of Chinese apothecaries marked with indecipherable Chinese characters, where nightmarishly frightening dead creatures floated in glass containers. "What's that, Grandma?" I would ask her, and she would reply in her Polish accent, "Oh, honey, it's just the Chinamen." Grandma remained cryptic, but even as a very small child my impression was "Primitive hocus pocus—get me out of here!"

Cut to a zillion years later. I'm living in Santa Barbara, which is a mecca for alternative medicine, and meeting people who went to doctors of Chinese medicine for herbs. I decided to try Chinese herbs, and remember getting my first sacks of roots and twigs and brewing them into tea called a "decoction." It was nasty tasting, but oddly addictive and remarkably effective, and after my first positive experience I became a convert to Chinese medicine—both herbs and acupuncture—and I eventually co-wrote a book on Chinese medicine.

Chinese medicine evolved from the belief that true health results from balancing the system as a whole, as your body and mind are interconnected and interdependent. Chinese medicine considers human beings and their environment to be part of the same system, or part of the whole. *Yin* and *Yang*, in constant flux, dictating balance. These constant fluctuations of energy occur within the eternal circle of nature. I mean that all occurrences have a consequence, positive or negative.

Meridians are invisible channels in your body through which *Qi* (the integration of *Yin* and *Yang* energies) flows. *Qi* continually flows through these channels to create the wholeness of your body. Because *Qi* permeates the universe, meridians connect your internal body with the outside universe as well.

In diagnosing and treating illness, Western medicine uses sophisticated scientific technologies to attempt to pinpoint the exact cause—whether bacterial, viral, cancerous cells, or another tangible cause. Chinese medicine doesn't aim to isolate tangible causes of disease in order to treat illness, because your *Qi* flows through the meridian system of your body. *Yin* and *Yang* energy form an infinite number of internal patterns within your body.

If the equilibrium of *Qi* is upset for any reason, the energy flow will slow, and any toxins and metabolic waste will not be sufficiently removed. When *Qi* becomes weakened, blocked, or stagnated, this energetic imbalance will result in illness and disease. To arrive at a diagnosis, the Chinese doctor compiles a complete picture of you as a whole being. After diagnosing a problem, the doctor designs an individualized treatment to get *Qi* moving and correct the imbalance that caused the problem. The goal is to rebalance a person's energy system, in other words restoring your body's optimum functioning. Chinese medicine healing modalities include medicinal herbs, acupuncture and acupressure, tuina bodywork (based on martial arts), *Qigong* (breathing/flowing movements to move energy), moxabustion (heat therapy), and cupping and scrapng (ridding your body of impurities with suction cups and scraping toxins from the skin).

I've been lucky to have cultivated relationships with several brilliant doctors of Chinese medicine, including Maoshing Ni, L.A.c., D.O.M., who goes by Dr. Mao and is the author of *Secrets of Longevity*. He is also the cofounder of The Tao of Wellness clinic in Santa Monica and Yo San University in Los Angeles. Dr. Mao told me, "The key to understanding Chinese medicine is to respect and assist your body's innate healing capabilities and to recognize the role of the spirit. The spirit guides the mind and the flow of *Qi* or energy. *Qi* in turn animates the body's functioning, enabling health, healing, and longevity of one's life. That's the secret to a healthier, sexier, and happier you."

Ayurvedic Medicine

My first experience with Ayurvedic medicine occurred when I was a hippie hitchhiker, living in Columbo, the capital of Sri Lanka. During that time my boyfriend got very sick with symptoms of malaria: sweating, shaking, chills, fever, and loss of appetite. We'd just come from a jungle camp where several girls had lain in shaking sweats on grass mats. We were too dumb to be scared, so we thought we'd let him sleep it off. When he didn't get any better, he finally went off to the local clinic.

At the clinic there was a long line of poverty-stricken barefoot villagers, the women in raggedy saris and the men wearing lungi and sleeveless T-shirts. Everyone carried a bottle, Coca-Cola bottles being the favorites. Slowly we got closer to the building where we hoped the doctors would be. Eventually we got to a huge room with eight exam tables, one doctor to each table. My boyfriend was cold, pale, clammy, and trembling when an elderly woman doctor in a sari examined him.

She spoke in Singhalese to an orderly who ushered him to a shed outside where there were three huge glass tanks of liquid, labeled A, B, and C. "So you need emulsion C, I see," the orderly said. "Give me the bottle." A dreary looking liquid was siphoned into a Coke bottle. "Take three times a day in one swallow." The orderly handed it to him and looked over his shoulder, calling in the next patient. Within a few days of gulping emulsion C, my boyfriend was fine.

Like Chinese medicine, many Ayurvedic practices predate written records and were handed down by word of mouth. Ayurveda is Sanskrit for *ayur* (life) and *veda* (science or knowledge) (i.e., the science of life). The purpose of ayurvedic medicine is to integrate and balance the body, mind, and spirit, to achieve happiness and health, as well as to help prevent illness.

The eight branches of Ayurvedic medicine include: internal medicine, surgery, treatment of head and neck disease, gynecology, obstetrics, and pediatrics, toxicology, psychiatry, care of the elderly and rejuvenation, and sexual vitality. If you've been to India, you'll have likely seen evidence in statuary and other artifacts that the ancient scholars were extremely interested in pleasurable sex—something I think is important for a well-balanced life, too. I think it's cool that Ayurvedic medicine doesn't beat around the bush about sex, but rather it explicitly says that sex is a major tenant of good health. It was also progressive of the ancient Ayurvedic scholars to have emphasized a healthy GI tract, with special attention paid to elimination of toxins.

Ayurvedic medicinal concepts revolve around universal interconnectedness, the body's constitution (*prakriti*) and life forces (*doshas*). As in Chinese medicine, Ayurvedic medicine teaches that all things in the universe (both living and nonliving) are connected, and every human being contains elements that can be found in the universe. If your mind and body are in harmony and your interaction with the universe is natural and wholesome, you will be well. Disease arises when a person is out of harmony with the universe—disruptions can be physical, emotional, spiritual, or any combination of these.

The body's *prakriti* (constitution) is defined as a person's overall health, likelihood of becoming imbalanced, and ability to resist illness and/or to recover from disease. *Prakriti* (your constitution) is your unique combination of physical and psychological characteristics and the way the body functions to maintain health. Your *prakriti* doesn't change over the course of your lifetime. Your *prakriti* is determined by how much of each basic element is intrinsic to you: space (*akasha*), air (*vayu*), fire (*agni*), water (*apu*), and earth (*prithvi*). The collection of your personal elements determines your *dosha*, or life force, which controls the activities of your body. The *doshas* are:

> **Vata:** Space and air. *Vata* controls movement and is responsible for basic body processes such as breathing, cell division, and circulation. *Vata* body areas are the large intestine, pelvis, bones, skin, ears, and thighs. If you have *vata* as your main *dosha* you're quick thinking, thin, and fast, but you're susceptible to anxiety, dry skin, and constipation.
>
> **Kapha:** Water and earth. *Kapha* is responsible for strength, immunity, and growth. *Kapha* body areas are the chest, lungs, and spinal fluid. If you have

kapha as your main *dosha* you're calm and have a solid body frame, but you're susceptible to diabetes, obesity, sinus congestion, and gallbladder problems.

Pitta: Fire and water. *Pitta* controls hormones and the digestive system. *Pitta* body areas are the small intestines, stomach, sweat glands, skin, blood, and eyes. If you have *pitta* as your primary *dosha*, like me, you have a fiery personality and oily skin, but you're susceptible to heart disease, stomach ulcers, inflammation, heartburn, and arthritis.

If you do get sick, Ayurvedic treatment is tailored to your individual constitution. Doctors of Ayurvedic medicine assume that their patients are going to be active participants because many treatments require changes in diet, lifestyle, and habits. Your doctor will first determine your primary *dosha*, cataloguing any imbalances by asking, observing, and checking your bodily output as well as speech, voice, and pulse. Ayurvedic treatment goals include eliminating impurities, reducing symptoms, strengthening resistance to disease, reducing worry, and increasing harmony in your life. Yoga, breathing exercise, meditation, massage, sunbathing, and changing your diet all help to reduce symptoms. Ayurvedic medicine also emphasizes mental nurturing and spiritual healing. Recommendations will include avoiding stressful situations that make you worry and using techniques that promote release of negative emotions, such as yoga, meditation, and massage.

Homeopathic Medicine

I'm new to the use of homeopathic medicine, but I find it exciting and am happy to know that there is another alternative to drugs. Homeopathy is based on three principles:

- Like cures like: Substances that cause certain symptoms are diluted and given to patients with those symptoms (comparable to how snakebite antivenom works).
- Minimal dosing: Medicines are prepared in extremely diluted forms.
- Single remedy: No matter how many symptoms you have, only one medicine is given and that is to address all of your symptoms.

Although homeopathy is the second most widely used system of medicine in the world, it's discounted by the scientific community as no more effective than a placebo (see antidepressants on page 91 and drugs on page 277 as examples of pharmaceuticals' efficacy). People are turning to homeopathy in droves because of the damage that pharmaceutical drugs have done to our collective health. Homeopathy has no side effects and can be used by infants and pregnant women. Although drugs are also given to infants and pregnant women, drugs have caused serious, fatal, and tragic side effects. Homeopathic medicines are natural, non-addictive, and holistic (addressing all symptoms). Like all medicines, homeopathy must be practiced by an enlightened doctor who is versed in this type of medicine.

When I notice a health issue, I don't rush to the nearest pharmacy. Rather, I investigate what I'm doing to cause the problem. Then I stop doing whatever it is I'm doing, and add whatever food, nutrients, or hormones that I need. If I'm sick or have a condition I want to address, I do the same, using Chinese, Ayurvedic, or homeopathic medicines whenever possible before turning to drugs.

So much of what is happening in commerce impacts our health in a negative way. Let's talk about our dangerously toxic world, as avoiding toxins is crucial to healing or maintaining health.

eight

Ultimate You Skill No. 7: Live a Detox Lifestyle

On May 5, 2010, a two-hundred-page document from scientists and medical experts on the President's Cancer Panel rocked the country by finally admitting that chemicals are killing us. They went so far as to say that three hundred contaminants, including industrial chemicals, consumer product ingredients, pesticides, and pollutants from burning fossil fuels, have been detected in umbilical cord blood of newborns. The report warned, "to a disturbing extent, babies are born 'pre-polluted.'" The report lamented that, "The American people—even before they are born—are bombarded continually with myriad combinations of these dangerous exposures." The scientists blamed weak laws, lax enforcement, fragmented authority, and existing regulatory presumptions that chemicals are safe. The panelists advised President Obama, "to use the power of your office to remove the carcinogens and other toxins from our food, water, and air that needlessly increase health care costs, cripple our nation's productivity, and devastate American lives."

The whole thing reminded me of the preposterous understating of common knowledge as when George Bush said, "Americans are addicted to oil." Even so, having mainstream acceptance does create a more conducive environment for change, so that much was good. But until such time as the government really does something to clean up the toxins in our food and environment, it's up to us to do something about the highly explosive, synergetic effects of the commingling toxins in our bodies.

What Toxins Do to You

We all have different toxic loads depending on accidental exposure, and/or whether or not we've intentionally endeavored to avoid toxins, or if life has just been a merry toxic free-for-all.

Sources of Toxins

Environment
Food (including packaging)
Medicine
Self- and home-care products

Poison overload interferes with vital organ and gland functions and damages your liver's ability to filter, break down, and eliminate toxic substances. Because many toxins are fat soluble, the chemicals that are too abundant to be eliminated migrate to the subcutaneous fat under your skin and remain there, smoldering, generating free radicals, and destroying mitochondria and DNA. These toxins create havoc by displacing nutritional minerals and enzymes that play crucial roles in biological functions. Prolonged toxic overload poisons cell membranes; causes genetic damage, endocrine problems (including reproductive issues), neurological disorders, and cancer. It can flip out your immune system, manifesting in allergies and sensitivities, escalating to extreme environmental sensitivities, severe autoimmune reactions, and adrenal burnout, and culminating in autoimmune conditions. The brain, which is 60 percent fat, also harbors toxins.

Get Educated About Toxins in the Environment

You may think that your toxic exposure isn't really that great because you eat organic foods and buy organic products. Unfortunately, the government, particularly the FDA, perpetuates the mentality that a little poison here and there won't hurt us. So even if we try very hard to avoid toxins, we are still going to be exposed through the environment. The FDA's ineptitude and corruption is another topic that I covered in depth in *Death by Supermarket*. For now, just know that the FDA isn't likely ever to protect the American people over the interests of corporations. This criminal protection of corporations has polluted our environment with more than eighty thousand chemicals to the point that even the government can't ignore it anymore (case in point, the President's Cancer Panel report). See page 261 for an appendix of environmental toxins.

Get Educated About Toxins in Food

See page 233 for toxins in factory-food products.

Get Educated About Toxins in Self-care Products

My grandma had her beauty tricks that were inexpensive and nontoxic. She used witch hazel to clean off her makeup and as a toner, and she deep conditioned her hair with mayonnaise. Years ago I gave up poisonous home care products. Cosmetics were another story. I avoided looking at the lists of chemical gobbledygook on the packaging for a very long time. But since I've urged people to purge their kitchens of factory-food products, I had to also sacrifice and toss all of my Lancôme and Chanel (except Chanel N°5, which is one of my "poisons").

Putting toxins on the skin, or breathing them is much more dangerous than ingesting toxins, because mouth enzymes can break some ingested toxins down and others can be processed by your liver (to some extent). People who use skin care products and wear cosmetics are absorbing five pounds of poisons per year through their skin. Throwing my favorite cosmetics in the trash was tough, but I did it. I now use witch hazel like my grandma, and I've found a lot of organic cosmetics to use that aren't going to infiltrate my organs with poisons. No animals have been tortured to test these products. You can avoid all of the toxins by using natural biodegradable, chemical-free, environmentally safe self- and home-care products that are kind to humans, animals, and the planet. See page 266 for an appendix of toxins in self-care products.

Get Educated About Toxins in Home-care Products

Toxic home-care products have been taboo in my personal environment for a very long time. In fact, when I turn on the TV I'm always aghast at the nice commercials for these poisonous products. Why can't we just open a window or burn a candle in the bathroom to eliminate odors rather than having a time-release blast of poisonous gas billow out every time we move a muscle? If it smells weird, like a rearview mirror deodorizing thingamabob or a chemically scented "essential oil" candle, it's not good to breathe—and furthermore it's not good for animals or the planet. See page 273 for an appendix of home and home-care toxins.

Get Educated About Toxins in Drugs, Protocols, and Procedures

Our system of medicine has gone way overboard in the prescribing of drugs. Children are not only born pre-polluted, but their own loving parents begin dumping drugs into their systems as soon as they are born until they reach adulthood. Adults are taking cocktails of OTCs for every little thing, and medicine cabinets across the land are cornucopias of prescription drugs. Elderly people are swallowing handfuls of pills every day. There is no reason for any of this. (Taking life-sustaining HIV cocktails is an entirely different subject.)

I once arrived at a summer gathering I had been invited to at the same time as an elderly woman with crinkly hair, swollen, veiny ankles, a puffy, heavily lined face, droopy eyelids. As soon as she spoke, I knew who she was, although I hadn't seen her in twenty years. The last time we met, she was a delightfully sexy, alluring, attractive, athletic woman. It was shocking, but I had an inkling just from looking at her, what had aged her. After the party, when I was washing dishes, I asked the host, who was a good friend of mine, about the woman. "I would venture to say that she takes a lot of drugs." My friend confirmed that she was a hypochondriac and took pills all day every day.

She's not the only person I know who has destroyed her or his appearance and health by taking too many drugs. I actually know quite a few people whose truly astonishing cocktail of daily drugs have changed them completely. And even if I don't know the person, I can spot a man across a crowded room and identify the pills he's on: antidepressants, statins, sleeping pills, beta blockers, antacids, and impotence pills. With women, I can tell if they are taking antidepressants, statins, sleeping pills, beta blockers, antacids, and osteoporosis pills. Like the woman at the party, their prematurely aged appearance, slack gray skin, thinning hair, edema, and other outward manifestations of aging are dead giveaways.

Medical interventions can indeed wage a full-on assault on your metabolism, with a breathtaking massacre of mitochondria, propelling you into accelerating aging. As much as I hate drugs, I do take them if unavoidable, but only extremely judiciously, and that is the way I wish doctors would prescribe them. I'm not suggesting anyone dump their prescriptions, nor am I criticizing anyone for taking drugs. I'm merely suggesting that you examine the amount of drugs you're taking or being urged to take, and question and even vociferously challenge any drug that's suggested or prescribed by your doctor. Sorry to say, but most doctors are prescription happy, and use that pad as the easy way to usher you to the door. My policy is to try natural healing methods first if possible, and to use drugs as a last resort. If you're already taking drugs, you may also want to ask your doctor if there are any that you can eliminate.

Another problem is that doctors today can go a little overboard on procedures, especially if that's how they make their income. Let me reiterate that I am not against medical procedures. But I do suggest you take extreme caution before you allow potentially dangerous medical procedures to be done to your body, and that you take immediate steps to alleviate any damage done to your body by doubling your efforts at living a detox lifestyle. And if you must spent time in a hospital, take your own food and water. See page 277 for an appendix of some toxins in drugs, protocols, and procedures.

The Detox Lifestyle

If you want to try to avoid illnesses resulting from toxic exposure, or even if you've been diagnosed with a disease, the best strategy is to be religiously dedicated to living a pristinely detox lifestyle, and allowing your body to either fight off disease or to heal naturally. A detox lifestyle is also an anti-inflammatory lifestyle. Chronic inflammation has been identified as the single mitigating factor in the development of accelerating aging/degenerative diseases.

I should warn you that your choice to live a detox/anti-inflammatory lifestyle is likely to be met with intense resistance, vociferous scorn, ridicule, sneers, and at the very least eye rolling. I've been subjected for a long time to the same treatment my grandmother endured from friends and strangers and doctors. As I write from the south of France, I'm getting the, "Oh là, là!" comments about my supplements. If it's not for my supplements, then it's for using BHRT, or eating my copious fat and cholesterol diet, or my many "strange" habits like running in front of sauntering smokers on city streets so I don't have to walk in the wake of their secondhand smoke. People have been irritated with me for refusing to drink city water, for turning down poisonous factory-food products, and for many other reasons. I'm accustomed to being the nut case and don't care what anyone thinks of me. If you're as committed as I am to fighting the Big Food, Big Diet, and Big Drug interests, then you have to take a stand.

Although detoxing is popular, I don't personally apply that approach to my life. The purpose of detoxing is to rapidly cleanse your system of toxins; it's something like spring cleaning. I don't do that, per se. Rather I eat and live in such a way to keep my toxic load as low as possible. I use chelation (explained shortly) from time to time, but I also drink cilantro and parsley juice every day and take sea algae supplements. There are times when we are exposed to toxins in factory-produced food, anesthesia, secondhand cigarette smoke, chemical exposure in third world travel, vaccinations, and so on. Going back to a detoxifying lifestyle will bring your body back into balance. I've never found it necessary to assault my body with detoxification, which can be harsh and draining on the system. Colon detoxes are harsh on the GI tract, which responds better to pampering.

The Basics of a Detox Lifestyle

Address inflammation.

Avoid all factory-produced foods (including animal products).

Avoid constipation.

Avoid obvious toxins in the environment, food, self- and home-care products.

Avoid toxins and carcinogens through drugs and medical protocols and procedures (when possible).

Avoid toxic fats (heat/chemical-processed and partially hydrogenated polyunsaturated vegetable oils).

Cut back or quit (with your doctor's supervision) prescription and OTC drugs.

Drink up to three cups of white tea every day (contains very little caffeine).

Drink detox teas that contain a combination of dandelion, burdock, alfalfa, red clover, slippery elm, golden seal, and silymarin (milk thistle).

Drink green veggie juice daily.

Drink plenty of purified water every day.

Eat enzymatic foods (see page 68).

Eat only good fats (see page 77).

Eat only real organic food, including humanely raised animal foods.

- Engage in any type of aerobic exercise for twenty to thirty minutes as often as possible to increase your heart rate to a moderate working level that makes you sweat a lot. If you are not used to vigorous exercise, walk at a fast pace.
- Get enough sun for vitamin D_3 if at all possible.
- Have chelation through IV or chelating capsules if blood tests show you have a high toxic load, and your enlightened doctor deems it safe for you.
- Increase your vigilance about your detox lifestyle when exposed to toxins.
- Sit in a sauna (preferably infrared), set at approximately 140°, for five to thirty minutes to eliminate contaminants through sweating.
- Take high-quality supplements, nutraceuticals, Chinese and Ayurvedic herbs, including niacin which releases toxins.
- Take probiotics daily until your GI issues are healed (not necessary to take indefinitely).

Chelating Heavy Metals

The presence of heavy metals in your system can cause weird symptoms that your doctor may shrug off or not know how to treat. Treating these symptoms before they go any further can ward off escalation into something more disastrous like a neurological disease or an autoimmune condition. So you really should not ignore any of these symptoms. If you are pooh-poohed by your doctor, find a more enlightened doctor.

Symptoms of Heavy Metal Toxicity

- Burning sensation on tongue
- Cold hands and feet
- Constipation
- Diarrhea
- Difficulty making simple decisions
- Facial (or other muscles) twitching
- Faulty memory
- Feeling bloated
- Feeling itchy
- Feeling out of breath
- Fluid retention
- Frequent urination at night
- Hair loss
- Headaches after eating
- Heartburn
- Insomnia

Irritability
Joint pain
Jumpiness/nervousness
Leg cramps
Metallic taste in mouth
Numbness and tingling in extremities
Ongoing depression
Sudden, unexplained anger/rage

Suicidal thoughts/attempts
Tachycardia
Tinnitus
Tremors or shakiness
Unexplained chest pain
Unexplained chronic fatigue
Unexplained rashes and/or skin irritation

Urine and hair analysis are noninvasive, inexpensive screening tests that will tell you if you have high levels of heavy metals. Once you know if you have high levels of heavy metals in your system, you can rid your body of heavy metals through chelation. A chelating agent is a compound that binds with heavy metals, pulls them from your tissue, and carries these toxins from your body via urine and stool. Ethylenediaminetetraacetic acid (EDTA) is the most common method of chelation. EDTA also pulls calcium deposits (plaque) out of arteries, and so it is an added benefit if you are at risk of a heart attack due to arterial build up.

The chelating agent, meso 2, 3-dimercaptosuccinic acid (DMSA), available under the brand name Chemet, can be taken in capsule form over a period of weeks. DMSA crosses the blood-brain barrier better than intravenous EDTA, so it very effectively reduces lead and mercury in the brain.

Chemet and EDTA are both prescription drugs that can only be obtained through a doctor. If you suspect you've been exposed or are suffering symptoms of heavy metal poisoning, seek the treatment of a physician who is trained and knowledgeable about toxins and chelation therapy. For more information on chelation therapy and physician referrals see the American College for the Advancement in Medicine: *acam.org*. NOTE: *Chelation can remove important nutrients so you should take a good quality multivitamin/mineral supplementation along with chelation.*

Natural Heavy Metal Chelators

Cilantro and parsley
Garlic
Chlorophyll

Magnesium malate or malic acid
N-acetyl-cysteine (NAC)
Spirulina and chlorella

Pick Your Poisons

When I say pick your poisons I'm not implying that the use of poisonous substances or food is okay in moderation. That's the FDA's stance (a little poison here and there). My position is to avoid all toxins as much as possible. As much as I can be fanatical, there are things in my life, like Chanel N°5, coloring my hair, going out to dinner occasionally, and drinking wine that I just don't want to give up. The point isn't to join a monastery, but to eat and live in such a way that you keep your toxic load as light as possible while providing rich nutrition to your brain and body—including bombarding your body with antioxidants—so you can enjoy the fruits of being healthy, sexy, and happy.

Think of your body as an ocean. You can either treat it to an oil spill, or you can flush, rinse, and nourish it with clean, revitalizing, refreshing liquids.

nine

Ultimate You Skill No. 8: Flush, Rinse, and Nourish

When I think of water, I think of the ocean, which covers 70 percent of the earth. Likewise, our bodies are 70 percent water. Our bodies need hydration every day because water is the principal constituent of all body fluids, is essential for proper metabolic functioning, and is necessary to flush toxins. There are a number of reasons why people don't drink enough water. One is that they would rather drink coffee or sodas. Some people don't want to weigh more when they get on the scale. A third common reason is that people simply don't want to run to the bathroom all day and night long. These are all self-defeating reasons. There are no redeemable qualities about coffee or soda; weight loss occurs more readily when the body is hydrated; and dehydration causes sluggish blood, which clogs microscopic vessels and leads to clotting (the definition of heart attack and stroke). Dehydration is a major cause of accelerated aging, so you want to stay hydrated.

In warm, humid weather, especially if you're exercising and sweating, it's extremely dangerous to drink too little water. A balanced diet of real, whole food will supply about 20 percent of your daily water requirements, then a good rule of thumb is to drink about one half of your weight in ounces of water every day. Bear in mind that your body can only assimilate eight ounces every fifteen minutes, so glugging an entire bottle isn't as efficient as drinking smaller portions. Keep in mind that drinking too much water can result in hyperhydration, which can actually be fatal. Drinking too much water leads to a condition known as hyponatremia, which indicates both diluted sodium and electrolytes. Electrolytes are minerals that are required by cells to regulate the electric charge across cell membranes. Hyponatremia behaviors resemble alcohol intoxication and can lead to seizures, coma, and ultimately death unless water intake is restricted and salt administered.

You also need to know what water not to drink.

Water Purification Systems

When I wanted to learn about water purification systems, I went to Ken Guoin, who has been involved in improving water quality for over thirty years. Ken told me, "The source water that is available to us today is the very same water that was placed here when the earth was formed millions of years ago. We're not getting any more and what's available is continuing to degrade." The fact that water scarcity is likely to be a major global issue in the very near future is frightening. But for now, we have an equally scary situation, as our city water supply is intentionally and inadvertently contaminated with arsenic, mercury, cadmium, fluoride, lead, aluminum, pharmaceutical compounds, herbicides, fungicides, industrial solvents (such as vinyl chloride, dioxin, benzene, acrylamide, and polychlorinated biphenyls), as well as disinfection by-products of the chlorination of water (DBPs), which are THMs (trihalomethanes) and HAA5s (haloacetic acids). As Ken said, "Nationwide, tap water is really good for only two things: putting out fires and watering our lawns." Bottled water is fraught with issues too. The bottled water industry is less regulated than our municipal water supplies. Ken calls it, "Free radicals in a bottle." Even if bottled water were clean, it sits all day in the delivery trucks baking in the sun, emitting xenohormones from the plastic into the water. In one year the United States produced over three billion empty discarded plastic bottles, which is something to think about. The very best solution is to install a purification system at home, and then carry your own water around in stainless steel containers.

Effective water purification systems aren't cheap, but if you consider the amount of money we all spend on bottled water, it adds up over the course of a year, or a lifetime. Since you can't live without water, and water is a primary source of toxins, a home system ends up being economical in the long run. The popular countertop water filtration systems may be the least expensive but they don't filter out all the toxins. All water purification systems, including countertop systems, use carbon water filters. The basic countertop carbon filter system removes chlorine and both inorganic and organic contaminants but is ineffective at removing fluoride, pharmaceuticals, and disinfection by-products of the chlorination of water. There's an enormous difference in the quality of the carbon or charcoal that is used in filters. Most inexpensive carbon filters are contaminated with aluminum and thus leach aluminum into the very water they filter. With all of this in mind, I have to discourage you from using these systems.

Coconut shell is the highest-quality carbon available and the one with the least amount of aluminum. When shopping for a countertop water filtration system, look for a filter made with acid-washed coconut shell carbon, as the acid wash process removes the aluminum in the carbon. But an even higher-grade filter is one that uses an acid-washed coconut shell filter and an additional copper and zinc filter. First of all, the additional filter increases the life of the carbon filter. This combined filter also has the ability to filter out nasty chlorine by-products and provide a bacteriostatic environment, which means it inhibits bacteria growth within the filter device itself. Ultimately this makes the water taste much better.

Reverse osmosis is considered the best system for overall water purification, as it combines a three-stage filtration system discussed above, as well as a microfiltration membrane. This system removes 95 to 99 percent of all contaminants from water (much more than the above described filter). However, in addition to removing contaminates, reverse osmosis also completely strips all minerals and trace minerals, leaving you with dead water. In times past humans drank water from wells, springs, brooks, and rivers that was rich in minerals and trace minerals. Minerals and trace minerals are essential to our body's operating systems as they regulate metabolic processes and help create enzymes, hormones, bones, tissues, teeth, and fluids.

Point-of-use water filtration systems, such as under the bathroom sink and in showers, provide extended health benefits. Because chlorine is vaporized when it comes out of the faucet, you end up breathing it when you wash and shower. Also, your body's largest organ is your skin, which is porous and absorbs toxins like chlorine. Toxins absorbed through your skin aren't broken down by mouth enzymes or filtered by your liver; instead these toxins go directly into your bloodstream and organs.

Ideally, systems—whether countertop, point-of-use, or whole house—should purify the water completely before passing it through a restructuring process to replace minerals. This system is now available. Please check my website for updates on all of these water purification systems.

Aside from city water, there are other drinks you should avoid:

Dead, Devitalized, Toxic Beverages

- City water
- Coffee
- Commercial beer
- Diet or regular sodas
- Energy drinks
- Enhanced water
- Juice (fruit is healthy but the juice is all sugar)
- Kool-Aid and other fake drinks
- Mixed alcoholic drinks
- Pasteurized and "ultra" pasteurized commercial milk and commercial "organic" brands like Horizon that are factory farmed

Healthy Beverages

- Coconut water and milk
- Green and white tea
- Herbal teas
- Mineral water
- Protein Smoothies
- Purified water
- Raw (live) beer
- Raw (live) milk
- Veggie juice
- Wine (organic)

Coconut Water

Coconut water is a natural, pure, nutritious energy drink. Coconut water hydrates and maintains the proper nourishment and fluid levels in your body. Coconut water is especially useful if you work out a lot, as it supplies electrolytes, calcium, potassium, and magnesium, which are lost during workouts.

Coconut Milk

The creamy milk that's pressed out of a freshly picked coconut is perfect for pouring over amaranth or steel cut oats in the morning. You can also use it in recipes in place of cow's milk. Coconut milk, an Ayurvedic therapy, has many of the same benefits as coconut water and oil. Coconut milk is anticarcinogenic, antimicrobial, antibacterial, and antiviral. The saturated fat in coconut milk contains lauric acid (also found in breast milk), which promotes brain development and bone health. See all the benefits of coconut on pages 47 and 48

Green and White Teas

Green tea is made from the leaves of Camellia sinesis. The leaves are minimally processed, so they are not oxidized. Regular green tea drinkers have lower risk of heart disease and certain cancers because of a compound called "catechins," and the tea is antiviral and antibacterial. Green tea extract induces thermogenesis (fat burning).

White tea is made of the bud and young leaves, which are sun or steam dried so the tea is also not oxidized. White tea has more antiviral and antibacterial qualities than green tea. It also contains anticancer catechins. White tea contains more of the relaxing, mood-enhancing amino acid theanine.

Green and white tea are lower in caffeine than black tea or coffee. However, green and black teas (even decaffeinated) contain high levels of fluoride so you're better off drinking white tea. CO_2 decaffination of tea is the safest and also preserves more of the flavor. If you are drinking decaf tea, buy organic.

Herbal Teas

Therapeutic herbal teas are delicious hot, but I like to make iced herbal teas and infuse them with citrus slices, melon, whole cloves, cinnamon sticks, and anything else that can impart flavor. See page 257 for an appendix of herbal teas.

Mineral Water

When I see people drinking sodas I wonder if they know they are drinking poison and are in denial, or if they really don't know. There are a lot of reasons why you should switch from soda to mineral water.

Hippocrates was among the first to preach the benefits of mineral water. Leonardo da Vinci was a big fan of the so-called "miraculous waters." I drink Pellegrino, though there are lots of good brands. So what's the difference between carbonated water and carbonated soft drinks? A lot.

95 percent of Americans each drink 56 gallons of soda per year. All sodas are made with city water, which has been treated with chlorine and fluoride that are known to kill cells and cause cancer. City water also contains trihalomethanes (by-products of the chlorination of water), lead, cadmium, and arsenic, which are all known carcinogens. Phosphoric acid is added to soda as a flavor enhancer and to inhibit the growth of mold and bacteria, which would multiply in sugary fluid. Phosphoric acid erodes tooth enamel and can interfere with the body's ability to use calcium, which can lead to osteoporosis. Phosphoric acid also neutralizes the hydrochloric acid in your stomach and interferes with digestion and absorption of nutrients.

Sodas also contain sugar, which feeds cancer cells and can contribute to high blood pressure, heart disease, diabetes, mood swings, depression, obesity, premature aging, and many more ailments. The health of our entire nation would take an immediate, dramatic upswing if sodas were eliminated and people switched to mineral water, or plain water.

While carbonated sodas are aerated with carbon dioxide gas, mineral water that comes from artesian wells passes through layers of minerals, including carbonates, and absorbs the carbon dioxide gas released by the carbonates. The result is a natural, delightfully delicious, effervescent mineral water. Mineral water is alkaline and helps the body maintain a homeostatic pH level in a world where we are bombarded with acidic insults—everything from secondhand smoke to fluoride in water (all chemicals and toxins are acidic, as is sugar).

Exercising is acidic because it produces lactic acid (the reason you feel stiff and sore after exercise). The alkaline bicarbonate in mineral water helps buffer that acidity—thus helping you recover from exercise by increasing the transport of lactic acid out of the muscles, reducing fatigue and improving athletic performance.

Epidemiological studies have linked drinking mineral water with lowered cardiovascular disease in various countries. And Hippocrates and Leonardo were right about mineral water improving digestion. The alkaline biocarbonate in mineral water prevents acid blood and bone leeching of calcium—so it is good for your bones!

Protein Smoothies

I don't drink smoothies because they don't fill me up. But I know a lot of people like the idea of grabbing a smoothie on the go instead of making breakfast. Protein powder is not real food; it's processed, and real, solid food is preferable. However, you could think of protein powder as a supplement, and so you could supplement your diet of real, solid food with protein smoothies from time to time. If I were going to drink protein drinks I would use organic free-range raw eggs as my protein source. Organic free-range eggs are not likely to be contaminated with salmonella, but I still must warn you that eating raw eggs can expose you to this deadly bacteria, so consume at your own risk. Raw egg whites contain inhibitors of the digestive enzyme trypsin, which are destroyed by the heat of cooking. Raw egg whites also prevent the absorption of the B vitamin biotin, so you'll have to factor that in if you use raw eggs. If you use powders, definitely avoid soy, egg (containing oxidized cholesterol), and most whey (also oxidized), and instead go for rice or cold-pressed whey.

The sea veggies (green algae) chlorella and spirulina can be added to smoothies. Use them together for maximum benefit. You can also find freeze-dried "green food" products that contain all-natural synergistically blended powders containing vitamins, minerals, trace minerals, enzymes, essential amino acids, and antioxidants. Green foods contain sea veggies as well as various herbs, fiber, bioflavonoid extracts (antioxidants), and probiotic cultures.

Essential fatty acid blends are formulated to provide a healthy daily dose of omega-3 and -6 oils. There are numerous healthy blends of EFAs at your health food store. If you're making power drinks, the easiest way to include good EFAs is to add one to three teaspoons to your power drink. People like to put bananas in protein smoothies, but consider that bananas are high carb and liquid carbs are already very high glycemic index, so I recommend berries.

Suggested Ingredients for Protein Smoothies

- Berries
- Blackstrap Molasses
- Coconut milk or coconut water
- Coconut oil (melted)
- Fermented honey
- Omega-3 oil
- Raw milk
- Raw organic, free-range eggs (or nonsoy protein powder such as whey, egg, or rice)
- Sea veggie (algae) powder
- Stevia
- Super green food

Raw (Live) Beer

Alcohol is derived from grain or fruit, which are carbs. Alcohol is toxic to cells and increases insulin levels, so drinking excessive alcohol accelerates aging. But I'm not a zealot, like I've said many times, and unless you are a recovering alcoholic or otherwise have a problem with alcohol there's no reason not to enjoy an occasional beer or glass of wine. Commercial beers are made with GMO ingredients, city water, and are pasteurized (heated to kill microorganisms), which kills life-giving enzymes. Unpasteurized "live" beer actually provides healthy enzymes. In fact, it is surprisingly nutritious food, as long as you don't drink a keg of it. Look for microbreweries that serve fresh, live beer on tap. You can take it home and it will last three days in the fridge, if you don't end up drinking it first.

Raw (Live) Milk

I had not had a glass of milk in ten years until my thyroid crash and my subsequent quest to be healthy again. At that point I wanted to know more about milk, so I read a lot about it. What I found really blew my mind. I learned that commercial milk products are a major contributing factor to the epidemic of disease, because they are the commingled product of thousands of diseased cows that have been bred to be milk machines. Factory-produced milk is tainted with everything the sorry cows are fed or injected with, from penicillin G and antimicrobial sulfonamides to antiworming agents and literally hundreds of drugs, including recombinant bovine growth hormone (rBGH), pesticide, herbicide, and GMO residues from feed, as well as aflatoxins, which are cancer-causing chemicals found in moldy grain.[31,32] If that isn't off-putting enough, because factory cows are fed an unnatural diet, their milk contains a high somatic cell count (SCC), which in simple terms means there's a lot of pus in factory milk.[33] Factory milk is sterilized through pasteurization, so it's dead pus, but still. The heat of pasteurization also kills good stuff like vitamins C, E, A, D_3 and B-complex; diminishes calcium and other minerals, making them harder to absorb; and reduces the digestibility and lessens the nutritional value of protein. Most important, the heat of pasteurization destroys the enzymes (see page 68 for more about enzymes).

On the other hand, real, whole, raw (unpasteurized) milk is one of the most dazzling of all living foods. It's such a complete food and so therapeutic, you could live on it if you had to. Whole, raw milk contains butterfat filled with vitamins A and D_3, which are necessary for the assimilation of calcium and protein. Natural vitamin D_3 prevents autoimmune diseases such as multiple sclerosis and rheumatoid arthritis in addition to osteoporosis. Natural vitamin D_3 is also linked to improvement in mood and relieving symptoms of depression. Butterfat is also the richest known source of conjugated linoleic acid (CLA), which reduces cancer and atherosclerosis risk, increases metabolic rate, and burns fat.[34]

Raw milk products also contain enzymes, without which life cannot be sustained. Because pasteurization kills enzymes, strain is put on the pancreas to produce the enzymes to digest it. Without natural enzymes in milk, lactose is indigestible for many people. Raw milk from a strictly grass-fed cow is also extremely helpful for people with gastrointestinal problems, even for people who think they are lactose intolerant because raw milk contains the lactase enzyme to help digest lactose. Most people with lactose intolerance got that way from drinking factory milk. Very few people are truly lactose intolerant.

Unfortunately raw milk is not legal in all states. If you can't obtain raw milk, there are many organic milk suppliers who operate humane dairies and pasture graze their cows, although all organic milk is pasteurized and many are ultra pasteurized (sterilized of enzymes as well as bad and good bacteria). You can find out if your state allows the sale of raw milk on realmilk.com and locate dairies on eatwild.com. In states that have outlawed raw milk sales, it's possible to purchase a share in a cow from which you are legally allowed to share in its milk production. I suggest looking at the standards found at rawusa.org.

Veggie Juice

Juicing veggies is a fabulous way to get a blast of instant nutrition. Why juice rather than eat veggies?

The nutrients in veggies are locked behind hard cellular walls. There are three ways to access these nutrients. One is to chew your veggies to mush in your mouth, but no one ever does that. Second, you can cook them but that will destroy some of the nutritional value. The best way to get your veggie nutrition is to juice nonstarchy veggies, which thoroughly breaks down the cellular walls.

Another reason to juice is that most people's digestive systems begin to weaken by the time they reach forty and nutrients aren't fully absorbed. Live liquid nutrients from juiced veggies contain enzymes that aid in the digestive process so that your body absorbs more of these vital nutrients.

When you consider that there are twelve thousand phytonutrients in one spinach leaf, you simply can't get this full spectrum of vitamins, minerals, enzymes, and nutrients in a supplement. It takes one to one and a half pounds of fresh veggies to make eight ounces of juice. If you drink fresh juice every day you're getting the phytonutrients of that many fresh vegetables.

Alkalinizing Benefits of Juicing

We live in an acidic world. Factory-food products, coffee, pharmaceuticals, sugar, secondhand smoke, fluoride in water, and all of the chemicals and other toxins we're exposed to are acidic.

The human body strives for a delicate pH balance. Maintenance of the delicate acid-base balance in the body is critical. The acid-base system is measured by what is known as the pH system. On a scale of 1 to 14, a measurement of 7 is absolute neutral. Water measures 7 on the pH scale, while a strong acid measures from 1 to 3, a moderate acid 4 to 5, and a mild acid 6 to 7. A strong alkali measures 12 to 14, a moderate alkali 9 to 11, and a mild alkali from 7 to 8. The human body strives to maintain a mildly alkaline state of approximately 7.4. This alkaline environment allows all the repair processes such as making new cells, membranes, tissues, enzymes, hormones, and neurotransmitters to take place. Normal metabolic processes, stress, toxins, acidic foods, beverages, and stimulants are acidic. In addition to providing your body with nutrients, drinking fresh juice helps your body maintain the homeostatic pH of your body.

Because many toxins are fat soluble, the heavier you are the more toxins you carry in your fat cells. Drinking juice causes these toxins to be released from cells back into your bloodstream where they are then eliminated. You may feel the effects of this blood toxicity the first few days you drink veggie juice with symptoms akin to a mild flu. After a few days, you will begin to experience an improvement in energy. From then on, you can see improvements in sleep, memory, concentration, vitality, skin and hair, some weight loss, fewer cravings for sugar, and, yes, less cellulite.

Select nonstarchy veggies of your choice. As you try different combinations, you'll find those that you prefer. If a certain veggie gives you a tummy ache, or you experience churning or gurgling in your GI tract, then either cut down on that veggie or try something else. The point is to enjoy the experience and to feel good all day as the result of flushing, rinsing, and nourishing your body with green juice. Avoid fruits in your juiced drinks, as fruit juice is pure sugar. Avoid carrots and beets, as they are high in sugar. Juice every part of the vegetable, including skins, rinds, seeds, and leafy tops.

It is ideal to drink your juice at room temperature within ten minutes after juicing. Some of the phytonutrients will oxidize and be lost after ten minutes. If you must store it, do so in a glass container in the freezer (leave room for expansion). Ideally you want to consume at least twelve servings of veggies per day in juice, which is about six cups of raw veggies.

To make fresh juice you will need a juicer. Please buy the blender version even if you have to scrimp and save for it. If you get the type of juicer that squirts out pulp you'll get so fed up cleaning all that mess that you'll be discouraged from blenderizing. The blender type is like a traditional blender only it has a very powerful motor so that the entire plant is pulverized. A regular blender can be used but it limits you to very soft veggies like mesculin salad and herbs or you can use denser veggies if you have the patience to chop them really fine. Still, if that's all you can afford, then definitely go for it. Add enough water and you can drink it all down.

Wine

Is wine a health food? Not exactly. But a glass of wine with dinner is a nice thing—and we're not zealots, remember? Of course, organic wine is the best. Nonorganic wine, especially California wines that are fertilized with boron-containing fertilizer, are contaminated with fluoride. Red wine contains a small amount of polyphenol (a plant compound) resveratrol, a cancer preventative agent that also improves cardiovascular health.[35]

Whether you're a man or a woman, and regardless of your age, being educated about hormone balance is going to give you an edge. Once you're educated, you can make your own decision whether to use bioidentical HRT when your hormones decline.

ten

Ultimate You Skill No. 9: Use Bioidentical Hormone Replacement if You Need It

If you have a desire to ignite a heated debate, forget religion and politics, and instead drop the subject of hormone replacement. The topic of hormone replacement is polarizing, and women generally fall into the anti or pro camps. I fall in with the pro-hormones group and consider bioidentical hormone replacement (BHRT) intrinsic to the *Healthy, Sexy, Happy* program. Hormone replacement is a complicated subject that many dense books have been written about. What you're going to read here is ultra simplified due to lack of page space.

You may be wondering why I would even consider using estrogen, when estrogen overkill damaged my thyroid. The fact is that I'm using estrogen as well as a full spectrum of hormones, and I intend to keep using them for the rest of my life. I could list them all for you, but I think it's best if you go into BHRT without any preconceived ideas of what is normal or optimal. I have numerous deficiencies that stem way back to my childhood sugar diet, through having been a teenage smoker, my high-stress lifestyle in the film industry in my thirties, my thyroid crash in my forties, and my ongoing demanding lifestyle as a writer and spokesperson for health! Every body lacking in hormones is deficient in a different way.

The reason I'm going to continue taking BHRT is that hormones are the chemical communication system on which every single metabolic process in your body depends. If one hormone falters, the rest falter, too, causing your entire system to go into an insidious but inexorable decline that propels you into accelerated aging. Eventually you're disabled by "age." I would very much like to see people become aware of the fact that we don't have to die a protracted death of "aging." We don't have to be stricken with diseases, incapacitated by drugs, crippled with pain, or lost in the oblivion of some neurological disease with nothing to look forward to but an appallingly impersonal hospital finale. (Again, because we're assaulted against our will by toxins, even the most health-minded, disciplined person can get sick. The purpose of this program, including BHRT, is to do everything we can to avoid that fate.)

I can't call BHRT a fountain of youth, but it is kind of miraculous. For the very first time in the history of humankind we can replace the missing hormones of our body's communication system in a fairly exact way and in so doing stay healthy and normal our entire lives. We don't have to nosedive into the abyss of aging. We can remain energetic, athletic, alert, sexy, and be as optimally healthy as we can be our entire lives. I'm not so delusional to think that BHRT will keep me young forever. We're all going to age and die. But it's how we age, and how we die that interests me. I would like to take care of business as usual until I die. And I would like for my death to be a celebratory experience, surrounded by loved ones in my own home. That's the way we were meant to leave this world. My program can help make that happen, but it's not going to be nearly as effective without incorporating BHRT when your hormones begin to decline.

For all the people who argue that BHRT is "unnatural," please tell me what's natural about having open-heart or brain surgery, being equipped with a colostomy bag, having chemo drugs shunted into your arteries, being irradiated, shooting insulin, or any of the other "normal" medical procedures or protocols?

Estrogen Dominance

My first hormone replacement experience was devastating, but that doesn't mean yours has to be. Doctors have gotten a lot more educated about hormone replacement, and they're a lot more cautious and individualizing in their prescriptions. BHRT is not cookie cutter. What happened to me was estrogen dominance. I was given way too much estrogen and, as I said, hormones are a balancing act. If one is too low or too high, the whole system is adversely affected.

The term "estrogen dominance" was coined by Dr. John Lee, a pioneer of progesterone replacement. He used it to describe a condition where there's not enough progesterone to balance the effects of estrogen in the body. Estrogen dominance is not just caused by overprescribing hormones. It is also the result of the absence of ovulation (pre-menses, perimenopause, menopause, pregnancy, the Pill, and ovarian dysfunction). And, although estrogen is a female sex hormone secreted by the ovaries (though men have some estrogen too), "estrogen mimickers" are now prevalent in our environment from chemicals (xenoestrogens) as well as from plants (phytoestrogens).

Estrogens are healthy, normal hormones in our communication systems. Environmental xenoestrogens are impostors that mimic the actions of estrogen and can alter hormonal activity in your body. Estrogen mimickers bind to estrogen receptors and disrupt endocrine functions. They are also linked to reproductive problems and cancer.

Sources of Xenoestrogens

- Antibacterial soaps and cleansers
- Artificial fragrances (air fresheners, perfumes, anything with artificial fragrance)
- Birth control pills and spermacide
- Car exhaust and indoor toxins (VOCs)
- Factory-food products
- Factory-raised meat and dairy
- Industrial pollution
- Paints, lacquers, solvents
- Pesticides, herbicides, insecticides
- Plastics (especially when heated)
- Self-care and home-care products
- Styrofoam cups

Sources of Phytoestrogens

- Isoflavones (found in high concentration in soybeans)
- Coumestans (found in alfalfa, clover, and other sprouts)
- Lignans (found mainly in flaxseed)

Symptoms and Conditions Associated with Estrogen Dominance

Acceleration of the aging process

Allergies, including asthma, hives, rashes, sinus congestion

Autoimmune disorders such as lupus erythematosis, thyroiditis, and possibly Sjoegren's disease

Breast cancer

Breast tenderness

Cervical dysplasia

Cold hands and feet (from thyroid dysfunction)

Copper excess

Decreased sex drive

Depression with anxiety or agitation

Dry eyes

Early onset of menstruation

Endometrial (uterine) cancer

Fat gain, especially around the abdomen, hips, thighs

Fatigue

Fibrocystic breasts

Foggy thinking

Gallbladder disease

Hair loss

Headaches

Hypoglycemia

Increased blood clotting (increasing risk of strokes)

Infertility

Insomnia

Irregular menstrual periods

Irritability

Magnesium deficiency

Memory loss

Mood swings

Osteoporosis

Polycystic ovaries

Premenopausal bone loss

Premenstrual syndrome

Prostate cancer

Sluggish metabolism

Thyroid dysfunction mimicking hypothyroidism

Uterine cancer

Uterine fibroids

Water retention, bloating

Zinc deficiency[36]

Estrogen Dominance and the Thyroid Gland

The hypothalamus in your brain tells your pituitary gland to release thyroid-releasing hormone (TRH). TRH releases thyroxine (T4), which then converts to triiodothyronine (T3). These hormones are necessary for the smooth functioning of metabolic processes. However, too much estrogen in the system results in excessive production of thyroid-binding globulin (TBG) by the liver. If the TBG levels are high it will bind to thyroid hormones, thus reducing the thyroid hormones available in your bloodstream. Although there are actually enough thyroid hormones in the blood, they can't be taken up by the body's cells as they are inactivated by TBG and can't be used by the cells for maintaining your body's metabolic processes. And like any other hormone imbalance, when one hormone goes missing, systems falter.

Because estrogen dominance leads to overproduction of TBG and the inactivation of thyroid hormones, it can lead to thyroid problems. Even if blood tests reveal normal levels of thyroid hormones in such situations, you may still suffer from classic low thyroid symptoms. A diagnosis of hypothyroidism should always factor in all of your physical symptoms.

Diagnosing Hypothyroidism

The body expects a certain amount of thyroid hormone. If thyroid hormone is in short supply, the pituitary will ramp up the production of thyroid stimulating hormone (TSH) in an attempt to entice the thyroid to produce more hormone. A constant assault of TSH may cause the thyroid gland to grow, forming a goiter. My thyroid was enlarged by the time I was finally diagnosed.

Blood tests typically measure levels of the main thyroid hormone T4 and TSH. If your thyroid is underactive, the blood level of T4 will be low, and TSH level will be high. However, pituitary failure can result in low TSH levels. Since the pituitary isn't making enough TSH, then the thyroid will never make enough T4. The question is what is too low and what is too high? If your blood levels seem to be in normal ranges, then you need to examine your symptoms to see if you really do have a low-functioning thyroid. It's likely that millions of people with mild to moderate hypothyroidism have not been diagnosed. The important thing for you is to find a doctor who doesn't stop investigating until you feel better—which will likely mean that you will be put on thyroid replacement.

Hypothyroid Symptoms

Abnormal menstrual cycles	Coarse, dry hair
Allergies worsen or appear	Cold intolerance
Brittle, ridged nails	Constipation

Depression (onset or worsening)	Irritability
	Memory loss
Dry, rough, pale skin	Muscle cramps, frequent muscle aches
Fatigue	
General weakness	No sex drive
Hair loss	Puffy face, extremities
Heavy menstruation	Retaining water
Herpes flare-ups, boils, acne	Weakness
Hoarse voice	Weight gain and/or difficulty losing weight
Infertility	

Many doctors prescribe synthetic thyroid hormones, and I've had unenlightened doctors tell me that my doctor is a quack because he put me on WesThroid, a bio identical combination of T3 and T4. I am not unfamiliar with the synthetic stuff, having taken Cytomel, which replaces T3. I experienced free-floating anxiety for a couple of years until I felt like I was going crazy. When I stopped the Cytomel, the anxiety vanished.

Even on bioidentical thyroid replacement, too low of a dose will not alleviate your symptoms; too high a dose can cause nervousness, heart palpitations, insomnia, and increased calcium loss from bone, increasing the risk of osteoporosis. So, again, balance is key.

Drug Hormones

When the subject of hormones is discussed in the media, drugs like Premarin are referred to as "hormone replacement." Let's be clear about this, because this so-called hormone is actually conjugated equine estrogen that's extracted from the urine of pregnant mares and combined with drugs. Premarin and other drug hormones are not FDA approved as "hormone replacement," but are FDA approved to prevent bone loss and to alleviate hot flashes.

When I was deciding whether to continue on BHRT, I never considered using an equine hormone/drug. There was no rational explanation to put drugs into my system, when I could use a hormone that matched what my body made. Let's look at some of these drug-hormones.

Premarin

I began BHRT five years before the controversy over hormone replacement was launched. In July 2000, the National Institutes of Health Women's Health Initiative (WHI), a taxpayer-funded study, was dramatically halted with much media fanfare. This study involved thousands of women on Premarin and a mixture of Premarin and Provera, (medroxyprogesterone acetate, which is synthetic progesterone).

I read about the study in the *New York Times*, but I didn't find it relevant to me. I'd already done quite of bit of analysis on the (actually kind of zany) world of medical studies. It's such a dramatic economic- and ego-biased method of investigation that you really can't take it too seriously. Invariably when you pick a study apart, flaws emerge. Aside from that, the WHI study was examining a drug-horse-hormone that I would not ever consider putting into my body.

In 1942, shortly after the "discovery" of hormones, Premarin was marketed for menopause. By 1972, Premarin was certified by the FDA as effective for "treating the symptoms of menopause," and in 1986, the FDA approved Premarin for treatment of osteoporosis. By 2000, almost fourteen million women were on these drugs: eight million who had undergone hysterectomies were on synthetic estrogen replacement therapy, mostly Premarin, and another six million who had not undergone hysterectomies were taking a combination of Premarin with an added synthetic progesterone, typically Prempro.

The initial WHI data revealed a high incidence of breast cancer, heart disease, blood clots, and stroke. Although the risks were less than one-tenth of 1 percent, researchers felt that the risks outweighed the drugs' benefits, which included a small decrease in hip fractures and a decrease in cases of colorectal cancer.

Millions of women quit taking these drugs and bottomed out with menopausal symptoms. But the drug companies didn't suffer one bit. They've made up their losses from the defectors with millions of more prescriptions for antidepressants—even though depression is not these women's problem. Other women have remained on these drugs, living in fear.

I once sat at lunch in a Wisconsin restaurant with a group of women and innocently began telling them that Premarin isn't good for human women because it's an equine, not human, estrogen and doesn't match the chemical composition of human estrogen. Slowly—from the pinched expressions on some of their faces—it occurred to me to shut up. These women were on Premarin and did not want to hear any negativity from me.

Even if Premarin were good for women, I would be against it because of animal cruelty. Premarin is derived from the urine of pregnant mares. These horses are confined to narrow tie stalls where they are forced to stand with catheters inserted into their bladders. Just because they're animals doesn't mean that having a catheter in the bladder doesn't hurt or cause infections. The stalls are too narrow to allow the mares to lie down or turn. The chronic lack of exercise can cause swelling of the legs, breakdown of the hoof structure, and colic. A mare may be kept pregnant for production for eight to nine years. Foals and older mares no longer able to conceive are slaughtered.

The side effects of horse urine–drug–hormones are well documented, and I could have easily provided examples for the women. But it would have been difficult to convince them that BHRT works very well, since there have been only a few studies done on it. Natural substances cannot be patented, so in order to receive a patent, drug companies must chemically alter natural substances—even if they work just beautifully and are the best and healthiest choice of treatment. The drug companies are concerned with profits, not necessarily with what works best. If a drug company were to fund expensive research on a natural substance, such as bioidentical hormones, they would not be able to patent it, and when these hormones went on the market, any other company could also sell them.

Side Effects of Premarin

- Blood clots
- Breast tenderness
- Depression, anxiety
- DNA damage that is cancer causing
- Estrogen dominance
- Eye problems
- Fluid retention, edema, weight gain, increased fat
- Gall bladder disease
- Glucose intolerance, insulin resistance
- Headache, migraine
- Heavy menstrual bleeding, cramping
- High blood pressure
- Increased blood clotting
- Increased risk of endometrial and breast cancer
- Leg cramps
- Loss of scalp hair, growth of facial and body hair
- Nausea, vomiting, cramping, bloating
- Pancreatitis
- Stimulates growth of fibroids
- Worsens endometriosis

Unlike BHRT, Premarin is prescribed in standard dosages and not individualized, which is also problematic. Some women are simply taking too much horse estrogen. Premarin can do what happened to me—cause an excessive increase in thyroid-binding globulin (TBG), which blocks thyroid hormone function. Some women are taking too little. All hormones (even if they *are* wrong) should be in balance with your system. In other words, hormones should be prescribed in physiological amounts. This means an amount that would be normal for your body to produce on its own. Pharmacological doses—above what a human body would normally make on its own—could have unknown side effects that may not show up for a decade or two.

If you are on Premarin and stop, it takes eight weeks for it to clear your body. BHRT is completely metabolized in six to twelve hours.

The major (often overlooked) issue with synthetic hormone replacement is that only two hormones are addressed—all the rest of the hormone levels are completely ignored, unless there is a very clear reason (like having the thyroid surgically removed) for replacing any other hormones. This causes further imbalances of the entire endocrine system, with a cascade of other metabolic imbalances.

The bottom line is that estrogen receptors do not operate as efficiently with horse-estrogen-drugs as they do with bioidentical human female estrogen. Also all drugs have side effects, and they all damage mitochondria and DNA. So it makes logical sense that horse-drug-hormones are going to cause problems.

I'm really going to go out on the very edge of a limb when I say that even bad hormones (like equine-drug hormones) appear to be better than none. If you compare older women on Premarin or Prempro to older women on nothing, the synthetic horse urine group seems to have aged much better on the outside. And the outside is a direct barometer to what is going on inside. I think that really says a lot for the body's *extreme desire to be hormonally balanced.*

Progestins

Progestins are chemical or drug imposters of progesterone, female steroid sex hormones, that come with side effects. Most progestins are made by taking natural progesterone and altering the chemical structure so that drug companies can patent it. Another type of progestin is made by altering a synthetic testosterone.

Progestins suppress the natural production of progesterone. They disrupt the brain's adrenal pathways, which can cause both immediate and/or insidious undermining of both adrenal and sex hormone function.

Known Side Effects of Progestins

- Acne
- Angina
- Anxiety, nervousness
- Breast tenderness
- Coronary artery spasm
- Depression
- Edema
- Facial hair growth
- Fatigue, which can develop into chronic fatigue
- Fluid retention
- Glucose intolerance (promotes insulin resistance)
- Hair loss on scalp
- Heart palpitations
- Insomnia
- Menstrual irregularities, spotting
- Migraine
- Nausea
- Skin rashes
- Weight gain

Side Effects Thought to Be Associated with Progestins

- Breast tenderness
- Coronary artery spasm, leading to heart attacks
- Gall bladder disease
- Increased risk of birth defects when taking the Pill
- Liver disease
- Pulmonary embolism
- Stroke
- Sudden or partial loss of vision

Did you know that cardiovascular disease is the number one cause of death in postmenopausal women? Premarin has been routinely prescribed for postmenopausal heart protection based on the assumption that estrogen protected women against heart disease. The WHI, which studied women on Premarin and sometimes Provera, found that these two prescriptions in combination *did not* protect against heart attack or other cardiovascular problems. The reason is that although Premarin alone raised "good" HDLs, when Provera was added the HDLs did not increase.

It's common knowledge to enlightened hormone doctors that estrogen must be "opposed" by progesterone for a portion of the monthly cycle, which is why women on Premarin are also prescribed Provera. In fact, all women should take progesterone to oppose estrogen for a portion of their monthly cycle, whether or not they have had hysterectomies, as the breasts also have estrogen receptors. However, it's not the conventional standard of care to prescribe Provera to women who have had hysterectomies.

The Pill

I'd be remiss if I didn't visit the Pill. I hate to disparage the Pill since I came of age during the time of the Pill and it was the coolest, most liberating thing to come on the scene for women ever. I have fond memories of being an eighteen-year-old hitchhiker in India, where I bought the Pill in pharmacies without a prescription, feeling grown up, confident, and hip. It would be years later that I understood that the Pill was behind the twenty pounds that I picked up between leaving high school in Japan and arriving in Goa, India. That was then, and this is now, and we know a lot more, including the fattening part.

Today's Pill comes in a variety of mixtures of low-dose estrogen and progestin, or sometimes just progestin. Besides preventing pregnancy, the Pill is prescribed for PMS and other hormonal problems to regulate the cycle. The Pill works by tricking the endocrine system and preventing the normal female cycle and ovulation from occurring. When you think about it logically, the idea of tricking the exquisitely delicate and complex endocrine system is counterintuitive. One would think that physicians sworn to "first do no harm" would have no part in something so bad for women.

Drug companies preying on young, innocent, gullible women is just wrong. The ads for birth control are among the sexiest most alluring on TV—total *Sex in the City*. Birth control is a fabulous example of how the drug industry can appear to be altruistic and caring. The truth is that the best birth control they can come up with is messing up young women's endocrine systems. And when a woman is in trouble as a result, the drug industry stands to profit further.

The Pill can precipitate chronic fatigue syndrome and/or fibromyalgia. It depletes the body of folic acid, B_{12}, B_6, and other B-complex vitamins, magnesium, manganese, zinc, and vitamin A. Babies born to women taking the Pill who happen to get pregnant have higher incidence of birth defects and birthmarks. The Pill causes copper imbalances, leading to copper toxicity—headaches, insomnia, depression, and PMS—which is often dismissed or attributed to what I call the "hysterical female syndrome," as many doctors automatically package these types of complaints into this neat little definition. The Pill can decrease testosterone levels and lead to low sex drive and lack of pleasure during sex. The Pill also contributes to estrogen dominance, thus you're at risk for all the symptoms listed above, including adrenal imbalances. After stopping the pill, it can take months to reestablish a normal cycle.

Risks Associated with the Pill

- Acne
- Antianxiety, antidepressant, sleeping pill usage
- Blood clots
- Cervical dysplasia, ovarian cysts, infertility
- Gall bladder problems
- Hair loss
- Headaches, migraines
- Heart attack
- High blood pressure
- Immune dysfunction, autoimmune diseases
- Loss of libido
- Mental and emotional side effects
- Other endocrine disorders
- Ovarian, breast, and uterine cancer
- Stroke
- Thyroid and liver problems and cancer

Condoms are hit and miss in terms of serious birth control, and in addition they have their own toxic issues (see appendix on page 266) but they are definitely a "pick your poison" in this world of STDs. There's now a nonhormonal intrauterine device (IUD) in the United States, marketed under the brand name ParaGard. An IUD is a small device that's inserted into a woman's uterus to prevent pregnancy. This type of IUD releases copper, which causes the uterus to become inhospitable to sperm, and can continuously work effectively for up to ten years. Women using this IUD may experience certain side effects, such as longer and heavier periods.

Sterilization surgeries are another alternative if you have all the children you want (or don't desire to have children). Tubal ligation for women and vasectomies for men are two examples.

Bioidentical Hormone Replacement

Bioidentical hormone replacement balances your endocrine system so that your body has the best fighting chance of combating accelerated aging, disease, and that awful death described earlier. Our medical system hasn't embraced BHRT and has for the most part rejected prevention and natural healing methods. Instead our medical system has become a business that focuses on treating disease once it occurs with drugs, surgeries, and procedures. This system has bogged doctors down with insurance bureaucracy, so they have no time to analyze the voluminous data from research that would in many cases support prevention and natural healing methods. Often doctors' only sources of new information are visiting pharmaceutical reps, the seductive ex-cheerleaders, prom queens, and jocks hired by drug companies to sell new drugs to doctors. Sloppy science and tunnel vision is also funneled into the medical community via the Food and Drug Administration, an incompetent and corrupt agency that's fueled by payoffs and cronyism.

There's a symbiotic relationship between Big Food, Big Diet, and Big Drug companies, a fun example of which is the selling of pink M&Ms for breast cancer research. M&Ms contain cancer-fertilizing high-fructose corn syrup, as well as petroleum-based dyes and other mitochondria-killing chemicals that actually contribute to breast cancer. This is a classic illustration of how the drug companies present themselves as altruistic. Let's all go out on breast cancer walks and eat breast cancer causing M&Ms while we funnel research money into companies that already have plenty of money to do their own research!

My goal throughout this entire book is to inspire women and men to seek out the truth. So far I have not seen the truth presented by pharmaceutical companies—and I give plenty of examples in *Death by Supermarket*. If you're interested in BHRT, you need to find an enlightened doctor who, through personal curiosity and the desire to help people, has made a point of learning beyond medical school. One such enlightened doctor is David Allen, M.D., an expert in bioidentical hormone replacement who told me, "When I was first thinking about prescribing hormones thirty-five years ago, I looked at the two alternatives, drug-hormones and natural hormones that matched the chemical composition of our body's own hormones. There was no question that I would prescribe natural hormones."

Hormone replacement is not experimental. Hormone replacement has been going on for thousands of years through the eating of animals' sex organs. Ancient practitioners of Chinese medicine collected the hormone-rich urine of adolescent boys and girls, dehydrated it, and used it to treat menopausal women and andropausal men (the lucky and spoiled emperors and empresses of the court).[37] To date, hundreds of thousands of clinical studies have been done on hormone replacement, and in the past thirty years, millions of women have benefited from the use of BHRT. Today, there is an ongoing fight: on one side, the prescribers, compounding pharmacists, and users of BHRT and on the other side, Wyeth, the company that makes Premarin and PremPro, the synthetic hormones found to cause heart disease, strokes, and cancer. Wyeth has launched a legal, lobbying, and PR campaign to malign BHRT and influence Congress to ban it (and eliminate their competition). It's extremely telling that Wyeth has a product containing bioidentical estriol, which it promotes heavily in Europe. Apparently American women don't seem to deserve real hormones, but European women do. Perhaps Wyeth understands that European women are a lot less likely to buy into putting horse pee drug hormones into their systems.[38]

BHRTs are made from plants and tweaked in laboratories to be exact matches of human hormones. They're healthy only when taken to replace the amount you cannot produce in your body and in doses that maintain normal blood and saliva levels. Hormone imbalances can cause serious health problems, as I experienced. Hormones have complicated pathways from their original production and through conversions into other hormones and uses in the body. Because it's an extremely complicated science, if you take hormones, it's essential to be monitored by an enlightened health practitioner who is knowledgeable and stays up to date in bioidentical hormone replacement therapy.

It's not possible to write about every single hormone in the endocrine system here, as there are more than one hundred. Following is a summary of just a few of the hormones replaced today with BHRT.

Estrogen

Our life expectancy has gone up, and so now we're expected to live a long, long time in a state of accelerated aging, with sex as a distant memory. That to me isn't living. And what's really alarming is that girls in their teens and early twenties are experiencing symptoms of low estrogen. Intensive exercise, eating disorders, stress, worry, and sugar are all factors that can result in low estrogen.

Low Estrogen Symptoms

Aches and pains (joints, muscles, tendons)	Bad taste in mouth, foul breath
Adult acne	Balding
Alzheimer's	Breast pain

- Burning tongue, roof of mouth
- Changes in body odor
- Cravings (sugar/carbs)
- Crow's feet
- Depression
- Difficulty concentrating, disorientation, brain fog
- Dizziness, light-headedness, episodes of losing your balance
- Electric shock sensation under the skin and in your head
- Exacerbation of any existing conditions
- Facial hair
- Fatigue
- Fibroids
- Fine lines around mouth (smoker lips)
- Fingernails are softer, crack or break easier
- Free-floating anxiety (dread, apprehension, doom)
- GI distress (tummy aches, gas w/pain, nausea)
- Gum problems, increased bleeding
- Hair loss or thinning on head, pubic area, or whole body
- Heart disease
- Hot flashes, night sweats and/or cold flashes, clammy feeling
- Incontinence (or going too often)
- Increase or decrease of headaches
- Increased allergies
- Increased tension in muscles
- Infertility
- Irregular heart beat
- Irregular periods
- Itchy, crawly skin
- Low sex drive
- Memory issues
- Mood swings, sudden outbursts, and tears
- Osteoarthritis, osteoporosis
- Painful sex
- Prolapsed uterus and bladder
- Recurrent bladder infections
- Sagging breasts
- Sudden onset of bloat
- Tingling in extremities
- Tinnitus
- Trouble sleeping (waking, not getting to sleep, waking too early)
- Uncharacteristic crankiness, bitchiness
- Unsettling memory lapses
- Vaginal dryness, itching, atrophy
- Weight gain, especially around belly, hips, butt

The argument against using estrogen always seems to go back to the WHI study, which showed an increase of breast cancer, coronary heart disease, and strokes in women on PremPro. What most people don't realize is that the women who took Premarin without the progesterone drug Provera had no increase at all in breast cancer. These women had 61 percent less plaquing in their arteries than the placebo group. Regarding the risk of clotting (strokes and heart attacks) with Premarin, and especially with Premarin and Provera together, subsequent research demonstrated that when bioidentical estrogen is used transdermally (applied to the skin) rather than taken as a pill (which forces the estrogen through the liver), there is no incidence of clotting.

We've already seen what happens when estrogen is too low or too high. But what about when it's nice and balanced? In that case estrogen reduces the risk of developing osteoporosis or colon cancer and alleviates the symptoms of menopause. Other benefits include youthful-looking skin, restored sex life, a keener mind, and a lower risk of developing Alzheimer's. Estrogen is important for brain health and is a natural antidepressant. It helps in the production of tryptophan, which converts to serotonin, a happy neurotransmitter. Estrogen also increases the sensitivity of serotonin receptors. In addition to keeping your bones strong, estrogen also maintains collagen, the fibrous protein that maintains that nice plump layer of support under your skin. Estrogen keeps your vagina lubricated and your genital tissue from aging, and it prevents your breasts from sagging and keeps you sexy and primed.

The three estrogens are estrone, estradiol, and estriol. Estrone is the least abundant of the three estrogens, estriol is the second most abundant, and estradiol is the most dominant of the three estrogens.

There are proponents of very high-dose estrogen replacement, which is an attempt to bring a woman's estrogen levels to the level of a twenty-five-year-old. I personally don't support this approach if you're not twenty-five. If you are, then it makes sense—and like I said, there are girls in their twenties with low estrogen. For older women, if estrogen levels are that high, then every other single hormone in the body would also have to be brought to that same level to match.

You need to be on an individualized dose of estrogen. It took me a long time to find a doctor who understood that regardless of what my blood levels looked like on paper, if I didn't feel good and still had symptoms of imbalanced estrogen, then my symptoms trumped the labs. I have often told doctors, "The best dose for me is one that would be appropriate for a two-ounce mouse." Since getting on low-dose, highly absorbable, transdermal Bi-Est, which is compounded for me, I've felt in balance.

A balanced diet with a lot of protein and saturated fat can also increase estrogen production.

Progesterone

The menstrual cycle is regulated by hormones. The estrogen level increases to stimulate the ovarian follicles. Under the influence of several hormones, a follicle grows and forms the egg. As the follicle matures, it releases the most powerful estrogen, called estradiol. The matured follicle ruptures, releasing the egg, which then forms endocrine tissue called the corpus luteum. The corpus luteum produces progesterone, which is essential to prepare the uterus to receive the fertilized egg, maintaining the uterus for pregnancy, and counterbalancing the side effects of too much estrogen. In the second half of the menstrual cycle after ovulation, if the egg isn't fertilized, menstruation occurs.

When the ovaries stop producing eggs, progesterone plummets. Many young women suffer from low progesterone due to lack of ovulation, and older women suffer from lack of progesterone when their ovarian function declines. Progesterone deficiency and estrogen excess have many symptoms in common.

Causes of Low Progesterone

Drugs	Insulin resistance
Estrogen dominance	Not exercising
Factory-food products (refined grains/sugar)	Unrelenting stress

Symptoms of Low Progesterone

Accelerated aging	Autoimmune disorders
Allergy symptoms	Backache
Anxiety, nerves, irrational fear	Balding (top of head)
	Belly is tender to touch
Arthritis	Bloating

Blood clots with period
Body hair
Breast cancer
Breast tenderness
Brittle nails
Brown spots on the back of the hands
Cervical dysplasia
Cold hands and feet
Constipation
Copper excess
Cracked heels
Cramps
Cravings, binges, eating disorders
Cystitis
Dark circles under eyes
Depression, anxiety, agitation
Dry eyes
Early onset of menstruation
Endometrial (uterine) cancer
Enlarged and tender breasts
Excessive and heavy periods
Fat around hips, butt, belly
Fatigue
Fibrocystic breasts
Fibromyalgia
Foggy brain
Gallbladder disease
Hair loss
Headaches
Hot flashes and night sweats
Hypoglycemia
Increased blood clotting (increasing risk of strokes)
Increased sensitivity to pain
Inefficient metabolism
Infertility
Insomnia
Irregular periods
Irritability
Low blood sugar
Magnesium deficiency
Memory loss
Migraines
Miscarriages
Mood swings
Osteoporosis
Panic attacks
Polycystic ovaries
Postnatal depression
Premenopausal bone loss
Premenstrual syndrome
Prostate cancer
Sex drive tanks
Swelling of feet and ankles
Swollen and reddish face
Tense muscles
Thyroid dysfunction
Uterine cancer
Uterine fibroids
Vaginal dryness
Varicose veins
Water retention
Weight gain

Many of these symptoms are fixable with progesterone. And even though progesterone is obtainable over the counter, it's not a good thing at all to self-prescribe hormones. You need to see your doctor and have your levels tested. Self-prescribing hormones is a sure way to imbalance the rest of your hormones.

Real progesterone doesn't have any of the side effects of progestins. For example, one of progesterone's important functions is to protect and maintain pregnancy, while progestins are contraindicated in pregnancy because of the risk of birth defects.

Pregnenolone

It's important to note that cholesterol is the mother of all hormones. A cholesterol rich diet is the best way to ensure that your body has the building blocks for hormone production. The first hormone made from cholesterol is pregnenolone, which is the precursor to DHEA, testosterone, estrogens, and cortisol. It's produced by the adrenals and exists in high concentrations in the brain. Because pregnenolone is made inside the cells' mitochondria, if you've trashed your mitochondria, your pregnenolone levels will decline.

Because pregneolone is the precursor to other hormones, if it's low, other hormones will likely be imbalanced as well. Too much of pregnenolone over long periods of time can overload the liver, so again, take this hormone under the direction of a qualified health practitioner.

Symptoms of Low Pregnenolone

- Copious, light-colored urine
- Cravings for salt
- Difficulty coping with stress
- Dry skin
- Feeling drained
- Flabby muscles
- General adrenal insufficiency
- Joint pain
- Loss of pubic and underarm hair
- Low blood pressure
- Poor color vision
- Poor memory
- Ridged, split nails

What Pregnenolone Does

- Buffers stress
- Enhances memory
- Improves energy levels
- Improves mood
- Lessen arthritis and rheumatoid inflammation
- Promotes myelin formation during nerve regeneration (assists in the treatment of multiple sclerosis)
- Reduces allergic reactions
- Restores hair and nails

NOTE: *Pregnenolone replacement is contraindicated in people with a history of seizures.*

Human Chorionic Gonadotropin

Human Chorionic Gonadotropin (HCG) can be used to stimulate testicles to produce testosterone. It's often used in younger men to increase testosterone. It can be used with men on testosterone therapy to prevent testicular atrophy. (When the testicles are not called on to produce testosterone, they can shrink.)

Testosterone

When moving out of the ranch in Santa Barbara where I lived for seven years, a crew of laborers came to help. At one point, I got the attention of a man who was about my size and asked him to get some guys to pack up the teak patio table. It was a table that I could barely nudge, much less lift. He effortlessly picked up the table, slung it onto one shoulder and walked away. I thought, *That's testosterone.*

Symptoms of Low Testosterone in Men and Women

- Bad moods, grouchiness
- Decrease in muscle mass (strength and endurance, both men and women)
- Fat gut
- "Fat" breasts (men)
- Gray hair
- Hot flashes and night sweats
- Less confidence in general, and feeling of "is that all there is?"

- Constantly fatigued—fall asleep after dinner or while watching TV
- Decreased energy, both men and women
- Decreased work performance
- Less athletic prowess
- Less *joie de vivre*
- Limp erections
- Lost height
- Sex drive plummets, both men and women
- Sparse beard
- Wrinkled, slack face

Bodybuilders, long-distance runners, cyclists, and other athletes have abused anabolic steroids to gain competitive advantage and improve their physical appearance by getting ripped/bulked up. Anabolic steroids are a group of synthetic steroid hormones that mimic testosterone and are used to simulate muscle and bone growth. The side effects of anabolic steroids are sterility, stunted growth in teenagers (caused by the closing over of growth plates in long bones), aggression, acne, irreversible connective tissue injury, and masculinization in women. Women run the risk of growing beards that do not go away after discontinuing steroids. Bioidentical testosterone is prescribed in physiologic doses (as it would be if made by your body under normal conditions). There's a huge difference between a physiologic replacement dose of testosterone and a pharmacologic dose of steroids.

Testosterone replacement for men reverses the problems listed above. The main risks are prostate hypertrophy (enlargement), balding, and excessive aggression. Men on testosterone need to have regular prostate checks and regular prostate-specific antigen (PSA) blood tests to screen for prostate cancer. Another danger is that testosterone can convert to estrogen. Estrogen levels should always be tested in men on testosterone.

Testosterone is a very interesting hormone for women. The right dose of testosterone can foster feelings of well-being and reduced levels of anxiety and depression.[39] For women, the proper dose of testosterone is also an aphrodisiac. But I want to remind you that testosterone must be prescribed with caution. Too much testosterone replacement in women can cause permanent hair growth on the face, balding, and anxiety. Everyone is different, but make sure you are aware of the risks going in if you're a woman.

Adrenal Hormones

Way back in the Preface I said that the three major factors of health and healing were brain, GI tract, and adrenal function. Adrenal hormone balance is so intrinsic to good health and well-being that the entire *Healthy, Sexy, Happy* program revolves around adrenal health. To learn more about adrenal function, please turn to page 191. For now, let's just look at a few adrenal hormones.

Hydrocortisone

Hydrocortisone, also referred to as cortisol, is an adrenal hormone that is depleted through burnout.

Healthy Levels of Cortisol

- Diminish inflammation
- Direct the body's systems
- Maintain blood sugar balance
- Maintain energy
- Maintain healthy blood pressure and fluid balance
- Regulate healthy immune response

Symptoms of Low Cortisol

- Aches, pains (especially neck and back)
- Allergies, asthma, sinusitis
- Autoimmune conditions
- Chemical sensitivities
- Dark circles under eyes
- Difficulty coping with stress
- Fatigue, especially in the afternoon
- Feeling burned out
- Hives, itching, skin sensitivity, overreaction to bug bites
- Hypoglycemia

Inflamed skin (eczema)
Low blood pressure, low fluid volume (dehydrate easily)
Low blood sugar
Muscle stiffness, joint pain, arthritis
Overwhelmed emotions (irritable, angry, panic attacks, blowing up)
Pigmented skin
Sugar and salt cravings
Sweaty palms
Weakened immune system/repeated infections (bronchitis and pneumonia)

Hydrocortisone replacement, sold under the name Cortef, is prescribed in physiologic doses as it would be if made by the adrenal gland under normal conditions. Cortef is beneficial during recovery from adrenal burnout. Hydrocortisone is the main hormone secreted by the adrenal glands and is responsible for maintaining your blood pressure, and your ability to process sugars, and how you react to stress and illness. Cortisol helps the body respond to stress. Hydrocortisone makes fatty acids available as an energy source and protects the brain by mobilizing and directing sugar to the brain.

One very good reason not to abuse Cortef is that if you're already burned out, overdoing Cortef is only going to make you worse by shutting down adrenal production of cortisol. The purpose of Cortef is to baby your adrenals so that they can repair and you can start to feel better.

Dehydroepiandrosterone

Dehydroepiandrosterone (DHEA) is an adrenal hormone that is the precursor for steroid hormones such as testosterone and estrogen. DHEA declines precipitously with advancing age in both men and women. Low levels of DHEA will put you into accelerated aging. DHEA replacement may improve artery flexibility and reduce blood sugar. It's one of the best hormones to quickly improve your sense of well-being and mood. It's also beneficial in the treatment of osteoporosis, and it may prevent certain cancers (including colon and prostate). DHEA restores an aging immune system and mediates inflammation, fatigue, and joint pain. The balancing hormone to cortisol, DHEA improves immunity, stimulates fat burning, improves energy, helps stop accelerated aging, alleviates chronic fatigue, and suppresses autoimmune diseases. Many people who are extremely exhausted are not making enough DHEA.

Healthy Levels of DHEA

- Better mood
- Faster fat burning
- Increased longevity
- Less risk of cardiovascular disease
- More energy
- More human growth hormone
- Shorter recovery time from exercise
- Speedier recovery from surgery or injury
- Stronger immunity

Symptoms of Low DHEA

- Age spots
- Balding
- Depression and anxiety
- Dry skin
- Fatigue
- Hair loss in armpits and pubic area
- Low sexual desire
- Sensitive to stress and noise

DHEA must be kept in physiologic doses, so you shouldn't rush out to buy it until you have had labs done to determine if you are deficient. NOTE: *Too high of a dose of DHEA can cause greasy skin and acne, balding, and facial hair growth on women.*

Brain and Other Hormones

People usually think of sex hormones when they think of hormones. But there are also hormones that affect your big dumb pet—your brain, and other metabolic processes that should not be overlooked.

Melatonin

The pineal gland is a pea-size organ situated in the brain that registers day and night by sensing light and dark and regulates the body's circadian rhythm—a daily rhythmic activity cycle, based on twenty-four-hour intervals. The pineal gland produces the hormone melatonin in periods of darkness, which makes you feel sleepy and aids in sleep. Our brain's ability to make melatonin decreases with age. If you're suffering from insomnia, melatonin is a good first step. While melatonin has been tested and found to be extremely safe in low doses, some people have a paradoxical reaction wherein melatonin causes them to feel energized or to have nightmares. Too much melatonin can also suppress female hormone production, which will lead to further imbalances.

Melatonin can also help reset your circadian rhythm offset by jetlag. It can increase human growth hormone and thyroid hormone by increasing the conversion of T4 to the active form T3. It can counteract excessive cortisol. But because it can decrease cortisol, it should be used with caution if you have an autoimmune disease and/or arthritis.

Melatonin is also an antioxidant. Moderate amounts of L-tryptophan or 5HTP, tyrosine, and melatonin taken at bedtime can help relieve symptoms of serotonin deficiency.

Symptoms of Low Melatonin

- Anger and aggression
- Anxiety, worry, fear, phobias
- Chronic pain
- Feeling extremely down and demoralized in dark weather
- Irritation
- Low self-esteem
- Mood disorders
- Obsession
- Premenstrual Syndrome
- Sleep problems
- Sugar cravings and bingeing
- Suicidal depression

NOTE: *The sublingual form of melatonin is optimal.*

Although I'm not giving doses in this book, I will tell you that the experts I've conferred with have agreed that 0.5 to 1 milligram is optimal.

Human Growth Hormone

Human growth hormone (hGH) is made abundantly when we're children and is the reason we grow. As adults, we need it to maintain muscle mass, but it begins a very early decline in our twenties and drops dramatically year after year. Between the ages of twenty and forty we lose half of our hGH production.

HGH is another controversial hormone, mostly because of its perceived abuses by professional athletes. Also its exorbitant cost has served to associate hGH with vain, aging movie stars. In my opinion, there's a very fine line between abuse, or "cheating," and personal responsibility to your body, and I'm perfectly comfortable sitting on the edge of this controversy. Look at elite athletes: they need hormonal support, given the way they punish their bodies during training and in competition causing dramatic accelerated aging. There's really no question that these people need some hormonal support. Is it abuse for them to replace the hormones that their bodies are using up like crazy? I'm not talking about people who turn themselves into circus hulks. But in many cases, I don't believe athletes are "cheating" by using hormones. I see many elite athletes' use of testosterone and hGH as a microcosm of what we all should be doing—being responsible to our health by assisting our endocrine systems, if and when we need it. Consider that athletes use up bodily fluids faster than normal, and so they need to drink water, right? For the energy they expend? Food. Nutrients? Vitamin and mineral supplements. Electrolytes? Veggie juice. Hormones? As my sister Nadine would say, "Ding, ding, ding!" And people may criticize those who use hGH and other hormones to stave off accelerated aging for being vain or "unnatural." Hormone replacement, especially human growth hormone, is still on the outer edge of health care, and you have to decide where you stand. In my opinion, the problem is not that hGH is unnatural or unfair, but more that it's not affordable for most. If we had real health care, we would be looking at ways to keep people from aging in an accelerated way by replacing hormones like hGH.

HGH helps balance all the other systems in our body and is the most powerful antiaging hormone to help keep organs healthy. You can increase growth hormone by getting adequate sleep (most of growth hormone is produced during sleep), staying lean, eating sufficient nutrition for metabolic rebuilding, avoiding sugar, alcohol, tobacco, and marijuana. The replacement of hGH accelerates repair and stimulates muscle building and fat burning. Because muscle mass dictates metabolic rate, you have more energy when you have more muscle mass. When your body produces hGH at night—or when you replace hGH—it increases melatonin, improves sleep, and stimulates fat burning. Your fat roll is the fat most likely to be burned off.

Symptoms of Low hGH

A lot of wrinkles	Gray hair
Anxiety and worry	Receding gums
Bloated face	Sagging cheeks
Bruise easily	Sagging, loose triceps, and inner thighs
Bump of fat below neck	
Cellulite	Severe nasal labial folds
Feeling exhausted	Slack muscles
Flabby tummy	Thin and/or dry skin
Furrowed forehead	Thin eyelids
	Thin, limp hair

HGH must be administered through an injection (though the needles are very fine), and as I mentioned it's prohibitively expensive for most people. Women need higher doses than men.

Sermorelin

Sermorelin is a reasonable facsimile of your brain's growth hormone releasing factor that stimulates the pituitary gland production and secretion of hGH. You may have seen ads for hGH releasers such as the amino acids L-arginine, L-glutamine, L-ornithine, glycine, L-dopa, as well as other substances and herbs. Given a perfect situation, when the body is in optimal health, releasers can sometimes elicit release of hGH from the pituitary gland. However, results through releasers are unreliable. High doses of amino acids are not recommended as they can cause kidney problems. (Remember, all things in balance.) Sermorelin is a more affordable option to hGH. It must be administered through injection. Still, not everyone has a positive response to Sermorelin. If you use Sermorelin, your doctor should require you to have labs drawn three weeks after starting to check your body's response.

Vitamin D

Vitamin D is really a hormone. Cholesterol is necessary for the body to synthesize sunlight into vitamin D, which is then used to absorb calcium for building bone.

(Vitamin D_2 is made in plants, but it is not as researched and its benefits are not as established, so our focus is on vitamin D_3.)

Definitive research has demonstrated that there is a seasonal correlation between vitamin D_3 levels and influenza. If you're in the sun, you're not as likely to get the flu. It's especially effective at preventing respiratory illness. Vitamin D also modulates neuromuscular and immune function, reduces inflammation, and aids bone growth and bone remodeling.

Sunblock inhibits vitamin D production. After the age of seventy the skin doesn't convert vitamin D effectively, even with adequate cholesterol intake. Vitamin D levels depend on skin pigmentation (darker skinned people have lower levels), altitude (the higher the altitude, the lower the level), and body weight (obese people have lower levels than thin people).

It's found in supplemented milk, Activator X, butter, wild-caught salmon, sardines, shrimp, cod, and eggs.

Symptoms of Short-term Vitamin D Deficiency

- Burning sensation in the mouth and throat
- Diarrhea
- Insomnia
- Loss of appetite
- Prone to colds and flu
- Vision problems
- Weight loss

Symptoms of Long-term Vitamin D Deficiency

- Breast, colon, ovarian cancer
- Dental problems (periodontal diseases)
- Depression
- Fatigue
- Low immunity with chronic colds and flu

Muscle pain
Musculoskeletal pain (deep throbbing in limbs)
Osteoporosis
Weaker bones, susceptible to fractures

The fear of malignant melanoma has everyone using sunblock now. That coupled with all the tall buildings and the fact that most people work inside, very few people are getting enough sunshine on their bare skin. If you got full exposure of ultraviolet B (UVB) sun rays for ten minutes, your body would make 10,000 IUs of vitamin D. The body is able to store vitamin D, but since we're not in the sun year round—and if you live north of Atlanta, the sun doesn't get high enough in the sky for UVB rays to reach you—it's really a dangerous situation.

Even doctors who abhor hormone replacement are now testing for vitamin D deficiencies, because its link to the immune system has been clearly demonstrated. You should be able to get tested with no problem. The old fear of vitamin D toxicity is unfounded. But as with any hormone, you want to have labs drawn to test and monitor your levels for your own good. You should never attempt to diagnose vitamin D deficiency yourself. People are starting to take vitamin D supplementation to the extreme and are pushing their levels too high. Make sure you get blood work done before taking vitamin D supplementation. See more about vitamin D on page 227.

Symptoms of Vitamin D Toxicity

- Bone pain
- Constipation or diarrhea
- Drowsiness or ongoing tiredness
- Dryness of mouth
- Headaches all the time
- High blood pressure
- Increase in amount of urine
- Increase in frequency of urination, especially at night
- Increased thirst
- Irregular heartbeat
- Itchy skin
- Loss of appetite
- Metallic taste in mouth
- Muscle pain
- Nausea or vomiting
- Severe tummy ache

Oxytocin

Oxytocin is a hormone, but it acts like a neurotransmitter in your brain. Most people associate it with childbirth and breastfeeding. But oxytocin plays a part in the pleasure of orgasm, and evokes warm and fuzzy feelings of bonding, contentment, trust. It also calms anxiety, especially around your sexual partner. Replacing oxytocin is free. All you have to do is have sex with someone you like, which is more likely to occur if you're hormonally balanced.

Many doctors refuse to even consider prescribing hormones. Others just aren't very skilled at it. BHRT is an art form, because it's so specific to each body. Even well-meaning doctors can mess up with BHRT. For this reason, make sure to vet your hormone doctor carefully, and don't be afraid to challenge labs with your symptoms. Symptoms always trump labs.

In 1964, when I was fourteen I had a front row seat at a Rolling Stones concert at the Balboa Bowl in San Diego. The Stones hadn't hit yet, and, to fill up the Bowl, the local radio station announced that admission was free. Mick Jagger, Bill Wyman, Charlie Watts, Brian Jones, and of course Keith Richards put their stamp of raw sexuality on me and hundreds of other impressionable girls that night. Flash forward 46 years ...

eleven

Ultimate You Skill No. 10: Sleep Eight Hours a Night

I'm standing in the Javitz Center in New York at the 2010 Book Expo looking up at a larger than life banner of Keith Richard's face on the book jacket of his autobiography, *Life*, and thinking, *Wow, that's creative Photoshopping*. We've all seen untouched photos of Keith Richard's road-map face, and it's not pretty. As it turns out, his accelerated aging is not just the result of the pharmaceutical grade amphetamines and opiates he used to stay up and come down. In *Life*, he writes, "For many years I slept, on average, twice a week." Yes, his drug use (that ended thirty years ago) and his notorious smoking are both aging, but one of the most damaging things you can subject yourself to is sleep deprivation.

Sleep is a necessary human physiologic need. Our autonomic or unconscious nervous system, which regulates the metabolic processes I've been talking about, is divided into the sympathetic and the parasympathetic nervous systems. During the day, we're predominantly in the sympathetic state, when the operational metabolic processes take place. Our nervous system transitions to the parasympathetic mode when we sleep, which activates the repair processes such as making new cells, membranes, tissues, enzymes, hormones, and neurotransmitters, thus it is truly *beauty* sleep. In addition, allowing your adrenals to replenish reserves lets you wake up with more oomph than what you went to sleep with. Everyone knows how much better they feel physically and mentally after a deep sleep. You're better equipped to seize the day.

People who avoid sleep are aging faster than they should because they don't give their bodies, and especially their adrenal glands, a chance to repair. Think of your adrenals as a savings account. You only have what you deposited into them. If you continue to spend adrenal reserves, your adrenals won't be able to keep up with the demand and your account will dry up, baby.

Sleep so Your Brain Can Repair

Your brain needs time to process the information from the previous day. It's like when your boss keeps walking into your office dumping piles upon piles of paperwork onto your desk so that you never seem to catch up. During the day, your brain retains everything you see and experience. At night, your brain repairs itself, makes new connections, and creates order out of the information you have taken in during the previous day. Rapid eye movement (REM) sleep, which is associated with dreaming, is the time when the brain integrates information taken in during the day and consolidates it into long-term memory. REM sleep occurs about every ninety minutes, and the periods of REM sleep get longer as the night progresses. Between the seventh and eighth hour of sleep is when we can experience a solid hour of REM sleep.

When you don't sleep enough, your brain carries a backlog of unprocessed information. Your brain simply goes on overload, and you either won't be able to get to sleep because your brain is frantically processing, processing, processing everything that is backlogged. Or, when you finally do get to sleep, your brain will launch vivid dreams in an attempt to process this stored information. These dreams can wake you up and keep you awake with whirling thoughts.

As a nation we all need a major nap, because accelerated aging is not just the result of factory-food products, diets, and drugs. Lack of sleep is a huge contributing factor. Sleep deprivation weakens the immune system, accelerates tumor growth, accentuates glucose problems, and impairs memory, problem solving, and performance.

What sleep deprivation does to your big, dumb pet—your brain—is very destructive. Sleep deprivation is one major reason people reach for stimulants. One thing leads to another and pretty soon all you're doing is eating crap and drinking Diet Cokes and your big, dumb brain is leading you around in a very unhealthy way.

Sleep Deprivation and Weight Gain

Weight management is confounded by sleep deprivation. If you constantly push past exhaustion, you're likely to begin to eat more. It may seem that you need more fuel because you're awake more hours, but in reality it's hormones that are dictating your hunger. Two hormones, ghrelin and leptin, check and balance each other to control hunger and fullness, respectively. Ghrelin, which is made in your gut, stimulates appetite. Leptin, produced in fat cells, signals your brain to stop eating because your stomach is full. Sleep deprivation drives leptin levels down, confusing satiety, while at the same time, ghrelin rises and stimulates your appetite. If you are sleep deprived for long periods of time, it's likely that you will gain weight.

Getting a Good Night's Sleep

Maybe you're reading this and thinking, I know about the need for sleep, but I can't sleep! If you suffer from insomnia you have my eternal sympathy. I know all about the downside of not sleeping. In fact I consider myself somewhat of an expert on insomnia. When my thyroid went, so did my sleep. It was a tortuous decade in which I searched for a sleep panacea. My overarching goal during my recovery was to achieve total health. Even though my sleep was really bad for a long time, I never stopped exercising despite how crummy I felt. I continued to nurture my body with a balanced diet of real food as well as doing all the other things I'm talking about in this book. People said I looked good, and I tried to console myself with what Billy Crystal's *Saturday Night Live* character Fernando Lama used to say, "It's better to look good than feel good." But it was very hard to believe. The emotional toll that insomnia takes on a person can't be discounted. When you're in a dejected state you'll try anything. And so I ended up following the advice of medical experts—and learning what doesn't work.

Sleep Hygiene Protocol—Not!

The cruel and unusual punishment called the "sleep hygiene protocol" that's inflicted on insomniacs goes like this: Remove the telephone, TV, books, and magazines from your bedroom. Do not do anything but sleep and have sex in your bedroom. Go for a ten-minute walk after dinner. At night, get ready for bed and engage in relaxing activities in another room of the house, such as reading, knitting, and watching TV, but do not work. When you feel sleepy, pee and then go straight to bed. Here's the bad part: If you can't get to sleep or awaken in the night and don't go back to sleep within ten minutes, get up, go into another room, and do your relaxing activities until you feel sleepy. Go to bed. If you don't sleep after ten minutes or awaken again, go to another room and do your relaxing activities. Get up at the same time every morning even if you haven't slept all night.

The protocol works, but only if you do it every night for the rest of you life. Yes, you do get back to sleep after engaging in "relaxing" activities in another uncomfortable and cold (compared to your bedroom) room of the house in the middle of the night. But you would likely eventually get back to sleep had you lain in wait under comfy covers.

After enduring this for a while, I decided the protocol was unhealthy to my mind, body, and spirit. Instead I developed my own protocol, which was based more on a Buddhist loving-kindness approach to the pain of my insomnia. Before you read my techniques, it's really important to grasp the fact that not sleeping is not natural, and you have your body, mind, and spirit's natural operating systems on your side. I believe this is what helped me, and I want to share everything I learned about overcoming insomnia with you. It's not just one thing, it's a constellation of factors and behaviors that lead to the calming of the entire integrated system of your mind, body, and spirit.

Eat Real, Living Food to Rebuild and Calm Your Brain

By this point in the book, you're educated enough about real food to understand what you need to eat to revamp your brain. If your insomnia is entrenched and you've been eating nothing but factory-food products for a period of time, it's going to take a while for your brain cells to turn over so that they are made out of healthy biochemicals. Having a solidly built brain that is flooded with happy neurotransmitters is imperative for sleep.

In addition to the balanced diet of real, whole food, there are other food factors that come into play for optimal sleep.

The Links Between Food and Sleep

When you sleep, calming neurotransmitters are regenerated. Insomnia causes a deficit of calming neurotransmitters. Chronic insomnia compounds this deficit until you do not have enough calming neurotransmitters to put and keep you asleep. Malnutrition is a major contributing factor to insomnia because any incoming building supplies will be used for immediate survival and nothing will be left over to make the neurotransmitters that will put you to sleep. If you're not eating complete proteins, it's likely that you're not getting the precursors to calming neurotransmitters. L-tryptophan, an essential amino acid in meat, poultry, and dairy, induces sleep by metabolizing into the neurotransmitter serotonin, which exerts a calming effect to induce sleep. L-tryptophan also metabolizes into the sleep hormone melatonin.

Eat Carbs

The pineal gland is a pea-size organ housed deep in the brain that identifies day and night by sensing light and dark. It regulates the body's circadian rhythm, a daily rhythmic activity cycle, based on twenty-four-hour intervals. The pineal gland produces the hormone melatonin in periods of darkness, which makes you feel sleepy and aids in turning on the nighttime repair and rejuvenation processes. Carbs are necessary to facilitate the transmission of amino acids into the brain which are metabolized into serotonin and melatonin. If you're suffering from insomnia, it may be as simple as adding in more complex carbs to your diet. (Complex carbs are real, whole carbs. Simple carbs are refined grains and sugars, i.e. factory food.)

Eat Foods Containing L-tryptophan

L-tryptophan is an amino acid precursor to serotonin, which converts to melatonin. Eating foods containing L-tryptophan helps both with sleep and depression. Turkey contains the highest amount of L-tryptophan of any food. If you are suffering from acute insomnia, eat foods containing L-tryptophan as often as possible for dinner.

Foods Containing L-tryptophan

Atlantic cod and perch	Meat
Baked potatoes with skin	Nuts
Bananas	Parmesan cheese
Beans	Pork chops
Beef	Roasted pumpkin, sunflower, and sesame seeds
Brown rice	
Cheddar, Swiss, and Gruyère cheese	Salmon
Chicken	Shellfish
Cottage cheese	Spirulina
Eggs (especially dried egg whites)	Steel cut oats
	Sunflower seeds
Fish	Tuna
Hazelnuts	Turkey
Hummus	Unsweetened dark chocolate
Kelp	
Lamb chops	Whole milk
Lentils	Whole yogurt

Eat Enough During the Day

I make a point of eating enough during the day, because I've found that if I don't, being overly hungry turns on my adrenals, and then I'm sunk. If I'm a little hungry at bedtime I have a glass of (preferably raw) milk and snack that also contains L-tryptophan. That said, going to bed stuffed is not only fattening, but keeps your body in a sympathetic state to digest and process all the food you have eaten.

Hydrate

I've found a direct correlation between not drinking enough water during the day and waking at night. Dehydration is stressful to your body, because if you're dehydrated, your body can't flush toxins. This disrupts the body's natural rhythms so that you either don't feel tired at bedtime or you feel fatigued but unable to fall asleep. Being dehydrated creates dryness (obviously) leaving you itchy all over. If you're really dehydrated the membrane around your brain can become too dry and you'll have headaches. It's better to have to get up to pee than to intentionally dehydrate your body, as dehydration causes sluggish blood which clogs microscopic vessels and leads to clotting (the definition of heart attack and stroke). Dehydration can lead to melatonin deficiency, so you won't have that sleep hormone lulling you into sleep.

Allow a Couple of Hours of Wind Down Time

Type A people who drive themselves love the sensation of the adrenaline rush, so they consequently live in a heightened state of sympathetic adrenal excess. Today with the barrage of information, images, demands, noise, and so on, it may be difficult for any of us to emerge completely from sympathetic dominance. Fears, anxiety, and skipping meals keep us in a sympathetic dominant state. We all need some quiet time to allow our brains to process the barrage of information that's come in during the day. Then when we get to sleep, the brain continues organizing in a more tranquil way.

Activities That Are Lullabies to Your Brain

People in our society are driven, working until they fall into bed, and where they stare at the ceiling, too wired to sleep. The reality is that your work will be there the following day, and you'll likely be more productive and definitely more pleasant to be with if you've gotten a good night's rest. Discovering the pleasure of an evening has enriched my life. I love my evenings! A luxurious evening of relaxing can actually be filled with activities that will lull you to sleep.

Take a Leisurely Walk

Walking is a great way to unwind and clear your mind. Go for a long walk—without your cell phone!

Have Sex

Just as adrenal burnout is the unhappy companion to all conditions, it's also the very unhappy companion to zero sex drive. If you've been driving yourself, and your sex drive is ancient history as a result, there's still hope. We're going to delve into adrenal fatigue in the following chapter, but for now, just know that a very important factor in healing your adrenals (and to getting to sleep) is spending time clearing your mind. One really great mind-clearing activity is sex.

It's not possible to reach orgasm if you feel fear or anxiety. Having sex to reach orgasm also facilitates the most delicious relaxation via the release of brain chemicals. With orgasm, women's brains release endorphins, but they also release oxytocin, which reduces anxiety, evokes feelings of contentment, calmness, and security.[40] After orgasm, men's brains release norepinephrine, serotonin, oxytocin, vasopressin, nitric oxide, and the hormone prolactin. Prolactin induces sleepiness, and the release of oxytocin and vasopressin accompanies melatonin, the hormone that regulates our body clocks.

Knit

Not exactly a close second to sex, you can knit for relaxation and mind clearing, but don't try to figure out complicated patterns. Only work on projects you can do blindfolded. And don't sew. Knitting is meditative; sewing takes brainpower.

Listen to Relaxing Music

My bedroom has an overhead sound system so I can listen to classical music, but I never turn on NPR or the news because I don't want to get stressed out before bed. The healing effects of music, in particular that of Mozart, have been studied, and the calming effects of music on the nervous system are well documented. Listening to music can significantly increase the concentration of melatonin in your bloodstream, but not just any music. Your nervous system is stimulated or calmed by music. Many types of music increase heart rate and respirations whereas classical music soothes.

Play with Your Pets

Playing with Charlotte Brontë and India (my whippets) calms me down, makes me giggle, and clears my mind. If you have pets, bedtime is a purrfect time to cuddle and play with them.

Practice Bed Yoga

The tendency to toss around and thrash legs is a classic characteristic of insomnia, but it doesn't lend to relaxation. Even if you don't practice yoga, you can learn to calm your body by lying in *Shavasana* (the corpse pose). Lie on your back with a pillow under your knees if you have lower back pain. Clasp the back of your head with your hands and pull gently, moving your chin slightly toward your chest to align your head and neck, and then rest your head on your pillow. Extend your legs hip distance apart and allow them to fall open naturally. Extend your arms at your side and relax your hands. Draw your shoulder blades down and away from your neck so that your chest is passively open. Close your eyes. Quiet your breath, listen, and focus on it.

Read a Non-agitating Book

When I was working on *Karma*, my psychological thriller about sex trafficking, my agent suggested a biography of a serial killer so that I could better understand the mind of a sociopath. I happened to read it in bed, and even though I only read a few pages before putting the book down for good, it took a long time to get those passages out of my head. Ever since I haven't read disturbing books before bedtime. Likewise, strumming through fashion magazines if you're struggling with your self-image probably will not help calm your brain. When I was deep in the thick of insomnia and worried about my career, I let my subscription to *Vanity Fair* lapse because I found it agitating in a deflating kind of way to read the articles and references to overnight mega sensational celebrities (like all the food celebs!). Read books and magazines that will soothe you, not upset you.

Take a Hot Bath or Shower

Take a hot bath or shower before you go to bed. Afterward your body will go into a cool-down mode, which is conducive to falling to sleep.

Revamp Your Bedroom

I've made my bedroom a very comfortable, luxurious, sexy, elegant place to be, with shades to block city light. I have sex in the bedroom and meditate there in the morning. In the winter I turn on the gas fireplace; in the summer I burn candles. Get rid of all the junk and clutter and anything negative like file cabinets with bills and tax documents inside that stress you out.

Some Tips for a Nicer, Sexier, More Comfy Bedroom

Invest in a New Mattress

If your mattress is lumpy or uncomfortable, for goodness sake invest in a new, quality mattress! Twenty-year-olds can sleep like logs on the floor; the rest of us don't do well in the gulag. When you replace bedding, buy nontoxic, hypoallergenic products.

Darken Your Bedroom

Light confuses your circadian rhythm, so your brain does not produce melatonin. Darken your bedroom and avoid blue light from computers, iPads, and cell phone screens, and TVs. I resorted to doing a Christo number on my bedroom windows with black felt and a staple gun until moving to a ranch in a rural setting where there were no barking dogs, city lights, or other distractions. Now I have black-out shades beneath the drapes. Investing in shades for your windows and eyeshades for your eyes can improve your sleep dramatically.

Keep Your Bedroom Temperature at 68°

This is the temperature that corresponds with your lowest body temp during sleep, though some people prefer it to be cooler. Start cooling down your environment before you actually get into bed.

Lose the Noise

Noise pollution is a ubiquitous problem of our time, but chances are there have always been noises that bothered human beings when they were trying to sleep. Music, however, decreases heart rate and blood pressure. If you can't sleep because of barking dogs, TV, traffic, or neighbors fighting, you can use music to mask noise and soothe your nerves. White noise machines also are fairly effective at masking discordant noise. I'm not a martyr by any stretch of the imagination and would not put up with snoring for two minutes. If snoring is keeping you awake while your partner gets a good night's rest, then there is absolutely nothing wrong with having your own bedroom.

It's not only the noise that keeps us awake that we need to concern ourselves with, but what noises we're listening to while we sleep. Our brains are wired for survival. The amygdala, which is the primitive part of our brain, is always on the lookout for danger. In his book *Life Unlocked*, Harvard psychiatrist Dr. Srinivasan Pillay writes about an otherwise emotionally stable patient who suffered from inexplicable fear and anxiety every morning when she woke up. She reported that her husband watched TV after she fell asleep. Dr. Pillay writes, "For about two hours, he would watch crime shows and action dramas that typically involved cars screeching to a halt or gunshots or people screaming, as well as frightening music." His patient's brain was registering all of that fear input. When her husband agreed to stop watching TV after she fell asleep, her fears vanished.[41] It's really important for mind, body, spirit health to think about what you're putting into your brain, even if you don't have insomnia problems.

Put Off Agitation Until Morning

I don't answer the phone after nine p.m. Whatever it is can wait until the morning. I don't want to get worked up and have something stressful on my mind. I also recommend that you don't pay bills or do other obnoxious things in bed, like have conversations with your partner about finances. When couples are busy all day, it sometimes seems that bedtime is the only time you have to discuss issues. Nevertheless, I've learned to say, "Let's talk about this in the morning." (Initiate sex and that will stop the conversation.)

Stuff That Can Wait

- Arguing
- Catching up on work
- Cleaning or puttering in your garage, basement, laundry room, backyard
- Discussing problems with kids or parents/grandparents
- Discussing your career
- Doing laundry
- Drinking caffeine
- Eating sugar
- Exercising

Paying bills
Playing video/computer games
Reading upsetting or scary books or magazines
Surfing the Internet
Talking on the phone
Watching TV or movies (especially violence)
Working on a project such as painting or sewing or anything creative that puts piles of work on your brain's desk
Working on finances and/or taxes
Writing agitating or even happily stimulating emails

Put Sleep on Your Schedule

Inability to fall asleep or waking abruptly can be the result of your adrenals inappropriately churning out stress hormones. This is generally the result of living on the edge so long that you're nearly always in a sympathetic dominant state, hardly allowing your autonomic nervous system to flow into the parasympathetic state. Constantly burning the candles at both ends disrupts communications between your pituitary and your adrenals. Eventually, your adrenals are so confounded that they begin to secrete the stimulating stress hormones cortisol and DHEA when you're actually trying to sleep.

Be Your Own Responsible Adult About Bedtime

Working into the evening, whether it be creating a Power Point presentation, folding the laundry, or paying bills, is generally motivated by fear of not measuring up in some way. Staying driven can also be a way to dull emotional pain. Of course, no one can just snap out of deep-seated fears. But you can begin to behave in a way that is more responsible to your body and brain, and these behaviors will ultimately help you to calm down, relax, and get to sleep.

Cut Yourself Some Slack

Before we talk about anything even remotely militant about bed rules, I want to emphasize that some of us simply don't sleep through a solid eight hours without waking and going back to sleep. There are lots of reasons people get woken up.

Historian Roger Ekirch explains in his book *At Day's Close: Night in Times Past* that humans didn't necessarily sleep uninterrupted all night long, due to threats to safety, vermin, smelly chamber pots, crowded conditions, hunger, and other irritants.[42] Now with alarm systems, comfy mattresses, indoor plumbing, and other creature comforts, the best we can do is set aside the time to sleep, set the stage, and relax. So before you even go there with bedtime schedules, remember that these suggestions are not meant to be followed like a grunt in boot camp.

Get Full Light Exposure

Our circadian rhythm is a twenty-four-hour cycle of metabolic processes that are linked to the rising and setting of the sun. In other words, light and darkness.

Unfortunately the artificial light that we are exposed to during the day confuses our brains. We stay up way past sunset, and even when we finally do go to bed we are surrounded by all sorts of little blue and red lights from appliances, clocks, computers, iPads, and so on. Try as much as possible to normalize your light situation by getting full sunlight exposure to your eyes, without sunglasses, for at least an hour every day. This will increase melatonin production.

Determine a Reasonable Bedtime

Going to bed as soon as possible after sundown is optimal because this is the time that your pineal gland registers dark and your brain will receive a sleep-inducing infusion of melatonin. The sleep hormone melatonin is suppressed when you are in light. Before electricity people went to bed when the sun went down and got up with the sun. If you are up late at night under the light of your laptop, iPad, TV, or the fluorescent bulbs in your office, release of melatonin will be inhibited. Determine what bedtime is reasonable for you and shoot for falling asleep around that time. It's also okay to decline evening out invitations if you really want to go home and wind down. I've gotten up early since the mid-1970s to work out, and I've said no plenty of times.

Go to Bed When Sleepy

Go to bed when you're sleepy or you'll run the risk of having your adrenals turn back on. It's good to have a regular bedtime.

Wake Within One Hour of a Set Time Daily

Habits are hard to break, right? Well, if you train your brain to go to bed and wake up at the same time, it makes sense that you're going to have your brain working for you to create a happy sleep pattern. That said, when I was suffering from acute insomnia I slept whenever I could sleep. Ultimately this kind and gentle approach allowed me to emerge from agitation and also provided the time for my body to enter a parasympathetic state to heal and regenerate.

Stop All Stimulants

Of course if you have insomnia, it doesn't make sense to use stimulants that will keep you awake (see page 82 for list of stimulants). Using stimulants keeps your body in a heightened state of sympathetic dominance with your adrenals over-producing stress hormones so that your body simply can't relax. Stimulants also deplete your body's balancing and calming neurotransmitters, creating the potential for insomnia. Following are stimulant no-no's before bed:

Alcohol: You may feel sleepy from a glass of wine, but when your blood sugar crashes it will wake you. Putting time between your glass of wine and going to bed is a good idea.

Caffeine: If consuming caffeine is causing your insomnia—whether from drinking coffee, tea, or sodas—then duh.

Exercise: Though exercise is an important part of a well-rounded lifestyle, over-exercising and exercising at night will both confuse and wake up the adrenals. Exercise is a stimulant, so you shouldn't exercise within several hours of bedtime.

Sugar: Eating sugar at night, including drinking alcohol, interferes with your body's circadian rhythm by stimulating your adrenal glands at the wrong time. (See page 17 for a refresher of adrenal involvement when you eat sugar.) When your adrenals are pumping out stress hormones, it will keep you awake. And while you're lying there, the fat roll around your waist will be inflating.

Eating sugar at night also suppresses the release of hGH by your pituitary gland. Remember, hGH is an antiaging hormone that accelerates repair and stimulates muscle building and fat burning.

Toss Sleep Drugs

Millions experience sleep disruption and that's why sleep drugs are huge moneymakers for pharmaceutical companies. Concluding that an occasional artificial night's sleep is better than nothing, insomniacs resort to Xanax, Halcion, Wellbutrin, Resterol, Sonata, Ambien, Lunesta, chloral hydrate, flurazepam—to name a few. You can become both physically and psychologically dependent on sleep medication. You may believe that you can't sleep without drugs, and you may actually experience physical withdrawal symptoms like anxiety and rebound insomnia. Sleep drugs can lose their effectiveness if used on a nightly basis, because the brain receptors become less sensitive to their effects. And also after "sleeping" with sleeping pills, brains have so much backlogged information waiting to be processed, that there is too much going on to allow for sleep. In as little as three to four weeks, sleeping pills can become no more effective than a sugar pill. The overall quality of your sleep can be reduced, with less restorative deep sleep and dream (REM) sleep. Especially with medications that last longer in your system, you may experience next day cognitive slowing and drowsiness (the hangover effect), which may be even greater than from sleep deprivation. Even if the medication is effective while taking it, insomnia returns once it is stopped.

Sleeping pills may all use various pathways in the brain to get you to sleep (at least a few hours in the night), but they all have one main objective: amnesia. If a sleeping pill can cause your brain to "forget" how crummy your sleep was, even if you get up in the morning feeling tazered, it's a physiological fake out. You think you've slept, and so you feel better about your sleep. This type of amnesia sleep doesn't provide the body with a true parasympathetic experience in which metabolic processes can operate optimally.

If someone is experiencing crippling insomnia, taking a sleeping pill is better than not sleeping at all, and those are the times when it's appropriate to hit your sleeplessness with a sledgehammer. Better than a sleeping pill is the lowest dose Valium you can take to calm down your nervous system. Benzodiazepines provide the best long-lasting sleep by slowing down the nervous system. Taking Valium is extremely habit forming and not a long-term or even nightly solution. The solution is calming your central nervous system for the long term. Ultimately natural alternatives are safer and lend equanimity to mind, body, and spirit.

Nature's Relaxants

Gamma aminobutyric acid (GABA)

L-theanine

L-tryptophan, 5-HTP, tyrosine, and vitamin B6

Magnesium citrate

Medical marijuana

Phosphatidylserine

Taurine

Valerian, passionflower, and hops

Use Bioidentical Hormones if You Need Them

Certain hormones are necessary for a smooth transition from the sympathetic to the parasympathetic mode.

Melatonin: The brain's ability to make the hormone melatonin decreases with age. Taking melatonin could be an easy fix if that's your problem. See pages 164 and 165.

Human growth hormone: Another hormone that is released primarily at night by your pituitary gland is the human growth hormone (hGH), which acts as the conductor orchestrating the repair processes and helping to rebuild lean body mass (muscles and bone). When your body does not regularly produce hGH, it does not repair as efficiently, and premature aging sets in.

Female sex hormones: Many women simply need a small dose of estrogen replacement to get back to their normal sleep patterns.

All the changes I made as I developed my personal health program chipped away at the ill health that had resulted in my insomnia. The most effective approach, however, was totally accepting insomnia and letting go of the stress, struggle, and anger from trying to control and manage it. This came about through self-compassion meditation. Along with meditation came the ability to completely let go of those adrenally stimulating inner dialogues, the replaying of stressful emails, phone calls, bills, or letters, upsetting conversations, or angry exchanges (which I try never to have, but no one is perfect). Self-compassion meditation was a revelation.

twelve

Ultimate You Skill No. 11: Practice Self-compassion Meditation

During my recovery, I was doing everything right in terms of food, supplements, exercise, and so on. There was just one thing standing in my way, and that was inner turmoil, that *blah, blah, blah* that we all have in our heads. I've always admitted to being driven but never really saw my attitudes about myself as *negative*, although I acknowledged that I've always been extremely hard and unforgiving on myself. In retrospect, the more my frustration mounted, the more agitated I became, the more self-demanding and critical I became, and the further away I drifted from the illusive psychological and physiologic tranquility I was seeking.

I started reading books on happiness and on Buddhism and Buddhist meditation. Then I met my teacher, Christopher K. Germer, Ph.D., author of *The Mindful Path to Self-Compassion: Letting Go of Destructive Thoughts and Emotions*, who introduced me to the *radical* concept of self-acceptance and self-compassion. He taught me a form of Buddhist meditation called *metta* (loving-kindness), which was developed by the Buddha as an antidote to fear.

Talking about Buddhism and Buddhist meditation is dicey because the last thing I want to do is come off as proselytizing, as that is not the Buddhist way. Plus, I don't consider myself a Buddhist. Also, people of various religions may balk because many imagine Buddhists worshipping the Buddha the same as people worship God. As Dr. Germer said in an email, "Many do worship Buddha nowadays and place flowers at the feet of statues. That's not what the Buddha wanted. But people are inherently devotional." Given that some worship the Buddha even though he was not, or never claimed to be, divine, I had to decide whether to sneak meditation into this book under some generic term or to present it the way it affected my life.

Let me just say that Buddhism is not a religion, it's a psychology. The Buddha figured out the way the mind functions and presented his teachings to those who were conflicted and burdened, wanting to know why and what they could do about it. Meditation is merely a practice that helps manage the mind. Meditation can be practiced by anyone, regardless of religious beliefs, in a quiet room in your home, office, church, synagogue, or temple.

I decided to openly write about my foray into Buddhist meditation because it really is a secular practice. I think if you read on, you won't be put off. I also have to add that some people may feel that hard-core Zen meditation is the only way! It's a matter of choice.

The Buddha

We live in confusing times, but when you think about it, all times were confusing and troublesome for those living during them. In his book *Awakening the Buddha Within*, Lama Suyra Das put it so well, "In the time of the Buddha, men and women were arguing, gossiping, judging others, losing their perspective, overreacting, sexualizing their experiences, chasing after greener pastures, obsessing about nonessentials, feeling lonely, and creating too many pipe dreams. Nothing has fundamentally altered." People from the beginning of humankind have felt the same pain. The Buddha, sometimes called the "Enlightened One," was born Prince Siddhartha Gautama in Nepal (563 to 483 BCE). His parents hid him from the harsh realities of life. He grew up, married, and had a child all within the confines of his rarified world as a coddled, protected prince. When he finally ventured out at age twenty-nine, he was shocked to see that in real life all humans age, get sick, and die, and that in the meantime, shit happens. He renounced his old life and lived the life of a wandering aesthetic, starving himself to emaciation. He realized this approach wasn't getting him anywhere and sought a "middle way" between the two extremes of hedonism and asceticism. At age thirty-five, while meditating under a tree in Bodhgaya, India, for forty-nine days and nights, he reached enlightenment. He then went on to share what he had learned about taming the insane and demanding human mind. The Buddha's main agenda was to teach the *dharma* (truth) about how to be free from suffering. Everything the Buddha ever said or taught was to alleviate suffering.

The Buddha Defined the Four Noble Truths

Life Includes Suffering (Symptom): Humans endure physical and psychological suffering—pain, aging, sickness, and death. Along the way we experience emotional pain.

The Desire for Things to Be Other than They Are Is the Cause of Suffering (Diagnosis): We either don't want what we have (aversion), or we don't have what we want (grasping).

We Can End Suffering (Prognosis): Ending suffering is possible, as are happiness and contentment. We can learn to live in the present moment without either regret for the past or worry about the future.

The Path to the Cessation of Suffering (Treatment): The Buddha taught concrete instructions for eliminating suffering, called the Eightfold Path, which in very simple terms is to be moral in what we say and do, and in the way we make our living, to focus our minds on being fully aware of thoughts and actions by developing understanding and wisdom of the Four Noble Truths, and by being compassionate toward others.

Before I began reading about happiness and Buddhist meditation, I'd read about meditation for another book I wrote (on adrenal burnout). One book, *The Relaxation Response* (1976), by Herbert Benson, M.D., Mind/Body Medical Institute associate professor of medicine at Harvard Medical School and director emeritus of the Benson-Henry Institute (BHI), made a huge impression on me, and I read it several times.

Dr. Benson pioneered meditation in the West by studying yogis and meditators. He discovered that meditation counteracted the fight-or-flight effect of the sympathetic nervous system. (See pages 203 and 204 for an explanation of the sympathetic nervous system.) We all know the term "fight-or-flight" now, and we've all experienced it. It's the response to stress that causes blood to be shunted to your heart, which beats harder and faster. It can happen any time of the night or day if a crisis or something exciting occurs. Immediately your muscles tense, arteries constrict, you breathe shallowly and rapidly. Our society has gotten into the syndrome of being in a constant fight-or-flight mode. Getting from home to work on the subway or freeway during rush hour is fight or flight.

Benson's research demonstrated that during meditation (relaxing and clearing the mind), the sympathetic nervous system tunes down and the parasympathetic nervous system eases on. Muscle tension melts and blood pressure drops, as can body temperature and metabolism rates.

Meditation affects brain waves, too. When you're awake but relaxed, your brain produces a pattern of smooth, regular electrical oscillations called alpha waves at a frequency of eight to thirteen cycles per second. When you're in a state of anxiety, your brain produces another waveform called the beta rhythm at a frequency of thirteen to thirty cycles per second. Meditation normalizes the central nervous system, reduces the body's need for oxygen, and changes brain waves from buzzing beta waves to tranquil alpha waves.

At the time, I found it all interesting, but I was too wrapped up writing two books back-to-back. I'd started doing yoga, though, which was introduced 5,000 years ago as a way to purify (prepare) the body for the higher state of consciousness in meditation. But even with these influences, it wasn't until much later that I started meditating on my own. When I did, I didn't know what I was doing. I simply sat with my eyes closed and concentrated on my breath. I practiced this way for one year, but I wasn't seeing a lot of progress in terms of my anxiety, insomnia, stress, and all the complex issues that continued to play out in my mind.

Stress

It may not have been called "stress" until Dr. Hans Selye gave it that term in the early 1950s, but stress by any other name still sucks, robbing us of joy before ultimately killing us. Stress is lethal because it depletes adrenal reserves, which are essential for metabolic processes to function optimally. Diminished adrenal function is just one more aging accelerant that contributes to the downhill slide of your physiologic systems. Another consideration is post-traumatic stress. I believe that everyone walks around with some degree of post-traumatic stress. For some it's a whisper of aggravation, for others it's a nuclear bomb constantly going off. Trauma, if not resolved, is a slippery slope to adrenal burnout (the unhappy companion to many other health problems).

Five Stages of Adrenal Burnout

By now you know that adrenal burnout is the unhappy companion to all other conditions. Adrenal fatigue doesn't happen overnight. Most of us want to grab as much as we can in life. In the course of our thrilling lives, adrenal fatigue creeps up inexorably in stages. And adrenal fatigue is the unhappy companion to insomnia.

Stage One: Adrenaline Rush

The limbic system of your brain translates sensory input into emotion. When your limbic system registers a major event, your adrenals release adrenaline, the fight-or-flight hormone. Some people love the adrenaline rush and drive themselves mercilessly. But the adrenaline rush can also be familiar to people who work nights, like say in an acute medical care or police work, or those who experienced frightening childhoods, or traumatic life experiences like combat, or even a prolonged, hostile divorce. These are all situations in which your adrenals would be repeatedly called on to secrete adrenaline due to insecurity and fear. You get an adrenaline response from all emotional or physical stress, but you also get the response from positive events such as winning the lottery, getting a raise, getting married, or driving off the lot in your dream car. During an adrenaline rush, you feel energized, alert, and sometimes euphoric. The rush is caused by the release of three factors: (1) a surge of energy from sugar stored in your liver and muscles; (2) a gush of the feel-good neurotransmitter dopamine into your brain; and (3) another gush, this one of the opiate (pain-killing) neurotransmitter endorphin.

During an adrenaline rush, you're buzzed and feel no pain. But inside your body, systems must work overtime. Look at every single president of the United States and how gruesomely they age. External aging demonstrates what's going on inside of your body.

Factors That Lead to Adrenal Burnout

- Blowing past exhaustion to keep working
- Breathing shallowly when tense
- Car, fire, or other traumatic accident

- Driving yourself relentlessly with no break
- Eating factory-food products
- Exposure to toxins
- Having to be a caregiver for a prolonged period of time
- Mentally replaying and reliving agitating inner dialogues
- Neglecting relaxing ways to calm your nervous system
- Not exercising or neurotically overexercising
- Partying all night (smoking, doing drugs, drinking)
- Purposely not getting enough sleep
- Remaining in a stressful marriage, relationship, job
- Skipping meals or chronic dieting
- Unrelenting fearful situations like combat, being a victim of a crime (and reliving it), the emotional aftermath of a traumatic childhood, a bad divorce
- Using stimulants to function
- Worrying, obsessing, ruminating

If stress is chronic, your adrenals will stop the adrenaline and instead release the hormones cortisol and DHEA to keep you going during chronic stress. (See pages 162 and 164 for healthy levels of cortisol and DHEA.)

The end of this stage is typically around age thirty. People complain about how their metabolisms have slowed down and left them with fat around their middle. Well, it's really not metabolism that's the root cause of your fat roll, but your adrenals. Your adrenal glands need rest to repair. If your adrenal glands are constantly on and not given the opportunity to rest and repair, they will begin to poop out. That's when you begin to notice a few nights of insomnia here and there, and then you have the accompanying fatigue and mood swings. Your sex drive slows and you begin to gain weight, retain water, and suffer from GI problems.

As you continue to drive yourself, your adrenals will first decrease DHEA production, which will cause you to have too much cortisol but not enough DHEA. This is not good, because DHEA buffers many of the negative effects of excess cortisol. For example, cortisol causes muscle wasting, but DHEA stimulates muscle *building*, essentially replacing what cortisol has broken down. Increased cortisol suppresses immunity, whereas DHEA increases immunity. Increased cortisol leads to increased weight gain, whereas DHEA leads to fat burning and weight loss.

What Excess Cortisol Causes

Emotional mood swings, depression
Fat tummy/fat roll around your waist
Gastritis (inflamed stomach lining)
Increased risk of high blood pressure
Increased risk of type 2 diabetes
Loss of lean body mass (muscle and bone)
Menstrual disorders
Recurrent infections
Slower wound healing
Tanks your sex drive
Thinning of the skin and connective tissue (outward signs of aging)
Water retention
Weight gain

Stage Two: Losing Your Edge

The second state of adrenal burnout leaves you feeling less energetic than you used to feel. When you started having a little bit of insomnia, you might have turned to caffeine or herbal stimulants, which are unfortunately touted as healthy alternatives to caffeine. Some people begin using street stimulants like cocaine. Maybe you're too busy to cook real meals, so you eat fast food. You start taking OTC and prescription pain relievers. You notice you're getting flabby. Some people start smoking or can't even dream of quitting at this stage.

Many of us push ourselves to the extreme by overexercising or working too hard out of unrelenting ambition. Some have been forced into this sympathetic dominant state by a harsh childhood, trauma, or bad circumstances. Regardless, people either engage in behaviors that force their bodies into a constant state of sympathetic dominance, or they are helpless to stop the adrenal demands, the psychological torments that keep them running mentally and physically.

Unrelenting pressure on your adrenal glands to secrete the stress hormones adrenaline, cortisol, and DHEA chips away at your adrenal reserve. The metabolic processes that take place while you are in a sympathetic state create acids as byproducts, which make your body more acidic. When your body is in a natural, healthy rhythm, the parasympathetic mode, which occurs predominantly at night, counteracts the sympathetic mode by turning on the repair processes. These processes rid your body of acid and allow repair processes to make new cells, membranes, tissues, enzymes, hormones, and neurotransmitters. It's easy to understand that if you prevent your body from repairing by remaining in a sympathetic dominant state too long you could end up progressing through the stages to the final state of adrenal burnout.

Stage Three: Who's That Person in the Mirror?

You have dark circles under your eyes. You're too fat or too thin, and you look much older than you feel you should. You can't sleep, so you lie awake worrying. You're not motivated to exercise and instead drink coffee and eat sugar to keep going. It still doesn't seem like a good time to quit smoking. You occasionally experience shortness of breath, chest pains, vertigo, palpitations, nausea, blurred vision, and environmental sensitivities, but you don't really pay too much attention. Some people begin to dabble in prescription drugs at this stage like Vicodin or Percocet that they've finessed or finagled out of their doctor.

Stage Four: Last Gasps

Now you are regularly bitching and moaning about being tired, fat, and sick of work. You suffer from brain fog, irritability, insomnia, nightmares, GI problems, allergies, asthma, headaches, migraines, musculoskeletal pains, back and neck pain, and dread. You depend on sleeping pills, antacids, anti-inflammatories, cholesterol-lowering medications, blood sugar–lowering agents and/or blood pressure medications, way too much coffee and caffeinated drinks, alcohol, and all the begged, borrowed, and stolen drugs you can get your hands on. You pee all night long. You believe that you could not function without antidepressants.

Stage Five: Burnout

You've reached the end state of accelerated aging and are either very overweight, or obese even, or prison-camp thin. Or you could have reached this stage because you were in a traumatic accident or injured in combat and face a long recovery.

Symptoms of When Your Adrenals Are Beat to Hell

- Anxiety
- Arthritis
- Autoimmune disease
- Cancer
- Chronic fatigue
- Colitis
- Depression
- Eating disorders
- Escalating allergies
- Esophageal reflux
- Fat tummy/fat roll around your waist
- Fatigue
- Fibromyalgia
- Gastrointestinal dysfunction
- Headaches and migraines
- Heart attack
- Hives
- Hypoglycemia and type 2 diabetes
- Hypothyroidism
- Inability to make healthy cognitive choices
- Infections such as recurring herpes, yeast, respiratory
- Infertility
- Insomnia
- Irrational fears
- Irregular menses
- Metabolic problems
- Mood disorders
- Muscle spasms
- Neurological diseases (multiple sclerosis, Alzheimer's, Parkinson's, etc.)
- Palpitations
- Panic attacks
- Premature heart disease
- Sciatica
- Severe debilitating environmental sensitivities
- Stiff neck
- Stroke
- Sweating (excessive)
- Temporomandibular joint syndrome (TMJ)
- Water retention
- Weight gain or weight loss
- Zero sex drive

Recovery from Adrenal Burnout

Recovery from total burnout is possible, but you really have to be determined. I'm grateful that I never reached the total burnout stage. However, I did experience a lot of health problems, including hypothyroidism. I knew that a huge factor in healing is sleep. However, even if you're not totally burned out, your sympathetic nervous system can get stuck in the ON position—the limbic system of your brain inappropriately tells your adrenal glands to churn stress hormones day and night, and you are unable to calm down and sleep.

Is Your Anxiety Caused by Something You're Doing?

You drink too much coffee, or use herbal or other stimulants.

You have heavy metal toxicity (lead, mercury, copper, cadmium).

You have high estrogen and low progesterone levels.

You have high testosterone levels (men or women).

You have low blood sugar.

You have low calcium and magnesium levels.

You have too low or too high vitamin B levels.

You take allergy medicines containing pseudoephedrine-like drugs.

You take anti-anxiety, antidepressant, and/or insomnia drugs.

You take Cytomel, a form of thyroid replacement.

You're taking too much of any type of thyroid medication.

After addressing any issues listed in "Is Your Anxiety Caused by Something You're Doing?" and turning off your sympathetic nervous system, you need to calm your big, dumb pet—your brain. The foundation is to build a solid brain and flood it with happy neurotransmitters by eating a diet of real, whole, living food and all the other things you've read about in this book. Of course, there's always the not-so-small issue of your psyche.

The "Self-Soothing" Antidote

In the 1980s I was working like a fiend in the film industry, which is essentially an impersonal, dog-eat-dog world. I dreamt up the concept of a phone-in service called 1-800-CALLMOM. You could call the 800 number and a nice little old lady would answer and remind you to eat breakfast, take a sweater, and just generally listen and sympathize with you. I thought (and still do) that it would do a blockbuster business. The reason 1-800-CALLMOM would do so well is that we all need a comforting, nonjudgmental mommy. Short of that, you do have recourse. Researchers, like Dr. Paul Gilbert, who wrote *The Compassionate Mind*, are looking at the brain from an evolutionary neuroscience perspective, and uncovering the sweeping benefits of developing a more compassionate mind through "self-soothing." Dr. Gilbert identified the following three "systems" in the brain.

Threat and Self-protection System

Our brain is fixated on primitive passions of lust, hunger, power, and the need to avoid danger. This system in the brain is involved in defensive emotions like anger, anxiety, disgust, and fight-or-flight behaviors.

Incentive and Resource-seeking System

Our modern dog-eat-dog way of life activates the incentive system where the emphasis is on autonomous, competitive striving, which doesn't leave a lot of room for socializing, deep bonding, a sense of community, and feeling safe. This system is associated with pleasure, excitement, achievement/reward, acquisition, and competition. The incentive system releases dopamine, which is a pain-relieving neurotransmitter, and so this behavior is reinforced, which is why people can drive themselves to burnout.

Soothing and Contentment System

When the threat and self-protection and the incentive and resource-seeking systems are overactivated, the soothing and contentment system is underactivated. Our brains have evolved over millions of years with these two systems discussed above, which run contrary to living a compassionate life. The "new" part of our brain, the neocortex, allows us to be self-aware, to reason and conceptualize, and to empathize with others. This new part of the brain is capable of generating the soothing and contentment system to foster peaceful feelings, well-being, social connectedness, and safety (what you would get if you called 1-800-CALLMOM). This "soothing system" apparently evolved with the need for bonding in mammals—and humans are hardwired to respond to love and kindness. Close, caring relationships can reduce fear, anger, and competitive striving. The soothing system releases the pain-relieving neurotransmitters, endorphins, and comforting oxytocin.

Self-soothing

Researchers assert that by understanding these emotion systems, we can learn to regulate our own stress better and in so doing evolve into a more humane society. Kind of like what the Buddha taught. Researchers have found that suffering is a given in people who are unable to be kind and gentle to themselves when things are going wrong. In writing about this research, Dr. Germer says, "The new brain can either inflame our primitive passions (for example, orchestrating a full-scale war just because we feel afraid), or help us disengage from these automatic reactions. In other words, our minds create heaven or hell, inside and out."[43]

Rather than criticizing, blaming, or hating ourselves, self-compassion training, which could also be referred to as evoking the "soothing system", can gradually change the brain. Learning to be compassionate toward yourself means that, like the little old lady on the line at 1-800-CALLMOM, you'll learn to be attentive, sensitive to your own distress, tolerant, empathetic, and most of all *nonjudgmental*. When you think about it, every moment of the day we are "training" our brains. So if you train your brain to suffer, then you'll suffer. If you train your brain on self-compassion by soothing your brain, then your suffering will decrease.

Metta Meditation

Not one single person who has ever known me would call me nonjudgmental. I'm extremely nitpicky with myself. As my body became healthier, the turmoil in my psyche became more evident. It's like I'd redecorated and cleaned my entire home and left a pile of garbage dumped in the living room. It was impossible to ignore. I set out to find a therapist who was a Buddhist and read about Chris Germer, who had traveled extensively in India, studied Ashtanga yoga, and had practiced Buddhist meditation for thirty years. He was also one of the founders of the Institute of Meditation and Psychotherapy.[44] I thought that was really neat, and I've since learned how meditation is exploding in the world of psychotherapy.

I spent a few sessions filling Dr. Germer in on my history and then said, "I just wanted you to have a basic understanding of who I am so that you could tell me about Buddhism and meditation." He explained the basics of Buddhism, how detaching from desire and clinging brought inner calm and peace, and said, "Mindful self-compassion is the foundation of emotional healing." He went on to explain that cultivating compassion toward yourself allows you to feel compassion for others.

Loving yourself is at the heart of true contentment and happiness. You learn to love yourself despite your history and failings, and you also begin to love others.

Dr. Germer explained that mindful self-compassion is the foundation of emotional healing. "Being aware (mindful) in the present moment when we're struggling with feelings of inadequacy, despair, confusion, and other forms of stress and responding with kindness and understanding (self-compassion). Mindful self-compassion also means holding difficult emotions—fear, anger, sadness, shame, and self-doubt—in loving awareness, leading to greater ease and well-being in our daily lives."

Dr. Germer explained that mindful self-compassion can be learned by anyone. "It's the practice of repeatedly evoking good will toward ourselves—cultivating the same desire that all living beings have to live happily and free from suffering. And as the Dalai Lama says, self-compassion is the first step toward compassion for others."

Dr. Germer led me in my first metta practice. "Metta" is a Pali word, translated loosely to mean loving-kindness. (Pali was the language spoken in Sri Lanka four hundred years after the Buddha's death when his teachings were translated from oral telling to written language.) Metta is loving-kindness meditation, which is a core practice to develop self-compassion. In metta practice you can also give love/compassion to others, to people you know, to your pets, and to strangers (all living beings). The ultimate goal is to free you of distraught, anger, tension, uptightness, anxiety, self-hating, and suffering so that you can experience love, peace, and happiness in a natural flow from your calmed down mind.[45]

The primary difference between metta and other types of meditation aimed at gaining mindfulness and taming the mind is that metta specifically targets the system of the brain that self-soothes. Metta intentionally bestows compassion on you. It's pure, unadulterated self-love, self-acceptance, and self-compassion, without any qualifications (I don't deserve. I'm being selfish. I should be thinking of others, not me).

When I practiced my first sitting with Dr. Germer and opened my eyes thirty minutes later, it was as if I had crossed over through a thin, thin veil of understanding. I experienced Samadhi (a Hindu word that loosely translates to "spiritually awakened" or "bliss" or "enlightened state"). It wasn't that I had spent forty-nine days under a tree fasting and meditating. It simply came over me as a gift. I left Dr. Germer's office and remained in this state all afternoon and evening. I did normal things, but everything around me was clear and the world was supernaturally beautiful. Time seemed slowed. My mind was untroubled by any negative thoughts, obsessing, ruminating. I meditated and my mind was still and tranquil. I felt pure joy. The state of Samadhi continued all that day and into the night. I remained aware but accepting of everything that occurred or didn't occur. When I meditated for the next week my mind focused with ease on my meditation phrases. I remained in a waning state of Samadhi for an entire week. Dr. Germer informed me that what I experienced was "beginner's mind," and not to expect it to happen again any time soon.

I wanted to understand more about metta meditation. I continued to meditate; I read Dr. Germer's book, *The Mindful Path to Self-Compassion*, and also attended a nine-day silent New Year's Buddhist meditation retreat at the Insight Mediation Society (IMS) in Barre, Massachusetts. Wanting to have the most profound experience possible, I left my laptop and cell phone at home. Because there is no talking or reading or any other distractions, I got into my head as if from a new door. I decided when I got to IMS that I wasn't going to be self-critical for nine days. After all, where in the world, in what situation, would it be safer and appropriate to try being self-compassionate and forgiving? When a negative thought would creep into my consciousness, I would merely dismiss it with the thought, *I don't need that now*, or *I'm done with that*. To my surprise, I found that I felt the happiest during the meditation sessions. I'm lucky to have had a solid foundation instilled in me by an experienced teacher like Dr. Germer, who taught me that meditation is not a competition and that just showing up is a good thing while on retreat. I had a few deep episodes of meditative bliss, a little meandering into who I needed to email when I got home, and episodes of screaming knees and sodden, paralyzed legs. After nine days of not being self-critical, the thought occurred to me: *If I could do that, what else could I do with my mind?*

The prospects are thrilling, and my life has taken off since then. The reason my life is so altered is because my brain is different now. I feel it in my emotions (much more controlled and even), my reactions (I don't knee-jerk react, and I don't make a catastrophy out of every little thing), and in my happiness level (I feel good the majority of the time). Most importantly my levels of compassion and understanding of others have gone way up. My sympathetic nervous system is able to turn down when I lie my head down on a pillow. I've learned to respond to stress in a radically different way.

It's not my imagination that meditation has changed my brain. If you think about the alert systems our government has in place now compared to pre-9/11 attacks, it's much like your brain before and after prolonged stress. Because of the plasticity of the brain, the more you use the areas of your brain that respond to stress, the more dominant those areas are going to become. It's like working a muscle. When you meditate you work out your amygdala so that comforting emotions dominate. Meditation trains the amygdala, which processes emotion, to feel pleasurable sensations of security and safety and to set aside fear and anxiety. It's really neat to feel control, happiness, and contentment blossom as you develop your practice.

Training Your Mind to Be Self-compassionate

A self-compassionate mind is not a natural state of being. For that reason, it requires effort, or "mindfulness." It's an about-face from what most of us do on a regular basis, which is to beat ourselves up, especially if we mess up—real or perceived.

Mindfulness means being aware. It's the ability to pay attention to the present moment without judgment or analysis. The Buddha taught that we could end suffering by being in the present moment, to accept and not resist.

Compassion requires responding in a kind way. It's the wish that all beings—including yourself—be free from suffering. The purpose of loving-kindness meditation is to develop loving-kindness—the wish that all beings—including yourself—be happy. When we direct compassion to ourselves, that is loving-kindness (metta). Compassion means that, when you feel bad and wish to feel better, you're not self-critical and demanding but loving to yourself. In short, self-compassion is saying something nice to yourself.

By practicing self-compassion, you activate your brain's soothing and contentment system. Your brain will gradually down regulate its threat and self-protection and the incentive and resource-seeking systems. Meditation actually changes the structure of the brain.[46] And when the part of your brain that is hyperalert to danger decreases, your sympathetic nervous system will stop sending inappropriate messages to your adrenals. Your adrenals will stop turning on at inopportune times (like the middle of the night), and you'll be able to calm down and sleep.

Practice Every Day

Other forms of meditation may use a mantra or require that you try to stay with your breath. Metta meditation is a simple meditation in which you repeat four phrases over and over.

May I be safe
May I be happy
May I be healthy
May I live my life with ease

You can add to these phrases, for example, "May I be safe, secure, and taken care of." However, Metta isn't a way to beg for certain things, like, "May I have enough money to pay my bills this month," "May I have a boyfriend," "May I have a bigger house," "May I have a better job," and so on. The purpose of metta is to give yourself simple, uncomplicated compassion.

To meditate, simply assume a comfortable position, close your eyes, and focus your attention on the phrases. Don't worry one bit about losing focus. It happens after one to two seconds to everyone, even those who are experienced in meditation. Just bring your attention back gently without condemning yourself. You can listen to Dr. Germer guide you through meditations on mindfulselfcompassion.org. Meditation is part of a well-rounded, balanced lifestyle. I hope you'll try it and experience the pleasure of a calmed mind.

Serious Physical Pain

Maybe you're reading this thinking, "Well that's great, but I'm not the Buddha, so I'm not that evolved, and I'm in great physical pain, so I can't calm down." I think it's really important to acknowledge that not all things work as well for all people. Some people simply can't "calm down," no matter how earnestly they meditate, accept, and forgive, because they are in pain. Pain and recalcitrant conditions can disrupt the quality of a person's sleep, as well as the quality of a person's life.

Neural Therapy and Micro-Dose BioModulation

As you know by now, I believe that the body is dynamic and desirous of mind, body, and spirit equanimity (optimal health/homeostasis). I regularly get questions from readers about health issues they're frustrated with, problems they feel they've done everything they can do for, yet these issues persist. Although I may not have all the answers, and I encourage people to continue to eat a diet of real, whole, living food, and to avoid toxins, I understand from my own health experiences that its natural to feel frustrated after trying so hard.

Jeremy E. Kaslow, M.D. is an immunologist, allergist, metabolic, and hormone specialist. One of the growing number of enlightened doctors in the U.S., Dr. Kaslow says, "I used to believe that if you ate all the essential nutrients, avoided substances that make your symptoms worse, and detoxified heavy metals, yeast, abusive relationships, and other toxins from your body and life, your body would heal itself. However, even when some individuals do everything right in these three areas, something seems to interfere with healing. I now understand that interference fields from scars and trauma disturb the instructions of the autonomic nervous system to heal the body."

Dr. Kaslow is referring to the theory that trauma can produce long-standing disturbances in the electrochemical function of tissues. We've talked about the autonomic system, the vast network of electrical circuits that control vital processes in your body. Your autonomic system regulates breathing, circulation, body temperature, digestion, metabolism, hormone formation, and all of the communications that hormones engage in. It regulates your heartbeat and enables your lungs to breathe automatically, even when you're asleep. Virtually every cell in your body is connected and influenced by your autonomic nervous system.

The autonomic nervous system has two divisions. The sympathetic nervous system is activated by stress to speed up your heart rate, make your body burn sugar for energy, tense your muscles, and in general increase your ability to fight or flee. The sympathetic nervous system links all of the cells of the body together, regulates the contraction and expansion of blood vessels, regulates the activity of the connective tissue necessary for regenerating body systems, and regulates the voltage (membrane potential) across the cell wall in every cell in the body.

The parasympathetic nervous system, by contrast, turns on all of the rejuvenating activities that occur when you're at rest. This includes promoting the repair and rebuilding of cells. But you won't be salivating over dinner, crying, urinating, digesting food, or eliminating when you're running from danger. As we've talked about, it's crucial to optimal health for your body to spend adequate time in the parasympathetic (resting) state.

When your healing is not progressing, it's possible that your sympathetic nervous system is stuck in an overly reactive ON state, which interferes with or impairs healing mechanisms.

Any type of tissue affected by trauma, including scars, nerves, or clusters of nerves called ganglions, can interfere with parasympathetic rest and repair. Infections, emotional trauma, and physical trauma (from any type of surgery, accidents, deep cuts, biopsies, childbirth, dental procedures, vaccinations, burns, tattoos, and so on) can all cause interference fields. General stress from illness, malnutrition, emotional stress, food allergies, pregnancy and other factors that the body perceives as trauma can also create interference fields. "Not all scars seem to cause interference fields," Dr. Kaslow explained. "However, if a scar occurs (as a result of elective surgery or otherwise) and there was emotional stress associated with the event that caused the scar, it's more likely to cause an interference field." A good example, says Kaslow, is breast augmentation. If the results are pleasing and there are no problems associated with the procedure or implants, there tends to be fewer problems in terms of causing an interference field. The same is true with facelifts. However, if a person is scarred, in pain, or traumatized, or the scar was associated with an infection or was delayed in healing, those scars almost always create interference fields. The reason that infections and lack of healing cause interference fields is because the inadequate voltage (healing energy) enables infections and delays the healing. Fibrous tissue, which is what a scar is, has lower voltage than other tissues. As a result, they are susceptible to interfere with healing.

Neural therapy involves the injection of Procaine (Novocain), a common local anesthetic, into specific areas. First explored and now used widely in Europe, when correctly administered this treatment can often instantly and lastingly resolve chronic longstanding illness and chronic pain by eliminating the interference that impairs healing mechanisms. Neural therapy when combined with homeopathic remedies, such as what Dr. Kaslow calls "Micro-Dose Bio-Modulation," is also often effective for other medical illnesses, including allergies, chronic bowel problems, kidney disease, male and female problems, infertility, tinnitus (ringing in the ears), and many other conditions. Neural therapy seems to reset the flow of information through the autonomic nervous system network. Dr. Kaslow uses the analogy of a computer that is malfunctioning. Rebooting the system often seems to enable the computer to reset itself and function again.

Dr. Kaslow says, "Because of the innerconnectedness of every cell through the sympathetic nervous system, any illness is an indication that the living organism as a whole has lost its ability to self-regulate itself and communicate in a completely healthful way. Organs never become diseased in isolation, but always as a symptom of the whole individual."

Down Time

I've only just recently come to understand the importance of down time—and I'm especially talking about vacations. In his book *Life Unlocked*, Dr. Srinivasan Pillay writes about vacations as "amygdala servicing." I asked Dr. Pillay to explain what we can get out of amygdala servicing vacations, and he emailed me, "The amygdala processes our emotions. Left to its own devices, it will process the most powerful emotions first. Fear is often that emotion, and at times of stress and anxiety—especially now when people are experiencing unprecedented levels of fear—fear takes over most the amygdala. In the absence of the continuous need to search for threat, vacations result in fear being displaced from the amygdala and positive emotions taking over. Positive emotions leave you feeling safer, more secure, and confident, paving the way for success in your endeavors. Amygdala servicing vacations also give the thinking centers of the brain a rest. The thinking brain may start to solve problems that it could not solve previously when it was being blasted by excessive fear."

If you go on unstructured vacations with little to do, your brain can become highly active, digging into the past to review threats and anticipating future danger. This "default network" is a survival mechanism to keep you from harm. But it works against you if you're not in imminent danger and are just trying to relax! Plan vacations centered around activities that you find positive and engaging. You don't have to save vacations for any particular season. Instead take breaks from the action whenever possible for however long you can fit it into your schedule. The goal is to regularly clear your mind with meditation and to add in as many amygdala servicing vacations as possible.

Hypnotherapy

Through Dr. Stephen Gilligan I met Carolyn R. Grothe, MS, MFT, who worked with me on insomnia with Ericksonian hypnotherapy. I asked Carolyn to explain how it works, and she emailed me, "Ericksonian hypnotherapy facilitates deep relaxation and connection to the body. It allows the brain to shift from an active, rational-thinking beta wave, into a quieter, more meditative alpha wave. In the state of hypnosis, as in mindfulness meditation, the part of the brain that is able to soothe the amygdala (the fear and anxiety generator area of the brain) is activated.

As the body relaxes, the racing thoughts quiet, and the fear center is calmed, the body's natural capacity to fall asleep can take over."

Prior to meeting Carolyn I had already come to the conclusion that it didn't feel right to revisit traumatic life experiences. I felt done with all of that and wanted to move on. Whenever I talked about trauma I felt worse and that bad feeling lingered, interfering with my happiness and my sleep. Carolyn explained why.

"In more recent years, there has been a movement in psychotherapy away from treating trauma by reliving the trauma. It was observed that, too often, the individual undergoing treatment was re-traumatized by reliving traumatic feelings and memories. No healing took place.

"The work of Stephen Gilligan, and others, has moved to a healing modality in which the traumatized individual is first anchored into a mental, emotional and physical state of safety in the present moment. The client is helped to connect with inner resources and positive states of feeling, as well as make a connection to the therapist as a safe and grounding resource in the present moment. From the perspective of the grounded observer, the client can revisit small doses of the traumatic experience at a time, bringing the memories and feelings into the present for healing and integration rather than going 'back' into simply reexperiencing the memories."

I hope that if you do not experience restful sleep through all of the other suggestions in this chapter that you'll at least give Ericksonian hypnotherapy a try.

The mere mention of exercise can get even the most sedentary person to run screaming from the room, so let's talk about it in depth and see what we can stir up.

thirteen

Ultimate You Skill No. 12: Exercise Regularly

I was twenty-four-years old before I did any kind of exercise at all. I'd been a sedentary smoker for ten years. After quitting smoking, I got interested in running. I didn't know a thing about training, stretching, or *anything* about exercise. The first pair of running shoes I bought were men's, because they didn't make running shoes for women back then. (We've come a long way, baby.) It wasn't socially acceptable for women to sweat, and people made grimacing faces when I'd finish a run with sweat running down my legs. I ran six miles nearly every day for twenty years. Every year on my birthday, I'd run ten miles. My life pretty much revolved around running. If I was invited out, it would cross my mind, *Is it worth staying up late?* I liked to go to bed early so I could get up at the crack of dawn and run.

Because running is injurious to the body, endorphins are secreted, which you'll remember are internal opiates that reduce pain and heighten pleasurable emotions. Dopamine follows, an excitatory, feel-good neurotransmitter. You can raise dopamine levels by using cocaine, marijuana, sugar, cigarettes, alcohol, and exercise. Ever since I discovered running, it's been a no brainer that exercise would be the healthy choice. I'm no exercise physiologist, but after all this time I know enough to share what I've experienced about exercise.

Exercise Is Anti-aging

Regular exercise stimulates the release of the longevity hormone, human growth hormone (hGH), from the pituitary. HGH accelerates repair of all tissues, stimulates immunity, and increases muscle building and fat burning—thus providing us more energy. Also, the reason people lose muscle mass is not due to "age," rather it's about moving or not moving. My Buddhist teacher, Chris Germer, calls it "congealing," which is so graphic.

When You're Sedentary You Congeal

Accelerated aging (look and feel worse)

Anxiety, depression, and tension

Can't make decisions

Decline in cognitive abilities (Huh? What?)

Decreased energy and more fatigue

Fat gain and muscle loss

Feelings of aging (losing *joie de vivre*)

Foggy brain

Increased risk for coronary heart disease

Less able to quit addictions

Sex drive vanishing

Sleep is not as good

Toxins accumulate in your body

Regular Exercise Builds Muscle and Causes Fat Loss

Helps to achieve optimal weight

Incentive to quit addictions

Lessens risk of coronary heart disease

Mental alacrity and sharpness

Mind is clear

Reduces anxiety, depression, and tension

Sleep better

Slows the aging process (because of hGH)

Sweating purges at least some toxins.

Yay! Sex drive is back.

You can make clear decisions.

You feel good! You've got *joie de vivre* and self-esteem.

You feel more energetic.

Consistency

If you're out of shape, you may be flashing on the times you tried to exercise and how it made you feel achy, tired, deflated, stupid, and fat. Now you're expecting me to say, "Exercise at your upper-working heart rate, for thirty to forty-five minutes three to four times a week." Not exactly. Some people like to exercise every day. Others, who have kids and a full-time job, can't do that. It's not possible by any stretch of the imagination. So why deflate your incentive? Just do something fun as many days as you can to feel good, look better, be happier, and live longer. The goal is consistency. If you're really tired and/or out of shape, you only need a little exercise to start rebuilding muscle mass.

Exercise Basics

We're no longer in the dark ages when it comes to exercise. There are gyms and yoga studios everywhere. You can catch yoga classes on TV, which is very cool! Just recently in Santa Barbara I hiked past people climbing on permanent rope and anchor systems that were installed for the public to indulge in rock climbing and rappelling. Even though many people are pretty well versed in exercise, it's nice to have the basics laid out as a refresher.

Exercise in the morning: Cortisol is naturally high in the morning, so that's a great time to exercise. Cortisol levels slowly come down throughout the day, so your body can shift into the parasympathetic mode. If you have trouble sleeping, definitely exercise before 2 p.m.

Exercise at your fitness level: Everyone is at a different fitness level. You may be out of shape, or recovering from an illness or injury, moderately fit, optimally fit for your age, ultra fit, or even extremely buffed and ripped. Once a person gets fit, she or he doesn't generally need a kick in the butt to exercise, and the reason is that exercise rocks. I think you'll be blown away when you see how many fun things there are to do that qualify as exercise. Also, remember to give yourself credit. Not everyone is a professional athlete, but we all have athletic prowess that we can develop. I couldn't win a competition, but I consider myself to be fit (though I'm always looking to improve).

Support your musculoskeletal system: You don't have to take up yoga, like I did. The jackpot, though, is if you can develop an exercise lifestyle that incorporates strength, endurance, and flexibility.

Strength

Unless you exercise moderately on a regular basis, you will begin to lose muscle mass after the age of thirty. After thirty, you can lose approximately 1 to 2 percent of your muscle mass every year. For most ambitious people, the mental image of a weakened old body is not a reality they look forward to. Staying strong means you remain a vital, active participant in life. Optimal physical functioning and longevity are both associated with strength.

What's more, weight-bearing exercise has been proven to impede bone loss. Bone mass reaches its maximum density between the ages of twenty-four and forty. After the age of forty, bone mass declines at about one half of one percent per year. Whatever exercise you chose, try to fit in some kind of weight-bearing activity.

Flexibility

As we age we lose flexibility (again, I'm talking to you twenty-year-olds). Just today I was in a yoga class in Los Angeles with three twenty-something girls who sat out most of the class because they simply could not flex. Increased flexibility improves range of motion, decreases risk of injury, eases creakiness, and prevents aches and pains. Yoga and Pilates are the best activities for gaining flexibility. If you choose another exercise, it is important—both to prevent injury and to increase flexibility—to stretch before and after you exercise.

Endurance

Although a significant decline in endurance occurs after the age of forty, regular moderate exercise can help prevent it (this applies to sexual endurance, too). One very important aspect of endurance is cardio-respiratory endurance, which refers to your body's circulatory and respiratory systems' ability to supply fuel during physical activity. You can improve your cardio-respiratory endurance no matter what your fitness level by exercising for a sustained amount of time, keeping your heart rate elevated. Improving endurance through exercise doesn't actually improve the condition of the heart itself, but it reduces the total workload of the heart. If you're out of shape, start slowly and work up to more intensity, until you can easily work out at your target heart rate. You can find your target heart rate by Googling "calculate target heart rate," which will direct you to numerous sites that calculate it. Walking is an excellent way to begin to build endurance. Start on a flat surface, and graduate to hills and walking faster. Keep your chest lifted and your chin up, and swing your arms, hand rising above your heart. To maximize building endurance, cross train—that is do something different as often as possible.

Training

All those years ago, I had no idea about training. I just went out and jogged around a football field with distance goals in mind—one mile, two miles, three miles. The following is what I've learned about training.

Hormones and Exercise

When you first begin to exercise, your adrenal glands produce adrenaline, which raises your heart rate and directs the blood flow to the muscles that are working. Adrenaline also releases blood sugar into your bloodstream to generate the initial energy to fuel your muscles. As you continue to exercise moderately, the hormone glucagon is released from your pancreas. Glucagon is the fat-utilizing hormone. During moderate exercise, glucagon releases fat from your fat cells to turn into sugar to burn as fuel. At the same time, DHEA is continually released. DHEA also stimulates your body to burn fat for fuel. Switching into fat-burning metabolism releases energy, so you'll lose body fat and feel more energetic.

You want to train up gradually, though, because jumping into radical exercise without training doesn't give your body time to ramp up glucagon production. However, it has plenty of cortisol to pump out. Cortisol, if you recall, breaks down lean body mass (muscle and bone) to provide your body with necessary sugar. So you may see weight loss by ratcheting up your exercise at an accelerated pace, but it will be due to muscle wasting, not fat loss. This is another balancing act, because ultimately you don't want a lowered metabolism and weight gain, which can happen. The more trained you are, the longer you can exercise without your body dumping cortisol into your system. That's why athletes train.

And here we talk about protein again, because your body needs a regular supply to make the hormone glucagon. If you don't have enough glucagon when you exercise, then guess what? Cortisol will rush in to break down lean body mass for sugar for energy. Less muscle mass equals aging, which translates to slower and less efficient repair. I'm talking about twenty-year-olds again, too, because aging is so rapid now. I see sedentary twenty-year-olds eating Fritos and drinking Diet Coke or Starbucks, and smoking, and I think, *Wow, you're going to look older than me pretty soon.*

Aerobic and Anaerobic Exercise

Aerobic exercise is relatively low intensity such as running on a treadmill or jogging, biking, or any activity that gets your heart rate to 70 percent of your upper working heart rate. Aerobic exercise burns 25 percent muscle and 75 percent fat. It also builds cardiovascular and circulatory strength.

Anaerobic exercise is serious resistance exercise that requires short bursts of exertion, like pumping iron, that stretches your maximum energy capacity, raising your heart rate to between 85 and 90 percent of your working heart rate. Anaerobic exercise burns 100 percent fat. It also builds muscle and bone. Hydration and cool downs help diminish the lactic acid build up caused by anaerobic exercise.

Your Working Heart Rate

Your heart rate tells you if you are exercising aerobically or anaerobically. The max heart rate for men is 220 less your age, women is 225 less your age. The target heart rate is 70 percent of your max. When the heart rate is faster than 70 percent, you are exercising aerobically. When it's less, it's anaerobic.

Maximize Breathing

Breathing is always stressed in yoga, and increasingly in other types of indoor aerobics classes. Air enters the lungs and oxygen is passed through the lining of the lungs, taken up by red blood cells that then carry the oxygen into circulating blood. Oxygenated blood goes to the heart and is circulated throughout the entire body. Your muscles use this oxygen to create energy. As it's being used, oxygen gives off carbon dioxide as a waste product. The carbon dioxide is released into the blood stream and returned to the lungs to be exhaled.

Interval Training

Interval training consists of intermittent high- and low-intensity exercises repeated in short sets. One reason I love yoga is that it is inherently interval training. Interval training is both aerobic and anaerobic. The anaerobic "sprint" can be as short as thirty seconds or as long as twenty minutes, followed by a corresponding recovery period.

Interval training is beautiful for busy people because you can cut your workout time to twenty minutes plus pre- and post-stretching. Bear in mind that all exercise comprises, to some degree, both aerobic and anaerobic exercise. Interval training just pushes the benefits of both.

Benefits of Interval Training

- Boosts energy
- Burns body fat
- Firms skin, reduces wrinkles
- Improves athletic performance
- Improves muscle tone
- Improves sex drive

How to Sprint (Interval) Train

- Warm up with stretching or easy movements for a few minutes.
- Hit it as hard as you can for twenty to thirty seconds until you are out of breath.
- Recover for ninety seconds.
- Feel your core body temperature rising.
- Feel muscle burn (due to lactic acid).
- Work so you're sweating by the second or third rep.
- Do seven to eight reps.

NOTE: *Some women don't sweat very easily or at all.*

Eat Right for Exercise

The entire *Healthy, Sexy, Happy* nutritional program could be summed up in one sentence: How to build up more than you break down. Accelerated aging is breaking down. If you're exercising without supplying your body with adequate building materials, you are going to break down faster than you're building back up.

Basic Nutrition for Athletes

Exercise creates a surplus of free radicals that you would not otherwise have in your system. The damage (breakdown) from these free radicals can launch you into accelerated aging if you don't supply your body with corresponding antioxidants. You'll end up doing more harm than good in the long run. If you're adding exercise because you don't want to stop eating factory-food products—and even if you end up thinner and looking perky—you'll see the consequences eventually. If you exercise, you have to be diligent about providing your body with real, living food—and plenty of it—and steering clear of toxins, stimulants, and emotional stress. Exercise (and the potential free radical damage) is a good example of why you need to seek complete balance throughout and not just pick and choose.

Protein and Fat

Just as we need to adjust our carbs, we also need to pay attention to protein when we exercise more or less, because muscle mass and bones are made of amino acids. If you're breaking down a lot faster than normal because you increase your exercise, then you need to eat more protein and fat to compensate. Protein and fat are also necessary to produce the fat-utilizing hormone glucagon.

Carbo-Loading

Even extreme athletes need to balance their meals to maintain optimal metabolic health. People believe that it's important to carbo-load before exercising because they will "burn" it off. True, you do burn off excess sugar as energy. However, you can't burn off the excess insulin that has been secreted in response—and insulin is implicated in every single degenerative disease of aging, not to mention that it's the "fat storing" hormone. Once insulin goes to work stowing away all that sugar, there won't be enough sugar in your bloodstream, and your brain will assume that you are in a time of famine and send a red alert to your adrenals to release adrenaline and cortisol. Adrenaline releases energy from sugar stored in your liver and muscles, and cortisol *breaks down* your own muscle mass to turn it into sugar. This influx of sugar into your bloodstream triggers the secretion of insulin, which immediately stores this new sugar away into cells. So ultimately your body chips away at lean body mass. If you're in the habit of carbo-loading, day after day, your adrenals continually will be responding to red alerts from your brain, secreting adrenaline and cortisol to manage your blood sugar. Eventually you can suffer from decreased muscle mass, fat around your middle, a flabby body, hypoglycemia, lowered metabolism, and accelerated aging—in part from having too much insulin in your bloodstream, which is as damaging as sugar.

The best diet for an athlete is a regular balanced diet of real, whole, living food that includes protein, fat, green vegetables, and some complex carbs. There are many studies that prove that athletes who eat a balanced diet outperform those who eat a high-carb diet.

Ditch the Sugar

I often marvel at how many young, overweight yogis I see in classes. If you eat properly before and after a hot yoga class, it's one of the fastest ways to lose body fat because it combines anaerobic exercise, heat (sweating to purge toxins), and interval training.

As I said before, interval training forces the muscles to use stored energy (fat) and also increases human growth hormone, which builds muscle. The more muscle mass you have the faster your metabolism. A lot of yogis are vegan and vegetarian, and these diets aren't optimal if you want a fit and toned body. Vegetarian diets are better, obviously, because they contain fat and protein from eggs and dairy. However, the typical vegetarian diet tends to be too heavily weighted in carbs—even if they are complex carbs. It may be possible to eat a healthy vegan diet if it were tightly controlled to provide the essential proteins and essential fatty acids necessary for hormone production and cellular renewal, but I'm rather skeptical. I'm not going to even try to explore the vegan diet because it is the polar opposite of my dietary philosophy. The problem with both vegan and vegetarian diets when combined with exercise is the natural tendency to eat refined carbs before and after.

Whether you're a meat eater, vegan, or vegetarian, if you eat sugar or any form of fructose (including a glass of wine or fruit) within a couple of hours of exercise, you'll increase somatostatin, which is the growth hormone–inhibiting hormone that turns off your internal production of growth hormone. For example, Gatorade, power bars, Red Bull, Snapple, and granola with chocolate chips and dried fruit are very bad ideas when exercising. If you are on a long hike, for example, a peanut butter sandwich on fresh, bakery-made whole-grain bread and water is a much better choice to refuel. For what it's worth, I've done my share of hardcore hikes, and I have never found it necessary to snack during a hike. It's more important to stay hydrated. For nutritional guidelines for all metabolic types, see page 62.

Electrolytes

Electrolytes are minerals that are required by cells to regulate the electric charge across cell membranes. Excessive loss of electrolytes happens through sweat, a factory-food diet, extreme exercising (especially if you're not trained), not drinking enough water, and too much or too little salt intake. A balanced diet that includes whole grains, dark leafy veggies, nuts, beans, legumes, whole dairy, fruit, some sea salt, and adequate water intake will supply your body with electrolytes. Sea algae is another good source of natural electrolytes.

Essential Fatty Acids

Essential fatty acids (EFAs) play numerous roles in human health. But if you are an athlete, EFAs can help reduce exercised-induced inflammation, and prevent and relieve joint and muscle stiffness and tenderness. See page 43 for more about EFAs.

Try Out New Sports and Activities

Once you've established exercise as part of your life, it's a good idea to branch out. I'd been a runner for about six years when I read an article in *GQ* that startled me with its revelations about running. I learned that I wasn't the only runner in the world who got winded climbing stairs and who had lost equilibrium. My interest was so peaked by that article that I started incorporating aerobics classes and weight training into my workout. I loved running, and I'm sure if I make it to that tranquil deathbed that I'll revisit fond memories of my very first runs around a track in San Diego, and later running in Burbank at 4 a.m. passing coyotes picking through garbage, running the Central Park and Hollywood reservoirs, in Detroit in the snow, the hills of Pacific Palisades, the median on San Vicente in Santa Monica, the foothills in Santa Barbara, through the surf in Manhattan Beach, Cabo San Lucas, Mexico, and Sydney, Australia, in the cities of Zürich, Paris, Rome, the chaotic streets of New Delhi, and on and on. Later, I made the conscious decision to stop running before I totally wrecked my knees, because I looked at the bigger picture of my life, in which I saw myself as athletic until the end. The drastic measure of forsaking a sport I was passionate about wasn't easy. I struggled for three years to find something to take the place of running. Quitting running turned out to be a blessing in disguise, because I ultimately discovered yoga. Among its other attributes, yoga can be as injurious as running, thus you end up with the endorphin and dopamine high, even if you're a beginner. In other words, it's addicting too.

The yogi scholar Patañjali, who lived about 150 years B.C.E. compiled the yoga sutras, which lay out the basic tenets of yoga philosophy and practice. Then in 1888, the Brahmin Sri Tirumalai Krishnamacharya was born in southern India, and became the most influential yoga teacher of our time by using the ancient yoga sutra texts and teachings from the Hindu bible, *The Bhagavad Gita*, to breathe life into the practice of yoga. Having effectively created a movement that has enchanted the modern world, he counted both B.K.S. Iyengar and the late K. Pattabhi Jois among his students.

"Yoga," a Sanskrit word from "yuj" meaning *to control*, *to yoke*, or *to unite*, is a combination of physical and meditative disciplines. As I said earlier, yoga was developed to prepare the body for the higher state of consciousness in meditation.

In the thirteen years I've been practicing, I've been influenced by several of my own significant masters of yoga, who formed my practice and my attitudes about yoga. I'd like to share them with you, because I see my yoga experience as a metaphor for acceptance. Yoga can do quite the number on your head if you let it, especially if you're competitive. For various reasons (age, injury, accident) we all have to accept limitations and find new ways of exercising, so it's best to have that in mind even if you're in love with what you're doing now.

Hatha Yoga

My very first yoga teacher, in April 1997, was Scott Blossom, L.A.c., who remains to this day my greatest inspiration. He came into my life when I was just becoming open to all things yoga and spiritual, and he could not have set a more dynamic example. Since we met, Scott has branched out into Traditional Chinese medicine,

Shadow Yoga, and Ayurvedic medicine, and I've continued to learn from him. Back then, Scott had only been practicing yoga for seven years, but being a twenty-seven-year-old with a graceful, lithe, strong body, he was already a master who blew me away by "floating" and doing all the otherworldly yoga asanas.[47]

Scott started me with Hatha Yoga. Hathayoga Pradīpikā is the classic Sanskrit yoga manual, written by Svami Svatmarama. It's believed to be the oldest surviving text on Hatha Yoga. The text was written in 15th century B.C.E. derived from Sanskrit texts dated around the eleventh century B.C.E. Scott guided me through the first excruciating six months. My muscles, ligaments, and tendons were so *tight* from all my years of running I could barely touch my toes—actually I don't think I *could* touch my toes. The idea of doing a foreword fold seemed like an impossible dream.

Sometimes still, I'll be in a pose and think of Scott remembering those early fundamentals that he taught me. I'll always consider him one of my masters. Just recently I met up with him at Kripalu in Massachusetts, where he worked with me on post-shoulder-surgery backbends.

Ashtanga

After Hatha, I graduated to another much higher level of yoga called Ashtanga, though I have to be clear that I didn't start until I was fifty, so I had built-in limitations. I kind of knew what Ashtanga was. But it was memorably intimidating to walk into a yoga studio and see people doing stuff that looked like part of a Cirque du Soleil performance.

The instructors were Michele Nichols, who is dark, lithe, and stunning, and her then boyfriend (later husband) Steve Dwelley, a truly evolved human being with extensive knowledge of yoga, as well as the accompanying wisdom and compassion. I knew Michele from other practices, though her primary focus is Ashtanga. Michele and Steve were close to Sri K. Pattabhi Jois, also known as Guruji, the Ashtanga master, and Michele had been the featured yogi in a photograph in a *New Yorker* article, "The Yoga Bums,"[48] and blew everyone away by continuing to practice Ashtanga, including doing standing backbends until two weeks before the birth of her twin boys. Michele and Steve were close to Guruji for good reason, as they are the real thing.

The morning I arrived for my first Ashtanga class, Michele set me up and explained that everyone practices at their own level in what's called "Mysore." "I am happy to teach you the primary series," Michele said. "But we ask that you commit or we don't want to spend the time with you." I agreed and got half way through the primary series in that session. Even though I couldn't do most of the poses, and ended up sweaty and sore, I was hooked.

Ashtanga is the traditional form of yoga from which commercialized "hot," "power," and "flow" yoga practices are derived. It's taught as a system that begins with the primary series—the same poses in sequence—and works through six series. I am not sure there is a living person doing the sixth series, but I'm fairly certain that it involves levitation and becoming invisible (just kidding!—but not really). Suffice it to say, if you've reached that level, you are no longer mortal.

The reason the practice is referred to as Mysore-style Ashtanga is that Mysore was the home of the late Pattabhi Jois, who as a young man learned the Ashtanga sequences from his guru Krishnamacharya and carried out his teachings in his hometown at the Ashtanga Research Institute.[49] Westerners flocked there to learn the practice under Guruji's tutelage. In the years before his death on May 18, 2009 at the age of ninety-three, Guruji regularly traveled his "final" world tour. I'd been practicing Ashtanga for almost a year when I attended his led classes at the Puck Building in Soho. It was two weeks after 9/11, and the positive energy was palpable in the room with 200 people doing headstands together, zoning out of the tragedy. A few years later I practiced at the Hollywood Roosevelt Hotel and actually got a few memorable adjustments from Guruji. Guruji's legacy has been passed to his grandson Sharath.

Ashtanga focuses on the breath called *ujjayi pranayama*, which is coordinated (linked) with movement and *asanas* (the Sanskrit word for "postures") that lead you into a meditative state. Ujjayi breathing is concentrated, controlled breath that makes a sound like the ocean. Of all the types of yoga practices, Ashtanga is perhaps the most injurious, and when the body is injured, a flood of opiate neurotransmitters is released in the brain, leaving you with a fairly significant high that lasts all day and into the night.

In Ashtanga the eyes focus on a *drishti*, a meditative point of reference, or gazing point, whether be it your hands or navel or somewhere above you. This helps develop the meditative focus throughout your practice. *Bandhas*, energetic locks, are practiced to foster awareness and generate internal energy and heat. During practice, the lifting of your pelvic floor, called *mulabhanda*, and the drawing up of your lower abdomen, called *uddiyana bandha*, also provide strength, heat, and energy. These techniques provide stability throughout your practice.

Mulabhanda for More Pleasurable Sex

Kegel exercises were developed by Dr. Arnold Kegel to build up the pubococcygeus (PC) muscles of the pelvic floor in women to help endure pregnancy and vaginal childbirth, and to prevent vaginal and uterine prolapse, and in men to treat prostate pain and swelling resulting from benign prostatic hyperplasia (enlargement) and prostatitis (chronic pain). Pelvic floor exercises help correct urinary incontinence in both men and women. This exercise increases sexual pleasure.

Mulabandha is the same as Kegels as you contract the muscles of the pelvic floor in a "lock" during your practice. Think of cinching the muscles that you contract to stop the flow of urine. The purpose of *mulabandha* is to provide a foundation for your yoga practice, but doing so over a period of time strengthens the pelvic floor. Strengthening the PC muscle increases sexual pleasure by tightening the vagina in women and helping men avoid premature ejaculation. Strengthening the PC muscle can resolve impotence, depending on its cause.

Krishnamacharya's Legacy

Practicing Ashtanga, even in my own limited way, enriched my yoga practice by giving me a foundation from which to explore other types of yoga. Krishnamacharya's legacy extends beyond Hatha and Ashtanga. For example, I've practiced Yin yoga on occasion, which requires a strong yoga practice, as it keeps you in asanas for long periods of time, strengthening and stretching you to the max. It's designed to open up the deepest, most neglected areas of your body to prepare you for long periods of meditation. Iyengar yoga was devised by B.K.S. Iyengar (who's now in his nineties and does a thirty-minute headstand every morning), another disciple of Krishnamacharya. Iyengar places emphasis on body alignment with the use of props: cushions, benches, blocks, straps, and sand bags. There are many other types of yoga—and covering them all would be a book in itself. But I did want to talk a little bit about American yoga.

When I went to India in the late sixties and was exposed to the trippy world of yoga, mysticism, and nirvana, it was all deliciously exotic but also insanely complicated. Since then, countless Westerners have swarmed to India and poured over ancient texts, studying, learning, and cherry picking the stuff that they wanted while tossing back what they couldn't assimilate or understand. Western yogis have devised their own forms of practice. Today it's not just Hatha, Ashtanga, or Iyengar. It's the Wild West.

PranaVayu Yoga

I met my next yoga inspiration, David Magone, in Boston. In 2001, David founded PranaVayu Yoga, which is an American school of vinyasa yoga (which means "breath synchronized movement"). Initially I started going to his class because his schedule worked with mine. By the time I arrived at his mid-day class, I was usually fairly amped up. His classes are packed, but when he walks in and starts talking, it's comparable to sinking into a hot tub. He's got a particularly effective mind-clearing way about him, and his opening talk sweeps the mind clean before you even begin practicing. It doesn't hurt that he is also very nice to look at, and like my other influences, a masterful yogi.

I asked David how he approaches a room full of people who are not versed in the Yoga Sutras (Hindu scriptures that are the foundational text of yoga), or Buddhism. "We all come from different backgrounds, but we're united in the fact that we all wish to be happy," he said. "With that basic understanding as my basis, I do my best to offer a complete set of teachings as nondogmatically as possible so that students can experience how regular yoga practice can lead to more happiness, health, and higher degree of openness." David explained that openness was related to the Buddhist concept of equanimity, or the extension of loving-kindness and compassion to all beings without exception. (We talked about Buddhist meditation in Chapter 12, and how it isn't a religion but a philosophy.) "Typically, when we extend our love and compassion to others we limit those emotions to our immediate sphere of close friends and loved ones, which by definition makes our openness limited. Buddhist philosophy encourages us to cultivate an unbiased openness by gradually extending those same feelings of love and compassion outward to our loved ones and perfect strangers, eventually our enemies, and finally all sentient beings throughout the universe as a whole. This process gradually helps us pull down some of the boundaries that we all unconsciously—or sometimes consciously—erect and creates a much deeper sense of openness and connection to others."

David's classes incorporate yoga poses designed to strengthen and stretch the body, traditional meditative techniques to calm the mind and develop a deeper sense of connection to others, and lessons from the Buddhist tradition that teach the behaviors that lead to happier lives. "The practice is built on the belief that people can make the world a better place by working toward the full realization of their potential as happy, healthy, and open human beings."

David, who has been meditating since 1995 when he was eighteen, wanted to be sure that the meditative practices and philosophy offered in PranaVayu Yoga were drawn from reputable, traditional sources. Through a friend, he was introduced to Khenpo Migmar Tseten Rinpoche, who is a Tibetan Lama and the Buddhist Chaplain at Harvard University. Lama Migmar took David on as a student, a collaboration took off between them, and now they teach together regularly. (I asked Lama Migmar why he meditated and he emailed me, "In simple words, I do meditation for peace and awakening." In my experience there is no bliss greater than yoga combined with meditation.) I hope you'll take inspiration in David's actions, as I truly believe that when the student is ready the teacher will come.

David's combination of serious yoga, guided meditative practices, and Buddhist-inspired philosophy drew me back to his class during the three years I lived in Boston. Practicing with David took my practice to another deeper level, for a couple of reasons. Part of the time I was recovering from bilateral rotator cuff surgeries. One of the major hurdles of any yogic journey is to come to a personal grasp of your limitations and to be able to accept them. Also, I began to fully appreciate the fresh contributions that Western practitioners, like David, have made to the American yoga culture.

Bikram

I recently discovered Bikrim yoga, which is a series of twenty-six postures developed by Bikram Choudhury from the Hatha yoga lineage. The series is designed to work every part of your body in a systematic, synergistic way (though this is typical of most well-designed yoga practices). Bikram calls his studios "torture chambers," because the heat is kept at 104° F.[50]

Depending on the practice and the mentality of the instructor, all yoga practices can fall prey to a fundamentalist vibe. In fact I had an absolutely *terrible* experience with a fundamentalist jerk who led an Ashtanga class. Yoga was developed to prepare and purify your body and mind for meditation, not as a forum for instructors to trot out their egos. Many of my Bikram experiences have been a little on the boot-camp side. I have my yoga preferences and quirks. I prefer to sit in a full lotus rather than cross-legged, and I have a habit of holding my hands in a yoga mudra—hand positions that seal energy—if I'm in a wrap or a bind. These are the kinds of habitual preferences you develop as your practice deepens. But there isn't room for individuality in Bikram. That isn't to say that it's a negative thing. Discipline is a cherished characteristic that we all can benefit from.

And Bikram is a wonderful path to discipline and can be a lot of fun if you let go of notions of doing your own thing. Bikram is meant to be structured. See more about exercising in heat on page 225.

Madonnathon

Another influence is Lynne Begier, who owns Back Bay Yoga in Boston. Lynne has also taken what she wants from the practice and made it her own. I wanted to mention her because she's another yogi who isn't taking herself so seriously that she can't have a good time. Her classes—like her Madonnathons—are nonjudgmental, challenging, and a blast. I revere yoga and have gotten a tremendous spiritual boost from my practice—but it doesn't always have to be taken so seriously.

Yoga and Weight Management

A few years ago, I went to a class in Pacific Palisades led by Billy Asad. I loved his challenging and exacting style so much that for the next few years I scheduled my West Coast trips around his teaching schedule so I could make his classes.

Billy developed his practice by studying Ashtanga, Iyengar, and Sivananda yoga (which is a slower paced yoga centered on *pranayama* (breathing) and full expressions of the poses). One quality that sets him apart from many yogis is that he's an athlete beyond yoga. Because he's accomplished at surfing, hiking, mountain climbing, and other athletic pursuits, he's looked at yoga as a way to strengthen and support the body outside of the yoga studio. His precision focus on yoga anatomy is a magnetic aspect of his practice, as yoga is about mind-body mechanics.

Because Billy eats the balanced diet of real, whole, living food that I advocate, he has a sexy, muscular body. He embodies what I've been saying about ideal body composition! So when he talked to me about helping people with weight management issues, I was very interested.

We've talked a lot about cravings and bingeing, and how to heal your brain through nutrition, neurotransmitters, and meditation. Yoga can be a huge part of healing your brain and turning off demands and cravings that lead people to unhealthy eating. I know from thirteen years of practicing yoga that no matter how much chatter is going on in my head, within a minute or two of practice my mind is serene and focused. And it's stays pretty much dead calm throughout.

There was a reason that ancient sages developed the practice of yoga to prepare the body, mind, and spirit for meditation. You are simply in a state of meditation without mental effort. This is the yoga phenomenon that Billy centers his yoga weight management philosophy on.

"With every practice, whether it's ten minutes or two hours, you create a birth and death," Billy told me. "You come in with baggage—the stuff of your life—and you surrender and move into the new you, and you start over again. You experience *tapas*, which is Sanskrit word that means 'purification through burning.' It doesn't mean sweating your butt off. Tapas is a stripping, burning, or death of old patterns and thoughts, and surrendering through your yoga practice. It's like shedding a snake skin." In his fifteen years of teaching, Billy has watched his students change and many of them gain control over unhealthy eating habits. "I see people heal themselves physically and emotionally through their yoga practice," he said. "We're using yoga as a way to change from the inside out so people start living a healthier life all around. A dedicated yoga practice is like a reset button, which has a snowball effect. Yoga releases stress and that's one of the main reasons people overeat. You find that you take better care of yourself and eat healthier. The word yoga is Sanskrit for 'yolk.' It's the union of body, mind, and consciousness. Along with this union is the mastery of the body. Ultimately you shed your old attitudes about body image and adopt a new healthier way of being."

Weight management occurs naturally through a gentle connecting of your mind, body, and spirit without all the strife associated with dieting and "weight loss." When equanimity is sought, the body shrinks (if necessary) and otherwise conforms to a pleasing, optimal body weight. If you've read this book through, you now have a better understanding that weight management is not about starving and seeking emaciation. I'm a lot more curvy than I was when I was a runner who didn't eat very much. And I sincerely hope you'll reject the prison camp thin ideal, and that you'll see where your body will take you.

Keep It Mellow

One popular practice that emerged from Ashtanga is power yoga. Unfortunately, some teachers get way too gnarly with it. Brian Kest, who has been practicing and teaching yoga since 1979, has a slant on power yoga that fits my mind, body, spirit philosophy. His classes are challenging, yet forgiving, with permission to practice in a way that restores rather than depletes you. In a class in Santa Monica, he led us through a pose called *Utthita Hasta Padangustasana*. You begin in a standing position, draw your right knee up, reach down your inner thigh to clasp your big toe with your right index and middle fingers, then you stand up straight and straighten your leg . . . and you get the picture. As we reached for our toes, Brian said, "I just taught a class of eight-year-olds and this is the part of the class where they laughed the most." When we began straightening our legs, he said, "And when they fell, they laughed the hardest." I loved this story because it illustrated what our attitudes toward yoga—or any other physical activity—should be: fun and happy. We don't need to take ourselves so seriously. When we struggle for perfection we end up feeling bad, insecure, and generally depleted. Let go of expectations, grasping, and clinging to find joy and renewal.

There are lots more yoga masters, and I wish I could mention every one of my influences, but I wanted to mention my significant teachers and influences so that you could understand how a yoga practice begins and evolves. There are times when my practice sucks, but I've never said, "I hate it." I'm doing things with my body that I couldn't even do as a child. I can go into a yoga class feeling exhausted and come out energized. Yoga makes me feel the way I felt when I got my second wind running. So the point is, if you reach a point in one sport that doesn't work for you anymore, there are plenty of other options. Just find something you love.

Hook Up with People Who Can Help You

Whatever your exercise of choice, it's neat to strive to learn more and to expand. Like in any endeavor, it's important to find mentors. You don't have to hire personal trainers; you can ask for help from someone you know who is more advanced in what you're doing. As you can see from reading about my yoga masters, I've pursued what I needed and have found people to help me on my yoga journey. Just recently—after thirteen years of yoga practice—I worked with yet another amazing yogi, Rebecca Pacheco, in Boston. After all these years, she pointed out two glaring moves that I needed to finesse. These small, conscious changes took my practice to an entirely new level.

Exercising in Heat

I've done a lot of hot yoga and marathon hikes on heat wave days in Santa Barbara. Sweating rids your body of heavy metals. However, exercising in very high temperatures can pose health risks. I've been in hot yoga classes where the heat goes up to 120° F. One day I decided to weigh myself before and after a hot yoga class to see how much water I lost. The studio was exceptionally hot and humid and my friends and I were all sweating profusely and in distress most of the class. Toward the end my blood pressure plummeted (my radial pulse was weak) and I couldn't drive home. Later, when I got home, I weighed myself and even after having drunk nearly two liters of water I had lost five-and-a-half pounds. That was over 4 percent of my body weight, which is way too much fluid for a person my size to lose, and it taught me a lesson.

Heat exhaustion results from salt and water depletion after prolonged exercise in heat. Early warning signs of heat exhaustion include flushed face, hyperventilation, headache, dizziness, nausea, arm or hand tingling, body hairs standing on end, paradoxical chilliness, losing coordination, confusion, uncharacteristically belligerent behavior (I *was* kind of grumpy), and low blood pressure. If you monitor your weight loss after a hot workout and you lose 2 to 3 percent of your body weight, you need to make sure to hydrate well before you go into a hot yoga room again. If you inadvertently lose too much water, you should fully hydrate and not exercise again for one to two days.

You also need to be aware that exercising in heat can raise your core body temperature. (An oral or even rectal temperature doesn't measure core temperature.) Any kind of exercise will generate free radicals, but extreme exercise in heat radically increases metabolic heat, which generates a landslide of free radicals. If you feel uncomfortably overheated—as the brain is exquisitely sensitive—you risk damaging neural cells with the increase in free radicals.

However, exercising in heat can also be beneficial if you take care to provide your body with enough water replacement as well as balanced nutrition, including plenty of antioxidants. All types of exercise oxygenate your tissues, however heat dilates your blood vessels, allowing for greater oxygenation and nutrition to your cells. To ensure that exercise in heat is beneficial and not detrimental, you should acclimate to heat by successively and incrementally increasing the level of your activity in heat. This will enable you to work out safely at temperatures that may have previously felt intolerable or even life threatening. Most people who enter into a hot yoga class are compelled, because of intolerance to heat and feelings of nausea, to sit out at least a few parts of the first few classes. Acclimatization markedly increases the amount of sweating, which allows you to cool off, but it also decreases the electrolyte content of sweat. Acclimatization significantly decreases risk of a heat illness.

NOTE: *Never drink out of plastic water bottles in a hot situation as heat causes plastic to emit xenohormones into the water.*

Exercising in the Sun: The Good, The Bad, and The Ugly

The Good: We all need some sun on unprotected skin so that our bodies can convert UV rays to vitamin D. Vitamin D deficiencies are linked to our epidemic rise in disease, especially cancer. Vitamin D is necessary for your body to utilize calcium, which is essential to building and maintaining a strong skeletal structure. So getting a little sun is a good thing.

The Bad: Too much sun exposure is called hypervitaminosis D. UV rays synthesize skin oils into vitamin D, which pulls calcium out of your tissues into your bloodstream. When that occurs, it can unleash the herpes virus, as well as canker sores and hives. To prevent outbreaks if you exercise in the sun or heat, take calcium lactate supplements. Also get enough vitamin F (contained in essential fatty acids in fish, walnuts, and sunflower seeds). Stay hydrated, and keep your potassium levels up by eating food rich in potassium such as apricots, raisins, figs, and bananas.

The Ugly: Melanoma. And wrinkles. (Enough said!) See page 271 for more on healthy sun block.

Over Exercising and Post-exertional Malaise

Over exercising is just as counterproductive to health as under exercising. There are those who use exercise as a way to dull emotional pain. Exercise to the extreme has just as many downsides as being sedentary. This is especially important for extreme woman athletes because there is more of a tendency not to eat enough to compensate for the accelerated breakdown that occurs when you rev your metabolism. So if you are exercising a lot and not eating, you are aging your body rapidly and sooner or later it's going to show up on your face. We've all seen it in woman long-distance runners: gaunt faces with severe nasal labial folds. If you must exercise to extreme, you also must eat.

Most people can over exercise for a certain amount of years before the metabolic breakdown catches up to them. If you begin to feel bad after exercise, or even sick the following day, it's a clear signal to ratchet back. If you're sick and trying to exercise and you experience a recurrence or increase in your symptoms, called "post-exertional malaise," then you're pushing yourself too hard. Anyone who is pounding his or her body with toxic stressors, not getting enough rest in between, is doing unhealthy things like over exercising or anything that might tip the scales can experience post-exercise malaise. The normal response to exercise is an antidepressant effect and feelings of invigoration. If exercise doesn't invigorate you then you need to reevaluate your exercise program.

All aspects of the *Healthy, Sexy, Happy* program are designed to preserve and rebuild you, not tear down. If you're tearing yourself down because of an inner drive to quell pain, then you need to address the emotional issues that are compelling you.

Sports Injuries

In the winter of 2009 I took a Wilderness First Responder course in Jackson Hole, Wyoming. During the course, the question of sports-related injuries came up. Most of the students were much more hardcore, extreme athletes than I've ever been. One by one they recounted litanies of abrasions, sprains, broken bones, broken backs, herniated discs, ruptured Achilles tendons, and ACL injuries. One guy even attended the course on crutches, having been rescued from near death after falling into a ravine. Anyone who participates in sports for any length of time will eventually experience an athletic injury. I have cartilage degeneration from running, as well as one spiral fracture (hiking), pulled hamstring connectors, and a torn rotator cuff requiring bilateral surgeries (yoga), and every imaginable strained muscle, to name just a few of my injuries.

Aside from serious injuries requiring surgery, dealing with the pain and inflammation of many sports-related injuries is best accomplished with RICE: rest, ice, compression, and elevation, along with a healing diet. OTC and prescription pain-killing drugs are too fraught with potential chronic side effects to take on an ongoing basis. But enlightened medicine is now offering miraculous alternatives to drugs and surgery for certain injuries. One enlightened doctor is my long-time friend, Allen Thomashefsky, M.D. When I have an injury—something that isn't likely to go away on its own—I go to see him, as his primary interest is getting people back to doing what they want to do.

Dr. Tom uses a nonsurgical proliferant regenerative injection therapy called prolotherapy to stimulate the body's own natural healing/growth cycle to repair. Novocain is injected into the injured site along with a proliferant solution of Sarapin (an herbal solution) and dextrose (sugar). Novocain is used to avoid the ouch-factor when the needle is tapped at the site to create a micro-injury. The combination of the micro-injury and the natural substances invigorate the immune system to rush in to repair. As Dr. Tom says, a "turbo-charged" alternative to dextrose is platelet rich plasma (PRP). Your body produces white blood cells and platelets that store growth factors. When your blood is harvested, concentrated, and injected into an injured site, these growth factors promote accelerated healing by turning on growth, activating DNA, and initiating cell repair and tissue regeneration.

Prolotherapy isn't exclusive to sports injuries, and Dr. Tom is just one example of the many doctors who are exploring natural methods of prevention and healing. You can find a doctor trained in prolotherapy at getprolo.com or aaomed.org. See page 203 for more on alternative pain therapy.

You may not be at risk of sports injury because you're sedentary. But being out of shape can lead to injuries due to lack of strength, flexibility/coordination, and endurance. Being intimidated by exercise is a roadblock you can overcome with determination, persistence, and will.

Exercises for the Out-of-Shape

- Aqua-exercises (in saline pool)
- Beach walking
- Bowling
- Gentle bike riding on a stationary bike or around the neighborhood
- Gentle hiking
- Hitting golf balls
- Hitting tennis balls
- Horseback riding (walking and trotting)
- Ping-pong
- Puttering in the garden
- Qigong
- Restorative yoga
- Roller skating
- Softball, shooting baskets
- Stretching
- Strolling
- Tai chi

Exercises for the Somewhat Fit

- Aqua-aerobics
- Beach power walking or jogging
- Bowling
- Cross-country skiing
- Cycling (indoors or out)
- Dancing
- Downhill skiing
- Elliptical treadmill
- Golf (nine or eighteen holes)

Horseback riding (more advanced training)
Ice skating
Jogging
Moderate hiking
More challenging yoga (Vinyasa flow, Yin)
Mountain climbing
Pilates
Ping-pong

Qigong
Roller skating, roller blading
Rope jumping
Serious gardening
Snowboarding
Softball, volleyball, football
Swimming laps
Tai chi
Tennis
Trampoline

Exercises for the Extremely Fit

Advanced yoga (Ashtanga, Yin, Bikram)
Beach power walking or running
Calisthenics (sit-ups/push-ups)
Competitive swimming
Cross-country skiing
Cycling (indoors or out)
Dancing
Downhill skiing
Elliptical
Extreme hiking and rock climbing
Golf (eighteen holes)
Heli skiing
Horseback riding (advanced training)
Ice skating
Mountain climbing
Muscle toning/fitness classes
Pilates
Power walking and long-distance walking
Rodeo
Rock climbing
Roller skating, roller blading
Rope jumping
Running
Serious gardening, ranching, or farming
Serious weight training
Snowboarding
Softball, volleyball, football
Tai chi
Tennis
Trampoline
White water rafting and kayaking

Psyche Yourself Up for Exercise

Since I bought that very first pair of men's running shoes, I developed a habit of psyching myself up for exercise. Every night before I go to bed I visualize my exercise the next day. When I wake up in the morning, I'm ready to go out and do it—no matter what. My intent is set in stone. I visualize myself hiking or doing yoga or whatever and how much I am going to enjoy it. Without fail, if I don't go through this process I face a nearly insurmountable psychological resistance.

You know the story I told you about not being self-critical during my meditation retreat? Well, you can do the same exact thing while you're exercising. Don't think negative thoughts about yourself. It will only defeat your intentions. Instead, reinforce positive beliefs about exercise. Remind yourself of how good it will make you feel and look. Tell yourself that exercise is *fun*. Then make it fun. Exercise has been a huge part of the enjoyment and pleasure of my life. Exercise epitomizes a lifestyle of health, sex, and happiness.

conclusion

Healthy, Sexy, Happy isn't meant as the be-all and end-all of our learning experience regarding prevention and healing. I'm sure there are subjects I could have covered, but I didn't want it to get too kitchen-sinky. This book is meant as an inspiration and roadmap for you to get on the path, if you weren't already, and a clarification if you are already health minded, but may have had some doubts and questions. I welcome comments and suggestions on my Facebook page, blog, and website, as I am always learning and indebted to the many people who have shared their healing/antiaging secrets with me over the years.

Many people today don't really know who they are because all they know is a mind, body, and spirit that have been fed factory food and are permeated with toxins. Sharing what I've learned, so that you can experience who you really are is my life mission. And now that you're educated, you don't have to blindly follow anything the food, diet, or drug industries try to sell you. You can make decisions for yourself. You have a plan and a program to follow to discover the real you.

Going through the years of my physical and emotional recovery, during which I developed the *Healthy, Sexy, Happy* program, taught me a lot about achieving optimal health. I never in my wildest dreams thought that I would be a spokesperson for health, sex, and happiness. But now I see that everything I've gone through has brought me to this point in my life. I hope that it's an inspiration to you too. Getting healthy physically and emotionally is the foundation. If I could do it, you can do it too. I sincerely wish you health, great sex, and happiness, because you know what? It's such a fun ride.

appendix one:

Toxins in Factory Food Products

Acrylamide: A cancer and nerve-damaging compound produced when frying, deep-frying, or extended microwaving.

Aflatoxin: Peanuts grow a carcinogenic mold called aflatoxin. Healthy peanuts are USDA organic and grown in a region where the soil is dry and aflatoxin has therefore not been reported as a problem. Maranatha organic peanut butter is aflatoxin free.

Aluminum: Found in canned food and foil lined containers. Linked to Alzheimer's.

Antibiotics and Other Drugs: Whatever CAFO animals are fed or injected with, we are going to ingest.

Aspartame: See page 23.

Bisphenol A or BPA: Toxic plastic chemicals used as can lining in brands of some infant formulas and water bottles and in all canned foods.

Caffeine: See page 87.

Corn: Just as cattle are fattened on GMO corn feed, so are we fattened on GMO corn feed. Corn is in just about every factory-produced food, including commercial milk.

Diacetyl: An extremely dangerous fake butter used in microwave popcorn that causes a terminal lung condition called bronchiolitis obliterans, (popcorn workers' lung).

Dyes Tartrazine (E102), Ponceau 4R (E124), Sunset Yellow (E110), Carmoisine (E122), Quinoline Yellow (E104), and Allura Red AC (E129): Used in factory foods. Dyes damage brain cells, resulting in a significant reduction in IQ.

Extrusion: Besides all the obvious problems that cereal has, like containing lots of sugar and being made of wheat that is stripped of nutritional value, cereal shapes are created through a high-pressure, high-temperature process called "extrusion," which creates neurotoxic protein fragments (even the health food store brands).

Fertilizer Residues: Overuse and abuse of chemical fertilizers (nitrate) harm the biological life of the soil. The residues including heavy metals present in the inorganic soils may pose serious health hazards. Excessive use of nitrates causes groundwater pollution and is linked to certain diseases in human beings.

Flavorings: Most flavorings, including "natural flavoring" are artificially made and contain MSG.

Fluoride: A carcinogenic that accumulates in the body and brain and contributes to bone disease as well as joint pains, teeth abnormalities, and neurological diseases.

Food Irradiation: The purpose is to kill pests, eggs, and larvae, and to stop ripening and sprouting to lengthen the shelf life of foods. Irradiation exposes foods to a high level of gamma radiation. The source of this radiation is nuclear waste. Irradiation has been linked to a dramatic increase in free radicals in the body, cataracts, reduced fertility, testicular tumors, kidney damage, premature aging, and death. Many spices are irradiated.

Genetically Modified Organism (GMO) Plants, Animals, Hormones: Genetic engineering, which is also known as recombinant DNA technology, is a two-step process. Molecular biologists use enzymes to dissect specific genes from the structure of DNA in living organisms. They then insert vectors (such as viruses and bacteria) into these genes to create desired characteristics, and insert these altered genes into the DNA of the organism they wish to alter. They are essentially creating new genetic DNA, which will dictate if a crop will be frost-, bug-, or drought-resistant and so on. This new crop is now "genetically modified."

Genetic engineering has created corn that resists insect infestation, Monsanto Roundup Ready wheat and soybeans, and fruits and vegetables that are devoid of nutritional value but don't rot. It has instilled "anti-freeze" genes into vegetables to extend the growing season, and created genetic pesticides within the DNA of crops, which essentially kill or ward off predators.

GMOs are not labeled, so you have no idea if you are eating genetically engineered organisms.[51] GMOs are suspected to increased the risk of food allergies and cancer, the creation of new, more virulent viruses, and antibiotic resistance.[52] Animals fed GMO feed refuse to eat it. When force-fed, animals develop stomach lesions and malformations of organs.

High-fructose Corn Syrup (HFCS): A manufactured sugar from corn and fungus. A major contributing factor in our epidemic of obesity, type 2 diabetes, and heart disease. It causes fatty livers, raises blood levels of cholesterol and triglycerides, makes blood cells more prone to clotting, and accelerates the aging process.

Hydrogenated/Partially Hydrogenated Oils: Polyunsaturated (liquid) fats that are intentionally molecularly altered so that they will be solid. They contain trans fats, which cause diseases like multiple sclerosis, heart disease, obesity, and allergies that lead to arthritis.

Mercury: Our waters are contaminated with the tons of mercury that spew from cement kilns and coal burning (for electricity). Mercury is in factory-produced food (including meat and produce) and in vaccinations and "silver" amalgam dental fillings.

Monosodium Glutamate (MSG): See page 25.

Nitrites/Nitrosamines: Extremely powerful cancer-causing chemicals used to preserve meat and keep it looking "pink." Exacerbated by frying.

Olestra: For goodness sake, this stuff is *weird*. Olestra attaches to valuable nutrients and flushes them out of the body. Olestra causes serious GI problems including fecal leakage. Please see *Death by Supermarket* for more on olestra.

Paraffin: Carcinogen in cosmetics and food.

PEG Stearates, PEG-12 Distearate, PEG-14M, and PEG-80 Sorbitan Laurate: Linked to cancer or other significant health problems.

Perchlorate: Byproduct of rocket fuel in over 90 percent of the U.S. lettuce and milk supply. Interferes with thyroid function can cause thyroid cancer and or hypothyroidism.

Perfluoroalkyls: Carcinogenic chemicals used to keep grease from leaking through fast-food wrappers. Perfluoroalkyls soak into factory food and are then ingested.

Pesticides (Including Herbicides, Insecticides, and Fungicides): Carcinogenic xenohormones in 50 to 95 percent of all nonorganic foods.

Phytoestrogen: See page 27.

Potassium Bromate: Increases volume of flour. Used to strengthen bread dough. Although countries like Britain and Canada banned the preservative as a carcinogen because significant evidence shows that it causes cancerous kidney and thyroid tumors in rats, it's still found in some baked goods in the United States. Potassium bromate is especially dangerous if the food product is not baked long enough at a high enough temperature.

Preservatives: Common preservatives in food are propionic acid, nitrates and nitrites, and benzoates. Nonorganic cosmetics may contain formaldehyde and formaldehyde-releasing preservatives as well as Thimerosal. Preservatives prevent botulism, mold, and bacteria, which give products a longer shelf life and protect people from illness. Unfortunately, many preservatives have dangerous side effects that cause cancers, hyperactivity, nervous system damage, and other problems.

Processed Vegetable Fats/Oils (Corn, Cottonseed, Safflower, Sunflower, Soy, Canola): These heat-, chemical-, and petroleum-solvent treated vegetable oils introduce and generate free radicals in your body.

Propyl Gallate: A stabilizer in packaged meats, dried milk, candy, potato chips, and baked goods. Causes prostate inflammation and tumors of the thyroid, brain, and pancreas.

Recombinant Bovine Growth Hormone (rBGH): Genetically modified growth hormones given to cows to turn them into super milk machines. It creates insulin growth factor 1 (IGF1) that can contribute to carcinogenesis.

Saccharine: A carcinogenic sugar substitute.

Salt (Stripped of Minerals): Factory food is loaded with mineral-stripped salt. Supermarket salt contains sodium chloride, with little or no minerals, sugar as filler, and may even contain aluminum.

Sodium Benzoate: A preservative in soda to prevent mold. This chemical can damage mitochondria in cells, which leads to neurodegenerative diseases. Causes hyperactivity in children.

Sodium Nitrate: Is used as a curing agent in processed meats like hot dogs, sausages, and bacon. Studies show that people who eat a large amount of processed meats have a 20 percent higher risk of colorectal cancer and a 16 percent higher risk of lung cancer.

Soy: See page 26.

Sucralose (Splenda): A chlorinated molecule. Chlorine is definitively linked to cancer, so why would you put that in your body?

Sulfites: Can cause reactions in asthmatics, and lead to death. A preservative used on raw potatoes, wine, and dried fruit.

White Refined Flour: Stimulates a similar insulin response as sugar. It is a cancer fertilizer that is stripped of vitamins and minerals. Contributes to disease, obesity, and the cold impersonal hospital death we talked about earlier.

White Sugar: Sugar is a white, crystalline stimulant that offers zero nutritional value. Refined white sugar is devoid of the vitamins and minerals necessary to digest and metabolize itself, your body ends up depleting vitamins and minerals from your diet or from internal stores in order to digest it. High-sugar diets result in cravings and bingeing, depression, and other mood disorders, in addition to a burning sensation on your tongue; acne; wrinkles around your lips; exhaustion; GI problems; thinning, graying hair; and recurrent colds and flu. Sugar is a cancer fertilizer and an immunosuppressant.

appendix two:

Supplements and Herbs

NOTE: *Dosing instructions are not included. See the Shopping at nancydeville.com page for updates on supplements.*

Acetyl-L-Carnitine: Used by all cells to produce energy. It also enhances the production of the neurotransmitter acetylcholine, important for learning and memory.

Acetyl-L-Carnitine Arginate: An amino-acid antioxidant that helps flush toxins from the body, has immune-boosting properties, reduces and prevents cell damage caused by beta amyloid (the substance found in the brain of Alzheimer's patients). May be beneficial for diabetes, cataracts, neuropathy, kidney failure, and skin conditions, helps block the accumulation of lactic acid.

Aged Garlic: Protects the brain against accelerated aging. Removes mercury from the brain and neutralizes its toxicity.

Aloe Leaf Extract: Has immune-enhancing and mucous membrane–healing capabilities.

Alpha-Carotene: Antioxidant and part of the carotenoid family, and is one of the most abundant carotenoids in a healthy diet. Some people can convert alpha- and beta-carotene into vitamin A for the maintenance of healthy skin and bones, good vision, and a robust immune system. Most cannot make the conversion, especially people with thyroid problems or blood sugar issues. Another reason a good multi is important.

Alpha Lipoic Acid: Called the universal antioxidant for its ability to increase the effectiveness or potency in other antioxidants including vitamins C and E, coenzyme Q_{10}, and glutathione. Counteracts reactive free radicals in the mitochondria and so it assists in slowing accelerated aging. Protects against mercury toxicity. Recycles itself and other antioxidants such as vitamin E back into their original form after they detoxify free radicals, and can reduce damage due to excess glucose in the blood.

Amylase: An enzyme responsible for the digestion of carbohydrates. Amylase breaks starch down into sugar. Present in human saliva, where it begins the chemical process of digestion.

Apple Cider Vinegar: Contains enzymes, acids, vitamins, mineral salts, and amino acids that have been a folk remedy for everything from acne to type 2 diabetes. If you can stand a glug of apple cider vinegar from time to time, go for it. Apple cider vinegar has a moderately alkaline effect on the body.

Ashwaganda: The Ayurvedic equivalent of ginseng. It improves adrenal function. It is a tonic for mental energy and a general system tonic.

B Vitamins: B vitamins, including folic acid, B_6, and B_{12}, may help lower blood levels of a substance called homocysteine that are linked to heart disease and stroke. Lack of these vitamins puts you at a higher risk of heart disease and memory loss that characterize aging. High dose B vitamins are now being studied as a way to delay the mitochondrial decay of aging.[53] B vitamins are cofactors important in mitochondrial reactions. B vitamins are water-soluble so they are excreted if not used, and the benefits should be felt immediately. If you can get weekly injectable B vitamins, go for it. I also like chewable B_{12}.

B_1 (Thiamine): Used in many different body functions. Deficiencies may have far-reaching effects on the body. Very little of this vitamin is stored in the body, and depletion of this vitamin can happen within fourteen days. Thiamine is essential to carb metabolism and a healthy nervous system. It is depleted rapidly by alcohol, which can result in memory loss.

B_2 (Riboflavin): Required by the body to use oxygen and the metabolism of amino acids, fatty acids, and carbs. Riboflavin is needed to activate vitamin B_6. It helps to create niacin and assists the adrenal gland. Used for red blood cell formation, antibody production, cell respiration, and growth. Protects skin, mouth, eyes, eyelids, and mucous membranes. It effectively diminishes migraines in some people.

B_3 (Niacin): Niacin helps the body make various sex and stress-related hormones in the adrenal glands and other parts of the body. Niacin is effective in improving circulation and improving cholesterol metabolism by reducing LDL cholesterol levels, lowering triglycerides, and raising HDL levels in the blood. Doses over 25 milligrams may cause a hot flash from the stimulation of rapid relaxation of tiny blood cells as they are flushing toxins and wastes out of cells.

B_5 (Pantothenic Acid): Stimulates the energy-making systems in the body. Plays an important role in the secretion of hormones, such as cortisol, because of the role it plays in supporting the adrenal gland. These hormones assist the metabolism, help to fight allergies, and are beneficial in the maintenance of healthy skin, muscles, and nerves.

B_6: Improves serotonin levels. Vitamin B_6 helps convert tryptophan to 5HTP and 5HTP to serotonin. Required for the balancing of hormonal changes in women as well as assisting the immune system and the growth of new cells. It is also used in the processing and metabolism of proteins, fats, and carbs, while assisting with balancing mood and behavior by helping to regulate the central nervous system. A natural diuretic and critical for healthy hormonal metabolism and neurotransmitters. Helps to repair DNA and protects the brain against glutamine toxicity (MSG, aspartame, and soy). Vitamin B_6 protects from high levels of the amino acid homocysteine, which is thought to increase with stress and play a major role in coronary artery plaquing.

B_7 Biotin (aka Vitamin H): Used in cell growth, the production of fatty acids, and metabolism of fats, sugar, and proteins. Plays a role in the Kreb cycle, which is the process in which energy is released from food. Necessary for healthy hair and skin, healthy sweat glands, nerve tissue, and bone marrow, and alleviating muscle pain. Biotin is necessary for fatty acid synthesis and the maintenance of blood sugar, and is especially important during pregnancy when biotin status declines.

B_{12} (Methylcobalamin): Known as the energy vitamin needed in the manufacture of red blood cells and the maintenance of red blood cells. B_{12} stimulates appetite, promotes growth, and releases energy (used in the metabolism of fats, proteins, and carbs). Necessary to form all blood cells, maintain healthy nerves and heart. It protects some genes from genetic mutation. Helps with clearing up infections and provides protection against allergies and cancer. It's often given to older people as an energy boost, to assist in preventing mental deterioration (thought to protect from Alzheimer's Disease), and to help with speeding up thought processes. If someone you know is diagnosed with Alzheimer's the first course of action should be measuring, and if necessary boosting vitamin B_{12} levels.

Beta-carotene and Other Carotenoids: Antioxidants that improve immunity. Beta-carotene is the beautiful red-orange color in plants and fruits, which is a precursor of vitamin A. Carotenoids are yellow, orange, and red pigments synthesized by plants, which are converted by the body to vitamin A. Available in apricots, asparagus, beets, broccoli, cantaloupe, carrots, corn, green peppers, kale, mangoes, turnip and collard greens, nectarines, peaches, pink grapefruit, pumpkin, spices, squash, spinach, sweet potato, tangerines, tomatoes, and watermelon.

Betaine Hydrochloric Acid: Research suggests that people with a wide variety of chronic disorders, such as allergies, asthma, candida, gallstones, and acne don't produce adequate amounts of stomach acid. If you're over forty with these problems, then your system may not be making enough hydrochloric acid so your food might not be able to exit your stomach efficiently. Trapped food will sit in your stomach or upper small intestine and cause tummy aches, bloating, cramping, gas, and constipation. Taking supplemental betaine hydrochloric acid can be the ticket. If you take too high of a dose, indicated by a burning sensation in your tummy, just drink a big glass of water.

Bioflavonoids: Also known as flavonoids, these are compounds that occur naturally in many plants. Used in conjunction with quercetin for allergies and sinusitis where it boosts the effect of quercetin in suppressing the inflammation of allergic reactions.

Blackstrap Molasses: Excellent source of calcium, rich in copper, which helps in the production of connective tissue and melanin (skin and hair pigment). An antioxidant that eliminates free radicals. Contains manganese, which is important for a healthy nervous system, and potassium, which helps sustain electrolyte and pH balance. Contains vitamin B_6, a nutrient that plays an essential role in cellular reaction and maintains healthy brain function. Is a good source of selenium, an antioxidant that prevents cancer and has anti-aging effects.

Boswellia: An Ayurvedic herb (the frankincense mentioned in the Bible) that is used to treat inflammation, respiratory, and GI problems.

Bromelain: A proteolytic (breaking down) enzyme found in raw pineapple that aids in the digestion of protein-rich foods. It is also a vegetarian alternative to animal sourced enzymes. Aids digestion by enhancing the effects of the digestive enzymes trypsin and pepin. It can also help to prevent heartburn or ease diarrhea, if either are caused by a deficiency of digestive enzymes.

Calcium: An essential mineral that plays a role in heart and muscle contraction, blood clotting, the conduction of nerve impulses to and from the brain, regulation of enzyme activity, and cell membrane function. It's needed to form and maintain strong bones and teeth during youth and adolescence, helps prevent the loss of bone. The first step in preventing or treating osteoporosis is to consume a calcium-rich diet. Calcium binds to and removes toxins from the colon, reducing the risk of colon cancer, and may help prevent migraine attacks (involved in nerve conduction).

Calcium is a natural calming agent that is depleted by stress and must be replenished. When calcium is diminished you feel more agitated. It is important to note that some women are chewing antacids to get their calcium. Antacids neutralize the very acid that is required to absorb calcium. The calcium carbonate found in antacids is also the very hardest type of calcium to absorb. See calcium and herpes on page 227.

Calcium Ascorbate: A natural form of vitamin C made up of 80 percent vitamin C (ascorbic acid) and 20 percent calcium. Ascorbates absorb best because they are less acidic. Calcium ascorbate acts as an antioxidant, builds the immune system so that your body can fend off toxins.

Carotenoids: Effective treatment for hay fever, a lack of carotenoids in the diet is thought to promote inflammation in your airways. A diet high in carotenoids might prevent the development of food allergies.[54]

Cellulase: Responsible for the digestion of fiber from fruits and vegetables, for breaking down lipids (fats), and the digestion of nutrients in the intestines.

Chlorella (Green Algae): One of the best detoxifiers, able to remove alcohol from the liver and heavy metals, in particular mercury, pesticides, and PCBs from body tissues. Chlorella can also absorb toxins from the intestines, improve bacterial flora in the gut, eliminate intestinal gas, and relieve constipation. Provides B vitamins for vegetarians and vegans. It's 60 percent protein, and is considered a complete protein because it contains every essential amino acid. Repairs nerve tissues, enhances the immune system, reduces cancer risk, improves digestion, promotes healthy pH levels in your gut, helps healthy bacteria to thrive in your gut, enhances focus and concentration, increases energy levels, normalizes blood sugar and pressure. Contains chlorophyll. Sea algae is a good source of natural electrolytes.

Chlorophyll: Binds to heavy metals and removes them from your body. Found in chlorella as well. If you can't digest chlorella then try liquid chlorophyll.

Cholesterol: Therapeutic fat, see page 48.

Choline: A memory nutrient. Fatigue, insomnia, accumulation of fats in the blood, and nerve-muscle problems can indicate a need for more high-choline foods (beef liver and eggs).

Chromium: A mineral that helps insulin to function as a blood sugar regulator.

Chromium Picolinate: An essential mineral and antioxidant found in very low concentrations in the human body. It's believed that chromium helps insulin bring glucose from the blood into the cells for energy. Chromium decreases insulin resistance in people who smoke cigarettes.

Cilantro: Chelates mercury, cadmium, lead, and aluminum from the brain and the central nervous system. Because cilantro is so efficient at mobilizing toxins out of the cells, it sometimes cannot complete the job (if toxic load is really high) to carry these toxins out of the system. It should be used along with chlorella.

Citrus Bioflavonoid Complex: Bioflavonoids are phytonutrients that stabilize cell membranes, balance hormones, and are anti-inflammatory.

Coconut Oil: Contains antiviral and antimicrobial properties that have been found to be effective in killing viruses that cause influenza, measles, herpes, mononucleosis, hepatitis C, and AIDS; the fungi and yeast that result in ringworm, Candida and thrush; parasites that cause intestinal infections such as giardiasis; and bacteria that cause stomach ulcers, throat infections, pneumonia, sinusitis, rheumatic fever, foodborne illnesses, urinary tract infections, meningitis, gonorrhea, and toxic shock syndrome.

Cod Liver Oil: Cold water fish contain polyunsaturated oil, which does not freeze in cold temperatures. Contains essential fatty acids docosahexaenoic (DHA) and eicosapentaenoic (EPA). DHA is essential for the proper functioning of our brains as adults and for the development of the nervous system and visual abilities during the first six months of life. EPA reduces inflammation and the risk for heart disease. Our bodies naturally produce small amounts of DHA, but we must get the amounts we need from our diet. Cod liver oil modifies immune reactions in the body, which helps prevent autoimmune reactions; helps cognitive ability and memory; protects against depression; helps cool and heal inflammation; and is extremely important for the development and function of the brain and nervous system.

Coenzyme Q-10 (CoQ_{10}): A fat-soluble vitamin-like substance, a coenzyme for several of the key enzymatic steps in the production of energy, and an antioxidant protecting against accumulation of harmful free radicals. Absolutely essential to the ATP production process so the high metabolic demands of the heart make sufficient CoQ_{10} levels a must. Researchers found that in most of the cases of heart problems, there was an associated deficiency of CoQ_{10}.[55] Helps regulate neurotransmitters like serotonin, and protects against glutamate and aspartate nerve damage (MSG, aspartame, and soy).

Colostrum: A distillate of mammal milk. When a mammal gives birth, before the onset of true lactation, colostrum is secreted. It is rich in antibodies, proteins that provide direction to the immune system, and lymphocytes, which are the main means of providing the body with immune capability.

Conjugated Linoleic Acid (CLA): Butterfat from the milk of grassfed cows is the richest known source of CLA, which reduces cancer and atherosclerosis risk, increases metabolic rate, and burns fat.

Copper and Zinc: These minerals are depleted by stress and must be replenished. They are best taken together; otherwise one could cause a depletion of the other. They are best in a ratio of twenty zinc milligrams to two copper milligrams.

Cordyceps: One of the most peculiar Chinese herbs. Its Chinese name is *Dong Chong Xia Cao*, meaning "winter worms and summer grass." Cordyceps is typically found only on the China/Tibet border. It is a fungus grown on the head of a caterpillar. It is a very effective adrenal burnout remedy.

Creatine: An amino acid that helps to supply energy to muscle by facilitating mitochondrial energy production.

Cryptoxanthin: Antioxidant also known as beta-cryptoxanthin, is a member of the carotenoid family, a group of flavonoids that provide color and flavor to fruits and vegetables. Carotenoids are proven antioxidants, and their role in protecting the body from free-radical damage has been well established. Researchers are just beginning to explore the benefits provided by cryptoxanthin.

Curcumin: An antioxidant flavonoid (plant compound with therapeutic effects) found in turmeric. Proven to reduce brain plaquing linked to Alzheimer's. A natural anti-inflammatory that cools down the brain's immune system and enhances detoxification.

Deglycyrrhizinated Licorice Root: If your sympathetic nervous system is regularly turning off your digestion leaving large amounts of food in your stomach, then your stomach may eventually stretch out. The high-tension ring-shaped muscle called the lower esophageal sphincter, which maintains constriction to prevent the stomach's corrosive digestive juices from escaping into the esophagus, will become lax. Your stomach contents, aided by gravity when you lie down, will gurgle up into your esophagus and cause problems. Before meals and at bedtime you can try taking deglycyrrhizinated licorice root. Licorice root accelerates the actions of the cells that provide a protective coating of the lining of the stomach. Licorice root has been shown to be comparable or better than the antacid Tagamet. Licorice root can raise blood pressure and alter potassium levels, so please don't take *licorice root*, take *deglycyrrhizinated* licorice root, which doesn't affect blood pressure or potassium levels.

Essiac Tea: Dates back to at least the 1920s. Essiac tea is composed of four or more herbs, including Sheep Sorrel and Burdock Root, which are known to kill cancer cells. The other herbs build the immune system, detox, and protect the organs.

5-Hydroxy Tryptophan (5-HTP): This amino acid is a more usable form of L-Tryptophan and can be obtained over the counter. 5-HTP is considered to be five times more potent than L-Tryptophan—so you don't need to take as much.

NOTE: *Don't take 5-HTP if you are taking serotonin-reuptake inhibitors such as Prozac or Zoloft. Contraindicated in people with interstitial cystitis.*

Flavonoids: A balanced diet provides flavonoids, which are compounds found in fruits, veggies, red wine, green and white tea that have diverse beneficial biochemical and antioxidant effects.

Folic or Folate Acid: A B vitamin used in the biosynthesis of adrenaline and cortisol and required for normal blood cell formation, growth, and reproduction, and for many important chemical reactions in body cells. Folic acid is required for DNA synthesis and cell growth and is important for red blood cell formation, energy production, and the forming of amino acids. Essential for creating heme, the iron-containing substance in hemoglobin, which is crucial for oxygen transport.

Gamma Aminobutyric Acid (GABA): An amino acid that increases the amount of calming neurotransmitters in your brain. GABA is nonaddictive. It needs to be taken as a powder (encapsulated) or in chewable tablets.

Garcinia Cambogia: Improves the release of fat from fat cells to be burned as energy.

Garlic: Contains sulphur, which oxidizes mercury, cadmium, and lead and makes them water-soluble. Garlic contains selenium, which protects the body from mercury toxicity. One clove per day is an effective dose (about 4,000 milligrams). Regulates cholesterol metabolism.

Ginkgo Biloba: An antioxidant plant extract with brain cell protecting properties. Aids blood flow in the brain. Reduces the risk of immune overactivation in the brain. Slightly thins the blood. NOTE: *Do not take ginkgo with other anticoagulants, such as aspirin and alternative blood thinners.*

GLA: Research suggests that GLA may reduce symptoms of nerve pain in diabetic neuropathy, reduce the symptoms of rheumatoid arthritis (pain, swelling, and morning stiffness), reduce general inflammation, lessen allergy symptoms, reduce ADHD symptoms, reduce symptoms of eczema, reduce high blood pressure, treat hot flashes associated with menopause in women who do not want to take estrogen replacement, reduce breast pain and tenderness and other symptoms of PMS, and help prevent bone loss.

Glandulars: Freeze-dried animal organs and glands, including liver, heart, brain, thymus, kidney, pancreas, adrenal, ovary, and testicle. Glanduars are basic genetic material of glands. Adrenal glandulars can help nourish and replenish fatigued adrenals. This is not proven in studies. However, animal glands were part of the diet of Dr. Weston A. Price's healthy primitive people.

Glutamine: An amino acid that helps balance blood sugar and liver function and increases the level of critical antioxidants. When taken at night glutamine helps alkalinize your body and increases level of human growth hormone, which helps balance all the other systems and is a longevity hormone. The cells that line the intestinal track need glutamine, and when it is present in proper amounts it speeds up the healing of intestinal problems.

Glycine: This amino acid is best known for diminishing sugar and alcohol cravings.

Grape Seed Extract: Reduces the risk of heart disease and stroke. Helps improve circulation, reduces varicose veins, repairs artery and vascular lining, and aids in resistance to bruising. Contains powerful antioxidants from its catechins. Improves lipid metabolism. Grape seed extract also possesses anticancer, anti-inflammatory, antibiotic, and antimicrobial properties.

Green Tea Extract: The most important of the catechins in green tea is epigallocatechin-3-gallate (EGCG), which is believed to provide anti-aging health benefits. Green tea lowers blood pressure, prevents the spread of prostate cancer, protects against all forms of cancer including lung cancer, and helps protect against sun damage.

Green Veggie Juice: Provides enzymes and fiber to aid peristalsis, and is alkalinizing, and loaded with antioxidants. See page 138.

Holy Basil: Supports adrenal function by lowering excess cortisol production. It also helps balance blood sugar.

Inositol: An antidepressant and is necessary for proper function of nerves, brain, and muscles in the body.

Iodine: A mineral that's important for thyroid metabolism.

Iron: A mineral that's critical for red blood cells to carry oxygen to your cells.

Krill Oil: Krill are tiny crustaceans that resemble shrimp that are food for fish, whales, squid, penguins, and seals. Krill oil is extracted from krill because of its rich supply of omega 3 fatty acids. Krill oil contains EPA and DHA, two chains of polyunsaturated fats that the body needs. Unlike fish oil, krill oil contains astaxanthin, a carotenoid (a red pigment found in salmon, shrimp, lobster, and other marine sources), which is an amazing antioxidant. Another advantage is that krill are at the bottom of the food chain so they're less likely to be contaminated with mercury or PCBs. Krill doesn't have a fishy aftertaste nor does it promote the dreaded fish burp.

L-Carnitine: Helps to metabolize fat from food into energy. Carries fuel into the cell and toxic waste out, so it "cleanses" your cells. Improves heart strength.

Lipase: Helps digest fats and oils. Undigested fats can cause weight gain, high cholesterol, and high blood pressure. Lipase helps your body better utilize omega fatty acids.

L-Theanine: A neurotransmitter precursor, found almost exclusively in the leaves of green tea (but can be obtained as a supplement). Supports the formation of GABA, an inhibitory neurotransmitter that blocks the release of the neurotransmitters dopamine and serotonin to promote a state of deep relaxation and calm, while increasing sensations of pleasure. Also stimulates the production of alpha brain waves, which are associated with deep states of relaxation and enhanced mental clarity. Supports healthy blood pressure levels, enhances concentration and learning, promotes mental clarity, and strengthens the immune system. It also increases energy levels while reducing anxiety.

L-Tryptophan: An amino acid that converts to melatonin and serotonin in our bodies and brains. Serotonin affects several central nervous system functions, including sleep, mood, aggression, pain, anxiety, memory, eating behavior, temperature regulation, hormonal regulation, and motor behavior. Tryptophan is converted to 5-HTP—an amino acid that is the intermediate step between tryptophan and the important brain chemical serotonin. 5-HTP is converted to serotonin and more serotonin more effectively activates the calming, mood elevating, impulse and appetite controlling serotonin neural circuits. L-Tryptophan can calm sleep disturbances and help lift depression. It's usually taken at nighttime for its calming effect but can be taken throughout the day for antidepressant use.

NOTE: *Don't take L-Tryptophan if you are taking serotonin-reuptake inhibitors such as Prozac or Zoloft. Contraindicated in people with interstitial cystitis.*

Lutein: Antioxidant, naturally occurring carotenoid.

Lysine: An essential amino acid that can't be made in the body so you have to eat it or take it as a supplement. Bolstered by vitamin C and vitamin A, lysine helps eliminate virus infections. Lysine is a natural remedy for cold sores, shingles, and genital herpes.

Magnesium Citrate: A mineral that's calming to the nervous system, it is involved in more than one hundred metabolic enzyme reactions in the body. Magnesium citrate is the more absorbable form of magnesium. It's an important cofactor in the production of neurotransmitters. Helps alleviate muscle spasms, fibromyalgia, allergies, constipation, and PMS and to relieve the muscle spasms in the intestinal tract that cause constipation. Magnesium maintains the heart muscle as well as the nerves that initiate the heartbeat. It protects the brain from strokes. Muscle spasms, cramps, and/or leg-twitching that keeps you awake may be the result of a mineral deficiency. Magnesium is a common mineral deficiency especially if you've been eating a diet of factory food. Magnesium can help soothe or even resolve your leg issues. You can take a bath in Epsom salts—hydrated magnesium sulfate—which is available in any drugstore. The magnesium is absorbed through your skin, and the hot water warms your core body temperature to make you drowsy. Magnesium deficiency seems to be carcinogenic, and in case of solid tumors, a high level of supplemented magnesium inhibits carcinogenesis, the process in which normal cells are transformed into cancer cells.

Magnesium Malate or Malic Acid: The tart flavor in green apples, grapes, wine, and unripe fruit. One of the most potent aluminum detoxifiers. Helps reduce aluminum toxicity of the brain, organs, and tissues of the body.

Manganese: A mineral involved in the health of connective tissues such as ligaments, tendons and bones and is the catalyst for numerous enzymatic reactions.

Marijuana (Cannabis): Marijuana is a remarkably effective, much less toxic, versatile, and affordable remedy than pharmaceutical drugs for numerous health problems. One of the preposterous reasons why the prohibition of marijuana has gone on for so long is that drug companies don't want to lose billions of dollars in profits from the sale of all the toxic drugs that suffering people are forced to take because they can't access marijuana. The pharmaceutical (drug-pushing) industry is a major contributor to the campaign for a "drug-free America," if that isn't a laugh in itself. If you're unsure about the ethics of marijuana use, you may find food for thought in the findings of studies estimating that one quarter of police officers, and 18 to 25 percent of attorneys and judges are alcoholics.[56] Marijuana has been used medicinally for nearly three thousand years.[57] There has been tons of research on beneficial uses of marijuana.

Some Possible Medical Marijuana Uses

Could be useful treating Crohn's disease and ulcerative colitis

Could be useful treating migraines, fibromyalgia, MS, spinal cord injuries

Eases nausea and vomiting associated with chemo and other toxic drugs

Eases pain

Eases PMS

Effective for treating insomnia for people who desperately need sleep (chronic fatigue and other autoimmune diseases, cancer, adrenal burnout)

Has been shown to have antispasmodic and muscle-relaxant qualities

May stop the spread of cancer, including breast cancer

Shown to alleviate opiate dependence, so can be used to help addicts through withdrawals and to kick drug habits

Stimulates appetite after chemo and in people with AIDS and anorexia

Treats glaucoma by easing eye pressure[58]

Uses Currently Allowed by the Government

AIDS	Epilepsy
Alzheimer's disease	Glaucoma
Anorexia	HIV
Arthritis	Migraine
Cachexia (wasting as with cancer and AIDS)	Multiple sclerosis
	Nausea
Cancer	Pain
Crohn's disease	Spasticity[59]

Many who argue that smoking marijuana is dangerous to your health are the very same people who advocate the heavy use of pharmaceutical drugs that are known to destroy mitochondria and DNA. A couple of hits of marijuana for a very sick person can alleviate a lot of suffering, and the free radicals associated with smoking pot can be ameliorated with a half a glass of green veggie juice and/or good-quality supplements containing antioxidants. With regular use, a tolerance will develop to the high that objectors object to, but the user will still receive the pharmacological benefits. Free radicals from smoking can also be minimized by using a vaporizer, ingesting marijuana in a cookie, using a sublingual spray, or eyedrops. However, researchers are thinking that tetrahydrocannabinol (THC), the active ingredient in marijuana, may encourage programmed death of cells that were verging on malignancy.[60] Although smoking marijuana *along with cigarettes* can triple your risk of developing chronic obstructive pulmonary disease (COPD),[61] I discourage cigarette smoking in the first place, and smoking marijuana *without smoking cigarettes* does not lead to COPD.[62] The same restrictions apply to medical marijuana as prescription drugs regarding driving, operating machinery, and making important decisions.

Marshmallow Root: Provides a soothing coating that protects the GI tract.

Multivitamin (Without Iron): For overall health of your metabolism, choose a quality multivitamin that does not contain iron. Too much iron in the bloodstream contributes to cancer and heart disease. Most meat eaters get enough iron from their diet. As you know, I encourage labs to check levels in the blood. If you are low in iron, then a multi with iron may be right for you.

N-Acetyl-Cysteine (NAC): An amino acid neurotransmitter precursor to GABA. An anti-inflammatory that can detox heavy metals as well as raise the level of glutathione, an amino acid antioxidant that protects against mercury toxicity. NAC binds to heavy metals and removes them from the body. NAC's antioxidant ability to neutralize free radicals and support the immune system can help slow down the aging process. It also boosts glutathione—an antioxidant—levels in the body. NAC has antimucolytic (antimucous) properties and has been shown to be exceptionally beneficial to repair mucous membrane damage in smokers.

Omega-3: Reduces inflammation in body and brain, reduces allergic response, improves the immune function, and repairs mucous membranes. Reduces risk of heart attack and stroke by slowing the build up of plaque in the arteries. Lowers blood pressure by making blood flow more freely and preventing blood clots, prevents arrhythmia, prevents the build up of plaque in the arteries, and reduces bone loss.

Pancreatin: A combination of three enzymes; amylase, lipase, and protease. This digestive enzyme mixture is used to treat conditions in which pancreatic secretions are deficient, such as pancreatitis and cystic fibrosis. It has been claimed to help with food allergies, celiac disease, autoimmune disease, cancer, and weight loss.

Papain: Responsible for breaking down proteins, papain is an enzyme present in papaya. Breaks down meat fibers. It has been utilized for thousands of years in its native South America.

Para-Aminobenzoic Acid (PABA): Aids in the metabolism and utilization of amino acids and is also supportive of blood cells. PABA supports folic acid production by the intestinal bacteria. PABA is important to skin, hair pigment, and intestinal health. Found in liver, mushrooms, spinach, brewer's yeast, wheat germ, whole grains, eggs, and molasses. It is crucial for detoxification.

Pepsin: Helps digests protein, and stimulates the liver to produce bile. In the stomach, the enzyme pepsin functions to break proteins into smaller pieces. Because pepsin can only break the bonds next to certain amino acids, proteins are only broken into these shorter chains, and not digested all the way to amino acids. That must be done later, in the small intestine. Most digestion and absorption of nutrients occurs in the small intestine.

Phosphatidylserine: A brain nutrient that helps rebalance pituitary-adrenal communication. If you wake up in the middle of the night wide awake with your heart pounding, your adrenals may be responding inappropriately. Phosphatidylserine influences your brain's messages to your adrenals to halt the inappropriate release of adrenaline, cortisol, and DHEA.

Phytase, Hemicellulase, and Xylanase: Specifically helps with releasing fiber-bound minerals from plant sources.

Potassium: A mineral that's depleted by stress and must be replenished. Potassium deficiencies can cause fatal heartbeat irregularities and/or cramps, spasms, and twitches anywhere in the body. If you are extremely active, a runner for example, you may find that you crave bananas. Eating a banana a day will help replenish potassium lost through demanding physical stress on your body.

Proanthocyanidins and Vitamin C: Antioxidants that quench free radicals and increase the strength of other antioxidants. Proanthocyanidins boost the immune system, protect from arteriosclerosis, enhance connective tissue health, reduce lipid peroxidation, boost the effects of vitamin C, lower cholesterol levels, reduce inflammation and edema, and lower your risk for cancer, stroke, and heart disease.

Probiotics: Commercial dairy and animal products are filled with antibiotics, which annihilate friendly flora in your gut. Probiotics are the opposite of antibiotics. Probiotics are the weapon of choice of the savvy modern hunter-gatherer. Reaching for probiotics right now is probably the smartest thing you can do if you have GI problems but are intent on improving your overall health. Probiotics are the natural, beneficial, live, friendly bacteria that will restore a proper intestinal balance of billions of colony-forming microbiological organisms in your gut—*Lactobacillus acidophilus* and *bifidobacterium*—that restore normal balance of friendly flora (bacteria) in your gut and mucous membranes. Probiotics can also help the body to produce cytokine cells, that can up-regulate (turn the immune system on) to fight infection, or down-regulate the immune system when not fighting infection, so that autoimmune diseases are not so easily developed. If you're suffering from yeast, leaky gut, gluten intolerance, or celiac disease, probiotics are of particular importance. Your gut needs healthy micro-flora to digest complex proteins like gluten. It's a ratio of about 85 percent friendly flora to 15 percent unfriendly bacteria. Friendly flora are the primary digestive activators for the complex gluten proteins.

Speaking of unfriendly bacteria, we have the mentality in this country of sanitizing everything. I have shunned hand sanitizers since they came on the market. And there is now scientific evidence emerging that point to the overemphasis on hygiene as one reason for the rise in autoimmune conditions. I think it's worth considering that human beings lived symbiotically with "bad" organisms for millions of years. Scientists don't really understand how it works. But rather than being clean freaks about our digestive tracts, the better approach would be to up your friendly flora.

Protease: An enzyme responsible for digesting proteins in your food (one of the most difficult substances to metabolize). Considered to be one of the most important enzymes that we have.

Quercetin: An antioxidant bioflavonoid (phytonutrient) that quells allergic reactions and decreases brain inflammation. Increased dietary intake of flavonoids particularly from quercetin-rich foods has been linked to decreased heart disease mortality and decreased stroke incidence.[63]

Resveratrol: An antioxidant found in red wine, grapes, raspberries, mulberries, and peanuts that is believed to help keep the heart healthy and ward off cancer and may also turn out to be a fat fighter, according to new research. At high doses, resveratrol may prolong life span and improve overall health. It can be taken as a supplement.

Royal Maca: The Peruvian equivalent of ginseng. Royal maca improves adrenal function. It improves virility, energy, staminia, and balances hormones.

Selenium: A potent antioxidant trace mineral, essential in several metabolic pathways. Plays a central role in the protection of tissues from the damaging effects of oxygen free radicals. Removes mercury from the brain. Selenium is critical for brain function. Deficiencies are associated with depression and suicidal thoughts. You can have your selenium and all micronutrient levels tested (go to spectracell.com).

Siberian Ginseng: Used for four thousand years and is well researched and widely respected. Siberian ginseng supports the body during times of stress. It was used in the past by Russian athletes and emperors for its ability to increase optimal mental and physical performance. Siberian ginseng supports the adrenals and is a general system tonic. For adrenal support it is considered superior to American and Korean ginseng.

Silymarin (Milk Thistle Seed): Provides protection for the brain against abnormal aging, inflammation, and immune overactivation. It also helps remove brain plaquing associated with Alzheimer's disease.

Spirulina: A blue-green algae that has been used to treat arsenic poisoning so if you must drink city water, you should consume spirulina. It contains essential fatty acids and is an antioxidant. Sea algae is a good source of natural electrolytes. It is 65 to 70 percent protein and like chlorella it contains all essential amino acids. Even though I know this to be true, I still can't endorse spirulina as a complete protein source, especially for pregnant and nursing women. Sea veggies are not a sustainable enough source to build bones, muscle, hormones, and so forth.

St. John's Wort: Has been used in Europe for decades to treat depressive disorders. It is thought to increase serotonin levels and lower cortisol levels.

Stabilized Rice Bran: If you're constipated, irritating laxatives like cascara sagrada can have long-term damaging effects on your colon. Instead, increase fiber in your diet by eating fruit, especially cherries and prunes, a lot more vegetables, nuts, and whole grains. The fiber attracts the toxins and pulls them out of your body before they can be reabsorbed or recycled. Or add stabilized rice bran to your diet.

Taurine: A neurotransmitter precursor, antioxidant amino acid that supports neurological development and helps regulate the level of water and mineral salts in the blood.

Tyrosine: This amino acid is a precursor to norepinephrine, epinephrine (adrenaline), dopamine, and thyroid hormone, which are the energy-providing hormones of the body.

Valerian, Passionflower, and Hops: Known for their calming effects.

Vanadium (Vanadyl Sulfate): A mineral that helps normalize and maintain insulin receptor functions. Without vanadyl sulfate you are more likely to have insulin resistance and type 2 diabetes.

Vitamin C (Ascorbic Acid): An antioxidant that is also used by the body as a building block for adrenal hormones. Vitamin C is depleted from the adrenal cortex when cortisol is being secreted. Vitamin C is required to make collagen (so that your skin stays supple and pretty). It's an important structural component of blood vessels, tendons, ligaments, and bone. Vitamin C also plays an important role in making the neurotransmitter norepinephrine. In addition, vitamin C is required to make carnitine, which is essential for the transport of fat into mitochondria—your cells' energy factories—where the fat is converted to energy and burned and gotten rid of! Vitamin C is also a highly effective antioxidant. Even in small amounts vitamin C can protect proteins, lipids (fats), carbohydrates, and DNA from damage by free radicals. Vitamin C may increase two more very important antioxidants, vitamin E and glutathione.

Vitamin D: See page 168.

Vitamin E: Vitamin E is a fat-soluble vitamin that improves circulation, tissue repair, healing, fibrocystic conditions, PMS. Protects cells from free radicals and oxidation, so it protects you from heart disease. A key nutrient required for strong immune response and an important fat-soluble antioxidant, vitamin E's preventive role in cancer has been well proven. Look for the term "mixed tocopherols," which are natural sources of vitamin E from food. "Alpha" and artificial sources of vitamin E do not have the same anti-cancer qualities.

Vitamin F: Omega-3 and -6 essential fatty acids. See page 43.

Zeaxanthin: Antioxidant, naturally occurring carotenoid.

Zinc: An antioxidant mineral. *Moderate* zinc supplementation can boost immunity to viruses. However, overkill can cause neurological damage, learning and memory problems, nerve damage, urinary tract problems, and other bad things. Zinc deficiency may be associated with increased risk of cancer. Zinc supplementation is associated with decreased oxidative stress and improved immune function, but again, caution is advised.

appendix three:

Therapeutic Herbal Teas

Alfalfa: A bland tea known to help with arthritis symptoms.

Allspice: Helps facilitate and promote digestion, bloating, burping, and gas. Helps prevent allergies, lowers blood sugar, relieves toothache and muscle/joint pain, improves mood and promotes relaxation.

Anise Seed: Aids digestion, freshens breath, soothes cough, improves bronchitis.

Birch: Antibacterial, anti-inflammatory, and antiviral properties. Contains betulin and betulinic acid that is currently being studied for its potential as an anti-cancer treatment. Birch also contains saponins, flavonoids, and tannins. May help alleviate joint pain related to rheumatoid arthritis and osteoarthritis, may be helpful in combating gout, and may help fight urinary disorders.

Blackberry: Has an antioxidant capacity that is much higher than any other berries. Also contains phenolic acid and flavonoids that help fight and prevent cancer. An abundant source of vitamins, antioxidants, minerals, and vitamins including vitamin A, vitamin C, and other minerals like potassium and calcium. Aids against lung inflammation, thrombosis, cardiovascular disease, and many others, and is a very good treatment for diarrhea and dysentery.

Blueberry: Blueberries provide significantly more antioxidants than other fruits. Fights aging, the formation of cancer cells, and other diseases.

Chamomile: Used to relieve anxiety, caffeine withdrawal, hyperactivity, insomnia, pain, stress, and as a digestive tonic helping to relieve colic, flatulence, indigestion, and irritable bowel. Used in some European hospitals to calm patients and prevent nightmares. Also used by women as a remedy for menstrual cramps.

Chrysanthemum: Provides a sweet-tasting brew that may help reduce body heat resulting from fever, help protect against liver damage, and neutralize toxins in the body.

Cinnamon: Has a calming effect and is thought to support healthy circulation and digestion.

Dandelion Root: Traditionally, dandelion has been used to support liver health, cure breast illnesses, bloating, disorders of the gastrointestinal system, aching joints, and skin conditions. The leaves contain large amounts of numerous vitamins, including A, C, D, and B-complexes, and minerals like iron, magnesium, zinc potassium, manganese, copper, choline, calcium, boron, and silicon. The root is roasted and used to make tea.

Echinacea: Has immune-stimulating properties. Echinacea promotes T cell activity and interferon production, and makes cells less likely to be invaded by viruses. Use it to treat colds, sore throat, fever, and flu by drinking several times daily. Echinacea mixes well with peppermint.

Essiac: Consists of four main herbs that grow in the wilderness of Ontario, Canada: Burdock Root, Slippery Elm Inner Bark, Sheep Sorrel, and Indian Rhubarb Root. Has very powerful health properties that boost the immune system, detoxify, and prevent or treat cancer, as well as heal minor illnesses.

Fennel: A digestive aid. Soothes upper respiratory problems.

Ginger: Improves digestion, nausea, lung congestion, and arthritis.

Ginseng: Many healing and energy-giving properties due to the presence of natural chemicals called ginsenosides. Restores appetite, aids digestion and respiration. Rejuvenating and works against fatigue, helps reduce physical and mental stress, aids the immune system, works as an aphrodisiac, helps counter arthritis, asthma, and diabetes, reduces the risk of cancer, lessens the effects of Crohn's disease, helps to relieve pain, helps modulate cholesterol metabolism, helps heal stomach ulcers and diarrhea, and is good for blood circulation.

Green Tea: Both green and black teas are from the same plant. However, black tea is fermented and contains more caffeine. Green tea leaves, rich in fluorine, help prevent dental decay by inhibiting the enzyme that causes plaque formation. A natural antioxidant, rich in vitamin C, with immune protecting properties.

Hawthorn: Known to lower blood pressure, reduce cholesterol, normalize heart rate, improve circulation, and is mildly sedative and antispasmodic. It is also used to treat depression and anxiety.

Hibiscus: Shown to help reduce high blood pressure and soothe menstrual cramps.

Kombucha: Made by fermenting sweetened black tea with a flat, pancake-like culture of yeasts and bacteria known as the kombucha mushroom. Contains a high antioxidant content. Boosts the immune system, detoxifies.

Lemongrass (Citronella): Lemony scent and flavor, with a hint of ginger. Known for its calming effect that relieves insomnia or stress.

Maté: Also known as yerba maté. A powerful antioxidant, nerve stimulant, rejuvenating tonic, helps promote regular bowel health, lifts the spirits, curbs the appetite, and helps relieve hay fever. Its caffeine-like constituent known as mateine does not seem to promote insomnia or nervousness the way coffee does. Rich in vitamins and minerals and maté has a pleasant earthy flavor.

Parsley: Used traditionally to treat high blood pressure, bring on menstruation, and for urinary problems as well as treating mosquito bites when applied topically.

Peppermint: Prized for its medicinal benefits and distinctive flavor. Treats irritable bowel syndrome, eases nausea and vomiting, controls flatulence and diverticular disorders, improves digestion and reduces heartburn, dissolves gallstones, reduces the severity of herpes outbreaks, fights bad breath, controls muscle aches and chronic pain, clears congestion and cough related to colds and allergies, controls mild asthma, and fights stress.

Persimmon: Rich in vitamin C. Chinese medicine believes that persimmons will regulate *Qi*, which is the life force.

Raspberry Leaf: Active constituents of raspberry leaves include flavonoids, tannins, and ellagic acid with substantial amounts of vitamin C, vitamin A, potassium, phosphorus, and calcium. Raspberry leaf tea aids indigestion; may help relax the uterus; may help in the treatment of leg cramps, morning sickness, and diarrhea in pregnant women; may help in post-partum recovery; helps alleviate cold symptoms and those of tonsillitis and the flu; helps in the treatment of canker sores and cold sores; may help in the treatment of gingivitis; and when applied topically, may help in the treatment and disinfecting of inflamed skin.

Rose Hips: A lemony tart taste and antiseptic properties, a natural source of vitamin C and bioflavonoids. Rose hips are considered a liver, kidney, and blood tonic, and a remedy for fatigue, colds, and cough.

Sarsaparilla: Used as a frothing agent in soft drinks like root beer and widely used as a spring tonic. It is used for gout, colds, fevers, rheumatism, arthritis, and flatulence. It is a diuretic herb that is believed to have the ability to remove heavy metals from the body. It is used as an anti-inflammatory and cleansing herb. Some women take it to help with menstrual problems and menopause. Some say it helps depression.

Slippery Elm: Contains antioxidants that help relieve inflammatory bowel conditions and often suggested for sore throat, cough, gastroesophogeal reflux disease (GERD), Crohn's disease, ulcerative colitis, and diarrhea.

Strawberry Leaf: Used to treat a multitude of symptoms from eczema to GI issues.

Rooibos (Red Tea): Herbal infusions made from a South African red bush. There are also green Rooibos teas that are delicious iced or hot and come in a wide variety of flavors. Rooibos tea is naturally caffeine-free, high in antioxidants, vitamins, and minerals and may help control allergies and fight colds. It is good for the skin and complexion and helps improve digestion.

appendix four:

Environmental Toxins

Arsenic: A carcinogenic heavy metal toxin, used in cigarettes.

Asbestos: Insulation used in construction from 1950 through the 1970s that releases fibers into the air that imbed into lung tissue and cause mesotheleoma.

Atrazine: Weed killer used on golf courses. It is a little chilling when I think that our childhood hamsters Chubsy Wubsie and Speedy Gonzales died the day after we allowed them to run around the backyard lawn with our Easter eggs (immortalized on 8-mm film). Weed killer kills!

Benzene: And other petroleum-based pollutants are emitted from vehicle exhaust. This carcinogenic chemical is used in cigarettes.

Beryllium: A carcinogenic metal used in cigarettes.

Bisphenol A: A carcinogenic in plastics and the lining of canned foods.

Cadmium: A carcinogenic metal used in batteries, shiny receipts, and cigarettes.

Chloroform: Formed when chlorine is added to water, and present in city water, swimming pools, laundry water containing bleach, industrial runoff and discards, municipal waste treatment plant discharges, and hazardous waste sites and spills.

Chromium: A carcinogenic metallic element, used in cigarettes.

City Water: See page 131. All bottled beverages, from beer, to nut milks, to sports drinks, are made with city water.

Dioxins: A carcinogenic compound that accumulates in animal fat and is found in commercial animal feed. Grassfed beef is lower in overall fat yet has more omega-3 fatty acids than meat from grain-fed factory animals. I personally choose to eat grassfed meat and to mitigate the toxic exposure with antioxidants, as I want the benefits of eating meat, and saturated fat.

Ethylene Oxide: A carcinogenic chemical used to sterilize medical devices. It is also used in cigarettes.

Fluoride: A carcinogenic chemical that accumulates in the body and contributes to bone disease. Found in water supplies and products made with water (i.e., wine, beer, sodas, reconstituted orange juice, soy, mouthwash, and toothpaste).

Formaldehyde: In kitchen cabinets and other plywood, and in the metabolizing of aspartame. Never consume aspartame. Don't use petrochemical-containing products for repair, maintenance, construction, or remodeling [e.g., pressed wood and plywood (formaldehyde and toxic glues), fiberglass (formaldehyde)].

Gamma Rays: Gamma radiation is electromagnetic radiation of high frequency (very short wavelength) that is a form of ionizing radiation able to cause serious damage when absorbed by living tissue and is therefore a health hazard. Flying in an airplane exposes you to gamma rays.

Heavy Metals: Arsenic, mercury, lead, aluminum, and cadmium are carcinogenic industrial pollutants in our environment.

Malathion: A man-made organophosphate (nerve agent) insecticide that is commonly used to control mosquitoes, fleas, ants, and a variety of insects that attack plants. Exposure may cause headaches, nausea, dizziness, weakness, cramps, diarrhea, excessive sweating, blurred vision, increased heart rate, skin rash (allergic reaction), vomiting, and central nervous system depression. A possible endocrine disruptor.

Nickel: A carcinogenic metallic element, used in margarine and cigarettes.

Noise Pollution: "Noise" is derived from the Latin word "nausea," meaning *seasickness*. We have to tolerate the chronic din of traffic, airplanes, jet skis, garbage trucks, construction equipment, lawn mowers, weed-wackers, leaf-blowers, subways, trains, etc. But my focus here is *loud* music, because this is something that can affect your health in a profound way. I've never liked loud music and find it painful to listen to. Because I've protected my hearing, I still have the perfect hearing that I had as a young girl. I recently begged and pleaded with the powers that be at a health club I belonged to to please turn down the music in the spinning classes that was excruciatingly loud even with earplugs. "Everyone else wants it loud to keep up their energy," I was told. If I complained in the class, multiple eyeballs shot daggers at me and the instructor turned sour and argumentative. It then occurred to me, *They don't mind the music because they already have hearing damage.*

I currently practice yoga in Santa Monica. One of my favorite classes blares rock-and-roll music that would otherwise hurt my eardrums if it weren't for the goofy wax earplugs stuffed into my ears. It's okay to be different—and to protect your hearing.

Noise Levels Are Measured in Decibels

Whispers: 30 decibels

Air conditioner at twenty feet: 60 decibels

Vacuum cleaner, crowded restaurant: 70 decibels

City traffic: 80 decibels

Subway, motorcycle, lawn mower: 90 decibels

Sports arena: 108 decibels

Rock concert or thunderclap: 120 decibels

Gunshot blast or jet plane: 140 decibels

Rocket launching pad: 180 decibels

With normal hearing you will feel annoyed at 55 decibels. Consider that rock-and-roll music was used to torture Panamanian dictator Manuel Noriega, Waco's David Koresh, and prisoners in Iraq and Guantanamo Bay, Cuba. Loud noise places stress on the adrenals, suppresses the immune system, causes learning disabilities and insomnia, and increases your risk of a heart attack. Moreover, *hearing aids are a certainty* in your near future if you listen to amplified music.

PCBs (Polychlorinated Biphenyls): Industrial chemicals that, although banned, still exist in our environment.

PFOA or C8: Used when processing polytetrafluroroethylene (PTFE), Teflon. This carcinogen remains in your system indefinitely.

Phthalates: Used to lengthen the life of fragrances and to soften plastics. They are estrogen mimickers (xenoestrogens) and pose particular health risks to children.

Polonium–210: A carcinogenic chemical element that gives off radiation, used in cigarettes.

Polybrominated Diphenylethers (PBDEs): Fire-retardant chemical used in the manufacture of computers, televisions, toasters, and other common electronics, has been shown to disrupt normal brain function. Be wary of foam that is misshapen and breaking down, use a vacuum fitted with a HEPA filter, don't reupholster foam furniture, be wary of old carpet and padding, avoid products with brominated fire retardants, and opt for less flammable fabrics and materials, like leather, wool, and cotton.

Secondhand Smoke: Tobacco smoke contains 4,000 chemicals that smokers exhale into the air as particles and gases, including nicotine, tar, benzene and benzo(a)pyrene, carbon monoxide, ammonia, dimethylnitrosamine, formaldehyde, hydrogen cyanide, and acrolein. When you breathe the exhaled smoke, you are "smoking." Gas can linger in the air and particles can accumulate on surfaces. Passive smoking is carcinogenic, increases the risk of respiratory disease, heart disease, stroke, and hardening of the arteries.

Tetrachloroethylene: A carcinogenic chemical used as dry cleaning fluid. Hang dry-cleaned clothing out to air. Preferably find a green dry cleaner that uses eco-friendly, non-toxic carbon dioxide methods.

Toxic People: Like chemical toxins, people toxins can get under your skin and smolder. You can suffer the same adverse health effects from toxic relationships including chronic fatigue, insomnia, and many other ailments. Toxic people aren't just those who are negative, angry, or difficult, but they can be cunningly manipulative, playing mind games and head-trips on you that cause your insides to churn and your emotions to seesaw. Because toxic people may not show that poisonous side to anyone but you, they can cause an extra internal battle of the continual "Is it me?" Toxic people can be complaining, blaming, emotional garbage dumpers, word vomiters, life-force suckers, narcissists, teasers, humiliaters, minimizers, trivializers (of your problems), gossipers, or any other type of user, abuser, or loser. As much as we want to love everyone and respect everyone, love and respect are due ourselves first. If associating with someone makes you feel toxic, you don't need validation, you just need to cut off the relationship nicely and move on. (Chelate that person right out of your system.)

Vinyl Chloride: A carcinogenic substance used in manufacturing plastics and used in cigarettes.

Volatile Organic Compounds (VOCs): Make up the air pollutant ozone. They are in most, if not all, household products and construction materials.

appendix five:

Self-care Toxins

Acetaldehyde/Acetone: Carcinogen found in nail-care products.

Acrylic Nails: Applying acrylic nails uses chemicals such as resins, formaldehyde, adhesives, and solvents, which may play a role in causing cancer and increase your risk of Alzheimer's disease.[64, 65]

Alcohol: Used in mouthwash, astringent, toothpaste, cleansers. Long-term exposure to alcohol can lead to oral sores and cancer.

Alkyl-Phenol Ethoxylades: May reduce sperm count. Found in shampoo and bubble bath.

Alpha Hydroxy Acid: Destroys skin cells, ages your skin, and renders your skin more susceptible to environment hazards, such as skin cancer. Found in anti-aging facial creams and lotions.

Aluminum: Linked to Alzheimer's disease. Used in antiperspirants.

Ammonium Glycolate: Increases risk of sunburn and skin cancer by intensifying UV exposure. A penetration enhancer that ushers other chemicals deeper into your skin, increasing your toxic load. Found in body products.

Benzalkonium Chloride, Cetrimonium Chloride, and Lauryl Dimonium Hydrolysed Collagen: Toxic allergens used in hair-treatment products.

Benzoic/Benzyl/Benzene: Contains carcinogens, is an endocrine disruptor, and may cause birth defects. Found in shower gels, shampoos, and bubble bath.

Benzoic Acid: Inhalation affects the nervous system and is moderately toxic by ingestion. Severe eye and skin irritant. Used as a food preservative and in pharmaceuticals and cosmetics.

Benzoyl Peroxide: In acne treatments, bar soap, facial cleansers. Highly toxic irritant.

Bronopol: May break down into formaldehyde, possibly forms carcinogenic nitrosamines. Found in body products.

Butylparaben: Linked to breast cancer, endocrine disruptor, found in body products.

Carboxymethylcellulose: Linked to cancer. Inhalation could cause chemical pneumonitis (inflammation of lung tissue). Used in cosmetics.

Coal Tar Dyes (FD&C Blue No. 1, Green No. 3, Yellow No. 5, Yellow No. 6, Red No. 33, and Others): Severe allergic reactions, asthma attacks, headaches, nausea, fatigue, lack of concentration, nervousness, increased risk of Hodgkin's disease, non-Hodgkin's lymphoma, and multiple myeloma. Used in bubble bath, hair dye, dandruff shampoo, toothpaste, and foods.

Condoms: Most condoms on the market contain N-nitrosamine and other carcinogens. Latex sensitivity can result in inflammation when latex condoms are used. Condoms also contain petroleum-based ingredients such as the spermicide non-oxydol 9, which are xenohormones to the body. [66-68] Condoms are one "pick your poison" that we have to put up with in this day of STDs. If you use condoms you need to up your antioxidants.

Coumarin: A carcinogenic, active ingredient in rat bait. Used in the manufacturing of deodorants, shampoos, skin fresheners, and perfumes.

DEA (Cocamide, Diethanolamine, Lauramide, Linoleamide, Oleamide): Used in shampoos, skin cream, bubble bath, shaving gel, conditioner, shaving gel, lotions, shampoo, conditioners, foods, deodorant. Blocks absorption of the nutrient choline, which is essential to brain development in a fetus. Carcinogenic.

Diazolidinyl Urea: Found in facial cleansers, shampoos, and conditioners. Linked to neurotoxicity and immunotoxicity.

Dibutyl Phthalate (DBP): Used to keep nail polish from chipping. Linked to cancer.

Dimethicone: A silicone emollient used in lotions and creams. May promote tumors and accumulate in the liver and lymph nodes.

Dioforms: Used in tooth-whitening products. Damages and weakens tooth enamel allowing more staining and discoloration to take place. CAUTION: While deemed safe by the FDA, look for clinically proven products, follow directions, and consult with an enlightened dental professional.

DMDM Hydantoin: Contains formaldehyde, which is linked to cancer, developmental and reproductive toxicity. Allergenic, can be an irritant to eyes, skin, and lungs. Found in manicure/pedicure products and hair treatment packages.

Ethylacrylate: Used in mascara. Linked to cancer.

Formaldehyde: Carcinogen and neurotoxin. Fatal if swallowed. Can cause spasms, edema, chemical pneumonitis (lung inflammation), and is extremely destructive to tissue of the mucous membrane. Degrades cellular structures leading to cellulite. Found in many nail care products, baby shampoo, bubble bath, deodorants, perfume, cologne, hair dye, mouthwash, toothpaste, hair spray, nail polish. Aspartame metabolizes into formaldehyde.

Fragrances (Synthetic): Some perfumes and fragrances contain carcinogenic/brain-damaging chemicals such as methylene chloride.

Glycolic Acid: Alters skin structure, allowing other chemicals to penetrate deeper into the skin and enter the circulation. Toxicant, neurotoxin, kidney toxicant, gastrointestinal or liver toxicant. Found in creams, lotions, cosmetics.

Hydroabietyl Alcohol: Human immune system toxicant. Unsafe for use in cosmetics according to the fragrance industry's International Fragrance Association. Found in styling gels/lotions.

Hydroquinone: A severely toxic and very powerful chemical. Banned in the United Kingdom, but still used in the United States. Alters the skin's natural structure inhibiting the production of melanin, causing blotchiness long term and making the skin more susceptible to skin cancer. Found in skin-lightening products and hair dyes.

Hydroxyethylcellulose: Used in cosmetics. Inhalation could cause chemical pneumonitis.

Imidazolidinyl Urea: Allergen found in deodorants, shampoos, hand creams, and some mascaras. Immune system toxin, respiratory toxicant, skin or sense organ toxicant, classified as toxic in one or more government assessments.

Isobutylparaben: Potential breast cancer risk. Itching, burning, and blistering of skin. Found in body products.

Isopropanol (Isopropyl Alcohol): Moderately toxic chemical. Used to clean/disinfect skin. Found in some body products.

Kajoic Acid: A chemical that inhibits melanin production, damages the skin, and makes it more susceptible to cancer. Used in skin-lightening products.

Lacquer: Can cause eyelashes to fall out. Found in mascara.

Lanolin: May contain carcinogenic pesticides such as DDT, lindane, dieldrin, and other neurotoxins. Can cause rashes. Found in body products.

Lye: Can dry and damage skin. Found in bars of soap.

Methyl Methacrylate: May cause inflammation to skin. Found in nail polish.

Methylisothiazolinone: Neurotoxin. Found in shampoo.

Methylparaben: Potential breast cancer risk and endocrine disruptor. Found in body products.

Mineral Oil: Clogs pores, locks in toxins, dries skin, inhibits your skin's natural oil production, possible carcinogen. Found in blush, baby oil, lotions, foundations, and creams.

MTBE: Gasoline additive. Possible carcinogen.

Padimate-O (PABA): Carcinogens may form in products that contain padimate-O. Found in cosmetics and sunscreens.

Paraffin: Possible carcinogen. Found in cosmetics and food.

Petroleum: Suffocates skin and traps toxins in body, clogs pores. Found in lotions, skin creams, and body gels.

Phenoxyethanol: Possible reproductive or developmental harm to fetus, potential for reduced fertility, classified as toxic and an irritant, risks to wildlife and environment through excretion of body product toxins and disposal of cosmetics.

Phthalates: Endocrine disruptor that accumulates in the body; proven damage to liver, lungs, kidneys, and reproductive systems. Appears in vinyl flooring, plastic wallpaper, perfume, hair spray, deodorant, nail polish, hair gel, mousse, body and hand lotion.

Polybrominated Diphenyl Ethers (PBDE): Toxic flame retardant. Residue found in breast milk.

Polypropylene: Possible carcinogen. Found in lipstick, mascara, baby soap, eye shadow.

Polyquaternium-7: Linked to cancer or other significant health problems. Found in body products.

Polyscorbate-60: Inhalation could cause chemical pneumonitis (lung inflammation). Used in cosmetics.

Polyvinyl Chloride (PVC): When produced, it releases dioxins linked to cancer, also affects immune and reproductive systems.

P-Phenylenediamine (PPD): Highly carcinogenic. Causes developmental and reproductive toxicity, allergenic, and can cause skin irritation issues. Used in hair dyeing, shampoos, and hair spray.

Propylene Glycol: Kidney damage, liver abnormalities, inhibits skin cell growth, damages cell membranes, causing rashes, surface damage, and dry skin.

Propylparaben: Potential breast cancer risk and endocrine disruptor; itching, burning, and blistering of skin; gastrointestinal or liver toxicity hazard. Found in body products.

Quaternium-7, 15, 31, 60, etc.: Toxic, causes skin rashes, allergic reactions, linked to leukemia, multiple myeloma, non-Hodgkin's lymphoma and other cancers. Found in body products.

Retin-A: Used to treat acne and skin aging. According to Samuel Epstein, M.D. one of the world's leading experts in cancer causes and prevention, Retin-A is safe, though it has the potential to make your skin more sensitive to sunlight, posing a risk for severe sunburn. CAUTION: Avoid tanning and use sunscreen when you cannot avoid exposure to the sun, avoid using while pregnant, cautious use with dermatitis or eczema.

Sodium Chloride: Eye irritation, hair loss, and dry and itchy skin. Found in shampoo as a thickener.

Sodium Hydroxymethylglycinate: Linked to cancer or other significant health problems. Found in personal care products.

Sodium Laureth Sulfate (SLES): A detergent and surfactant that may produce eye or skin irritation and found to contain low levels of the carcinogen 1,4-dioxane. Found in shampoo, toothpaste, bubble bath, body wash, soap. Related and equally dangerous ingredients are sodium lauryl sulphate, sodium laurilsulfate, sodium dodecyl sulfate.

Stearalkonium Chloride: Toxic and causes allergic reactions. Used in hair conditioner.

Sunblock: Sunlight consists of ultraviolet UVA and UVB rays. UVB rays affect the outer layers of skin, causing sunburn. UVA rays penetrate deep into the dermal layer of skin; overexposure to UVA rays leads to eye damage, immune system changes, cataracts, wrinkles and premature aging of the skin, and malignant melanoma. Sunblock blocks the UVB rays necessary to produce vitamin D. A little sun on the skin is a good thing. Most brands of American sunscreen offer protection from UVB rays but not from UVA rays. Only 15 percent of sunscreens sold in America block both UVA and UVB radiation. The vast majority of sunscreen products contain toxic synthetic chemicals that penetrate the skin, are powerful free radical generators, have strong estrogenic activity, and accumulate in body fat stores. Chemicals to avoid include benzophenone, octyl-methoxycinnamate, oxybenzone, para-amino-benzoic acid (PABA), dioxybenzone, parabens, and titanium dioxide. These chemicals not only hurt humans, but are also rinsing into the ocean and harming sea life. Right now only brands whose active ingredient is zinc oxide can safely shield your skin from both UVA and UVB rays. However, zinc oxide doesn't rub in, and so you'll have whitish residue on your skin. To get around this, manufacturers are creating zinc oxide nanoparticles that have the ability to be absorbed. Nanoparticles penetrate the deep layers of your skin, carrying toxins directly into your bloodstream where they lodge in your organs. The best you can do right now is to continue to use zinc oxide sunblock and put up with the white residue on your skin. There are sunblocks being developed that are safe for humans, animals, and the environment, and I will continue to research sunblock and provide updates on my website.[69]

Talc: Carcinogenic when inhaled, may result in fallopian tube fibrosis. Found in blush, condoms, baby powder, feminine powders, foot and body powders.

Toluene: Poison, respiratory irritant, causes hallucinations, bone marrow changes, linked to liver and kidney damage and birth defects, endocrine disruptor and carcinogen. Found in nail polish and cleaning products.

Triclosan: A toxic carcinogenic chemical found in antimicrobial soaps and toothpaste. Creates toxic fumes.

Triethanolamine (TEA): Allergen and toxic with long-term use. Restricted in Europe due to known carcinogenic effects.

appendix six:

Home-care Toxins

2-Butoxyethanol: A solvent in carpet cleaners and specialty cleaners linked to blood disorders, liver and kidney damage, and reproductive damage from long-term exposure.

Benzene: Found in crude oil, gasoline, and cigarette smoke. Inhalation of high levels can increase risk of non-Hodgkin lymphoma, and leukemia in children. Used in detergents, drugs, pesticides, and adhesives.

Bleach (Sodium Hypochlorite): When bleach is mixed with acids (found in toilet bowl cleaners), it reacts to form chlorine gas. When it is mixed with ammonia, it creates chloramine gas, a toxic substance. Sodium hypochlorite is acutely toxic to fish, and binds with organic material in the marine environment to form organochlorines, toxic compounds that persist in the environment.

Electropollution: Electromotive forces (EMFs) and extremely low frequency fields (ELFs) are unavoidable problems. Electricity is the phenomenon arising from the existence of charge. Most elementary particles of matter possess charge, either positive or negative. Two particles of like charge, both positive or both negative, repel each other; two particles of unlike charge are attracted. Alternating current (AC) is a flow that repeats in a cycle. The number of repetitions of the cycle occurring each second is defined as the frequency, which is expressed in Hertz (Hz). The frequency of ordinary household current in the United States is 60 cycles per second (60 Hz). The frequency of the human brain runs one to two cycles of AC per second while sleeping or resting and 18 to 22 cycles per second when using intense mental concentration. The electromagnetic frequencies of televisions, microwave ovens, electric blankets, hairdryers, computers, cell telephones, radios, and all of the appliances and electrical devices in our environment are not compatible with human cellular function. The current from these appliances disrupts a healthy human electrical current and can actually cause cellular mutation.

ELFs are also a contributing factor to electropollution. ELFs affect people in their own households where ELF wave–emitting devices (for example, televisions, fluorescent lights, electric blankets, and microwave ovens) are present.

Get rid of your microwave. Heat food in the oven or cast iron skillet. There are numerous models on the market of stainless steel electric kettles to boil water. Never use electric blankets and only use heating pads for short periods of time when absolutely necessary. Keep electrical devices such as TVs, radios, video recorders, bedside clocks, and microwaves at a three-feet distance. Electric wall plugs should be three feet from your head when sleeping as they emanate an electric field if there is something plugged in.

EMFs from Cell Phones: Cell phones expose you to electromagnetic radiation known as radiofrequency (RF) energy. Studies done by Swedish and other scientists on the dangers of cell phones link usage to brain cancer.[70]

Never have the phone to your head when the connection is being made as the zap you get is much more powerful. Never carry your cell phone near your breasts, ovaries, or testicles. Keep it turned off whenever possible. Don't sleep with it near your head if you're using it as an alarm clock. Use a corded landline if one is available, and text rather than call if possible. Just as with headsets for normal telephones, the headsets for cell phones come in corded and wireless variants. Almost all of the modern cell phones support corded headsets.[71]

Ethoxylated Nonyl Phenols (NPEs): Endocrine-disrupting chemicals used in cleaning products.

Methylene Chloride: A possible human carcinogen found in a wide range of paint strippers and similar products.

Naphthalene: A carcinogen used in mothballs and moth crystals.

Petrochemicals: Known carcinogens made from gasoline byproducts.

Some Products Made with Petrochemicals

- Adhesives and sealants
- Agrochemicals
- Condoms
- Construction chemicals
- Corrosion control chemicals
- Cosmetics raw materials
- Drugs
- Electronic chemicals and materials
- Epoxies
- Explosives
- Fertilizers
- Flavorings, fragrances, food additives
- Flooring and insulating materials
- Inks, dyes, printing supplies
- Luggage
- Packaging, bottles, containers
- Paint, coatings, resins
- Pesticides
- Plastics
- Polymer additives
- Recording disks and tapes
- Soaps and detergents
- Solvents
- Specialty and industrial chemicals
- Specialty and industrial gases
- Specialty and life sciences chemicals
- Surfactants and cleaning agents
- Synthetic fibers and rubbers

PFOs Perflurooctanotane Sulfonate: A fluorocarbon used in producing repellents and surfactant products, like stain-resistant fabric.

Phospates: Provides nutrients for algae and other aquatic plants as phosphate-rich wastewater enters the environment, becoming detrimental as they overfertilize aquatic plants and cause stepped-up aging processes in waterways.

Phthalates: Accumulates in the body. Damages liver, lungs, kidneys, and reproductive systems. In vinyl flooring, plastic wallpaper, and in children's toys, as DEHP, BBP, and DBP.

Silica: A carcinogen when breathed. Used in abrasive cleansers.

Tanning Beds: Sunlight consists of ultraviolet UVA and UVB rays. UVB rays affect the outer layers of skin. That's where you feel the sunburn. UVA rays penetrate deep into the dermal layer of skin, and overexposure to UVA rays leads to eye damage, immune system changes, cataracts, wrinkles, premature aging of the skin, and skin cancers. Tanning beds and sun lamps generally emit 93 to 99 percent UVA radiation. This is three times the UVA radiation given off by the sun.

Toluene: A reproductive toxin, which is used as a solvent in numerous products, including paints.

Trisodium Nitrilotriacetate (NTA): A carcinogen used in laundry detergents.

UVA Rays From Nail Salon Dryers: Drying your nails at the salon under the UVA light will accelerate photoaging on your hands and feet with age spots, wrinkles, and loss of elasticity. Ten to twenty years of mani-pedis will expose you to cancer-causing UVA rays.

Vinyl Chloride: Used to create PVC (polyvinyl chloride), a known carcinogen. Found in toys that kids chew.

Xylene: An extremely toxic ingredient, reproductive toxin, and neurotoxicant found in graffiti and scuff removers, spray paints, and some adhesives.

appendix seven:

Medical Toxins

Acid Blockers: Acid blockers or proton inhibitors that range from mild antacids, which neutralize stomach acid, to the powerful proton pump inhibitors that prevent stomach cells from producing stomach acid. We know them as the little purple pill, Nexium, Pepcid, Aciphex, Protonix, or Tums. While millions of people take these medications daily, few understand that the long-term health complications related to acid blockers are many, and very severe. They include nutrient deficiencies, increased risk of stomach cancer, low immune function, poor digestion of proteins, osteoporosis, heart disease, depression, pernicious (gradual onset) anemia, osteoporosis, poor eyesight, paralysis, severe neurological problems, and dementia to name a few.[72]

The stomach is a vat of acid because acid is required to break down proteins (meat, fowl, fish, eggs, cheese, nuts, and legumes) into their smallest units of amino acids. When acid production is neutralized or cellular function inhibited, food can't be digested. Instead it will remain in the stomach. With the aid of the bacteria present, undigested carbs ferment, undigested fats rancidify, and undigested proteins putrefy. All this gives rise to gas, bloating, and indigestion, and with a lack of unabsorbed nutrition, ultimately malnutrition.

Immune cells require protein from the food we eat so when protein digestion fails, there is inadequate protein to produce a strong immune system. A poor immune response can lead to any health problem from a simple cold to cancer and anything in between. Poor protein absorption resulting from the use of antacids causes the body to steal protein from joint surfaces, causing arthritis.

Calcium plays a major role in bone remodeling and is dependent on the presence of stomach acid for absorption. No stomach acid means no calcium absorption, so downing Tums for calcium supplementation is an absurd but great marketing ploy. Tums, which is calcium carbonate, neutralizes stomach acid. But taking the calcium in Tums without the other necessary cofactors, including magnesium, phosphorous, boron, manganese, vitamin D_3, vitamin K, vitamin B_6, and folic acid, causes calcium to end up in soft tissues such as arteries, tendons, and joints.

Vitamin B_{12} absorption is dependent on a protein made by the stomach cells—the same cells that secrete stomach acid and the same cells that are destroyed by acid blocker medications. So if you don't digest protein because it is putrefying in your gut because you are blocking stomach acid, you also are not absorbing B_{12}. (An important fact to know is that B_{12} is only found in animal products.)[73]

High levels of the amino acid homocysteine are a major contributing factor to heart disease and Alzheimer's disease. A lack of stomach acid results in B_6, B_{12}, and folic acid deficiencies, which are necessary to decrease homocysteine levels. Folic acid deficiencies also contribute to cancer. The eyes rely heavily on protein for proper function, therefore acid blockers are directly related to poor eyesight.[74]

Acid blockers should only be taken for a short period of time if you have a lesion that needs to heal.

AIDS Cocktails: Causes mitochondrial toxicity and damage that decreases the number of mitochondria.[76] This is a "pick your poison" for people suffering from AIDS. The side effects of these drugs can be ameliorated by Chinese herbs. Please see my blog (under "Health") to read an excerpt from *Ancient Herbs, Modern Medicine*, the book I wrote on Chinese medicine, entitled "HIV: Chinese Medicine Seeks to Treat Disease Without Side Effects."

Anesthesia: Neurotoxic, may cause structural or functional changes in the nervous system including cognitive difficulties and fatigue. [75] If you must have anesthesia, drink green juice before and after and otherwise follow the *Healthy, Sexy, Happy* program.

Aspartame: In addition to their inherent side effects, many drugs are coated with aspartame. See page 23 for more on aspartame.

Bisophosphonates: A class of drugs aimed at preventing bone fractures and offsetting bone loss associated with menopause, including Fosamax, Boniva, Novartis, Reclast, and Actonel. These drugs mimic, to some extent, the effects of estrogen on bone in that they work by inhibiting bone resorption (the process by which old bone is removed to make room for new bone), but unlike estrogen, these drugs have no ability to build new bone. Large, placebo-controlled trials show that these drugs can indeed increase bone mineral density and reduce the risk of vertebral, hip, and other nonvertebral fractures in women with osteoporosis in the short run. After trials lasting up to ten years, doubts are emerging about the long-term safety and efficacy of bisophosphonates because they not only inhibit osteoclastic bone resorption, they also inhibit the bone-building or osteoblastic bone formation. Researchers have found that among those who had taken oral bisophosphonates for five years or more the rate of esophageal cancer doubled from one in 1,000 to two in 1,000. Other researchers followed nine women with osteopenia or osteoporosis, who had been taking Fosamax for three to eight years (some had also been taking Premarin) and had developed nonspinal fractures (to the lower back, ribs, hip bones, and femur) while performing normal daily activities such as walking, standing, or turning around. The locations of these fractures were unusual for women with osteoporosis, and none of the fractures was related to a fall or other trauma. The fractures occurred earlier in the women taking both Fosamax and Premarin, suggesting an additive effect on bone resorption. Use of these medications has recently been linked to cases of jawbone decay or osteonecrosis of the jaw or "dead jaw," which is a rare bone disease in which the jawbone deteriorates and dies. To repair jawbone damage, a painful surgery is required to remove dying bone tissue.

Chemotherapy: Causes oxidative stress, damaging mitochondria.[77] If you are on chemotherapy, you need a broad spectrum of antioxidants. I suggest reading Dr. Russell Blaylock's book *Natural Strategies for Cancer Patients*.

Impotence Drugs: All three drugs currently on the market prevent the breakdown of the chemical that causes blood vessels in the penis to dilate, which allows more of the chemical to remain and build up, so erections are better and last longer. After orgasm, blood vessels contract and the erection goes down. Consider that 70 percent of men who have a cardiovascular event and 100 percent of men who have been diagnosed with diabetes have experienced erectile problems for years prior. What does that tell you? Instead of eating and living in ways that create serious health problems and then taking a pill so you can have sex, wouldn't it be better to take care of your overall health and have sex naturally? All drugs have side effects. Side effects of Viagra include headache, flushes, nasal congestion or runny nose, malaise, nausea, changes in blood pressure, irregular heartbeats, visual disturbances including rare cases of blindness, and chest pain. Viagra may cause stickiness of blood platelets. Laboratory studies suggest that taking Viagra may negatively affect sperm function and possibly male fertility.[78]

Men who take Pfizer's sildenafil (Revatio or Viagra) or similar drugs for erectile dysfunction increase their chances of hearing impairment. Impotence drugs such as Viagra and Cialis can increase the risk of eye damage in men who have a history of heart disease or high blood pressure. Following the *Healthy, Sexy, Happy* program including using bioidentical testosterone and other hormones, as well as practicing pelvic floor exercises (see page 220) will restore erections naturally, depending on the cause of your problem.

Interferon: Accelerates the normal oxidative aging of mitochondria and DNA.[79] See Chemotherapy.

Magnesium Stearate/Stearic Acid: A hydrogenated fat used to bind medicinal tablets and make them smooth. Used in most supplements including many "high quality" professional brands. May contain phosphatidyl choline, which collapses cell membranes and selectively kills T-cells, which weakens your immune system.

Mammograms: First let me express my respect for anyone who has undergone breast cancer and my reverence for their choices. Every one of us has to make our own choices when it comes to cancer diagnostics and treatments.

For years I've personally questioned the use of mammograms as a way to detect breast cancer. It seemed counterintuitive to smash our delicate tissue between cold metal plates and then beam our gorgeous body parts with radiation. Like most women, I love my breasts and I don't want to lose them. That is the single reason why the mammogram industry has flourished and why this industry is making billions of dollars every year.

The key to surviving breast cancer is early detection. In cases where a tumor was discovered early, 95 percent of women have survived. This commonsensical fact is used diabolically by the mammography industry to make billions every year. The horrible truth is that mammograms have contributed to the epidemic rise in breast cancer because radiation is carcinogenic. If the FDA would admit to this, this industry would be inundated with class action lawsuits, and if you don't understand that those with the deepest pockets own the FDA, then you have been living on Mars.

I first started questioning mammograms intuitively, and then began to read about studies done here in the United States, in Canada, Scotland, and Sweden that concluded that mammograms did not reduce breast cancer deaths. What does that mean exactly? Well, it means that women were dying of breast cancer, but with the advent of mammograms women knew they were going to die sooner rather than later—but they died anyway.

Meanwhile, women's breasts were being irradiated, which damages DNA and cells, and exposes benign tumors to radiation. More cancer tumors develop as a result. With each mammogram, your risk of developing cancer increases 1 to 3 percent, and this risk is accumulative. And mammograms have a 90 percent false positive rate and so have resulted in unnecessary biopsies, breast surgeries, radiation, and chemotherapy. To add insult to injury, mammograms smash existing tumors and exacerbate metastases.

If you want to read more about why you should have a mammogram, you can pick up the scary propaganda in your doctor's office courtesy of the billion-dollar mammogram industry. If you're interested in further education, don't just take my word for it. Go to my endnotes and look up the three articles cited there.[80]

You do have recourse to mammograms. One is an MRI scan—which gives a clear picture of the breast but is expensive and is not paid for by insurance. (If insurance companies paid for medical modalities that actually helped people stay well rather than modalities that contributed to disease, they would ultimately save money, but the insurance industry is just another industry that is in the pocket of big drug and big medical corporations.)

Thermography, a noninvasive, pain-free, infrared image of the breasts is based on the premise that before the growth of abnormal cells can occur, the body must produce an increased blood supply to the growth area. Thermography measures the heat generated by the microcirculation near any abnormal growth. For that reason, thermography can detect abnormal occurrences in the breasts *before* the actual tumor develops. You can find a thermography clinic at iact-org.org.

Painkillers: All drugs are poison to your body and all drugs have side effects. Prescription synthetic or semisynthetic pain drugs such as Fentanyl, Stadol, OxyContin, Demerol, Hydrocodone, MS Contin, Percocet, Lorcet, Dilaudid, and Zydone are addictive, and we all know it and don't need another primer on addiction. Regular use of nonsteroidal anti-inflammatory drugs, or NSAIDs such as Actron, Advil, Aleve, Bayer aspirin, Ecotrin aspirin, Excedrin, Motrin, and Nuprin can cause heart disease, stomach ulcers, and even severe hemorrhage resulting in death. Over use of acetaminophen (Tylenol) causes liver damage and is the most common cause of acute liver failure in the United States, requiring liver transplant.

See page 202 for treating pain with neural therapy.

Plastic Surgery: I'm sure I will be asked if I've had plastic surgery. All I'm going to say on the subject is, I'm sixty years old, what do you think? Plastic surgery has taken off since I first moved to Hollywood. People are fascinated with the secret society of nip/tuck. It *is* kind of a mysterious world. But what *isn't* mysterious are people's attitudes about plastic surgery. (Plastic surgery originated to help people with facial deformities, which is not what I'm discussing here.) Generally, there are four attitudes about plastic surgery:

The Aging Gracefully: Some people don't mind the outward signs of aging and are happy with themselves just the way they are and would not consider any type of plastic surgery. Others would secretly like to explore plastic surgery but the social set they live in perpetuates a condemning attitude about such frivolous pursuits.

The Malcontent: People who want to look completely different than who they are (the Michael Jackson syndrome) and have mutilating surgeries. If you're not happy with yourself, you will likely not be happy with your plastic surgery results, and you will likely continue to have surgeries until you are very unhappy.

The Overhaulist: People who live a sedentary lifestyle, eat factory-food products, smoke, gobble handfuls of prescription and OTC drugs, are adrenally burned out, and sick, and then go in for plastic surgery as an overhaul. This is not a candidate for great plastic surgery results, though there are plenty of surgeons who will operate on this type of patient. Reputable surgeons (who are not desperate for money) will turn this person away. Reputable surgeons, for example, will not perform surgery on someone who smokes.

The Fit and Healthy Tune-upper: Plastic surgery is appropriate as a tune-up to go the last fraction of the distance when a person has done everything already to be fit and healthy, inside and out. There are also instances when someone may want something a little more radical than a minor adjustment. An example is the "Mommy Makeover." The best candidate for these more radical procedures is still a fit and healthy person. A woman who completely lets herself go her entire life and then once the kids leaves home thinks, *I'll go in for a makeover!* is not likely to have great results.

Prescription and OTC Drugs: A new study confirms what we have all suspected for a long time, that 85 percent of drugs are not only useless, but the toxic side effects and/or misuse of prescription drugs make these drugs a significant cause of death in the United States.[81] In fact, it's been known since the 1960s that drugs cause mitochondrial damage, and that's the reason all drugs come with side effects. Taking massive amounts of drugs on a prolonged basis is going to affect your health on a fundamental level, and can cause side effects—everything from liver and kidney damage to turning your hair white—that are irreversible.

If you take a lot of drugs these side effects (symptoms of mitochondrial damage) will age you, hasten your demise, and can in some cases have immediate *fatal* adverse effects. All classes of psychotropic drugs have been documented to damage mitochondria, as have statin medications, analgesics like acetaminophen, and many other drugs.

In addition to trying natural healing methods instead of prescription and OTC drugs, you may have success stopping certain eating and lifestyle behaviors that may be the cause of the symptoms you are trying to treat with drugs. I use drugs from time to time. I never finish a prescription, as my goal is to nip things in the bud and then quickly rush in with antioxidants, therapeutic fats, and other nutrients to finish the job. I believe this is the way medicine should work but unfortunately we have one side of doctors who aren't versed in natural healing methods, and the other side of alternative people who vilify all drugs. They can and should be used together.

Silicon Breast Implants: Readers are sure to ask me my opinion on this as well, and it's another controversial subject. So here is my honest opinion. You can have either silicon breast implants with a silicon shell or saline implants with a silicon shell. I believe that in the warm soup of a woman's body silicon emits xenoestrogens. Are there studies? No. It just makes sense. And it seems to make sense that some women who may be immunocompromised (even if they weren't previously aware) could suffer acute effects of having implants in their bodies. Other women—and there appear to be millions of them—have healthy immune systems and seem to be okay with implants.

In addition to the risks of having silicon in your body, I've talked to numerous women over the years and the consensus (except for one woman) is that having implants means multiple surgeries over the period of their lifetime, until the implants are taken out. Hardening around the implant (encapsulation), rupturing, and shifting are the common problems. I'm not even going to go into the severe deformities and crippling autoimmune conditions because you can easily find photographs online, which plastic surgeons vehemently deny and ridicule. If a woman has implants for many years with seemingly no problems, she still should have the implants changed because after ten or fifteen years the shell will be completely assimilated into the body, leaving the silicon encased in scar tissue. My ultimate opinion is that if a woman feels healthy enough, or if implants are necessary because of mastectomy, tubular breasts, other types of deformity, or other serious issues, then breast implants could fall under the category of "pick your poisons," with the looming caveat that you have to be extra diligent about being pristine with other toxins and committed to future surgeries.

Stem cell assisted fat transfers to the breasts: The newest procedure to be FDA approved, though it was developed in 2004 by Dr. Kotaro Yoshimura of Tokyo, Japan. A plastic surgeon performs liposuction and divides the fat. Growth factors are extracted from one half of the fat (and the balance is discarded). The stem cells are mixed with the remaining fat and then injected into the breasts. This procedure works well for women with horrifying-but-true-bodily-mystery-fat rolls.

If you're going in for plastic surgery, prepare for it by following the *Healthy, Sexy, Happy* program. Start consuming green juice (with added spirulina and chlorella) as soon as you can after surgery. Take probiotics, theraputic fats (Activator X, GLA, cod liver oil, and coconut oil), as well as extra antioxidants.

Silver Amalgam Fillings: A huge mistake that was inflicted on millions of people, including me. Having grown up on a sugar diet, I have plenty of fillings. Twenty years ago I had all my mercury fillings removed and replaced with porcelain. Silver fillings are in fact 50 percent mercury, and mercury poisoning can cause myriad illnesses such as Alzheimer's disease, multiple sclerosis, Parkinson's, and other progressive degenerative diseases. Mercury poisoning can damage your brain, heart, lungs, liver, kidney, blood cells, hormones, and cause hair loss, fatigue, enzyme abnormalities, and suppress your body's immune system. If you have cavities filled, request porcelain instead of silver fillings. If you're suffering from an untreatable, illusive illness, have your hair or urine tested to find out the level of toxic metals, including mercury, in your system. Even if you aren't sick already, it's optimal to have your silver fillings removed by a dentist trained in mercury removal. Go to iaomt.com to find a trained dentist. Drink cilantro and parsley juice (with added spirulina and chlorella) every day to rid your body of mercury. Consider IV chelation.

Sleeping Pills: See page 185.

Statins: According to *BusinessWeek*, statins are "the single biggest market in the $492 billion global prescription drug business."[82] Dr. Russell Blaylock writes in his newsletter that the makers of statin drugs donate millions of dollars to university research, which provides incentive for the universities to produce evidence that statins are effective in reducing heart attacks.[83]

This is far from the truth. Still, these drug pushers have convinced people to take statin drugs for the rest of their lives and would like to see *children* taking them. Statin drugs, which switch off the enzyme in our liver called HMG Co-A Reductase that is responsible for making cholesterol, are fraught with side effects. It's no wonder because the human body is designed brilliantly and putting in drugs that are counter to the design process results in major imbalances. Statins deplete the body of the essential molecule coenzyme CoQ_{10}. A lack of CoQ_{10} weakens the heart muscle and can lead to congestive heart failure, muscle weakness, neurological disorders, and even death. Even more alarming is that statin drugs suppress vital immune cells called helper T-cells, which help protect us against from cancer as well as fungal, bacterial, and viral infections. By taking statins, you are lowering your immunity! Dr. Blaylock writes, "Recently, a new paper was released in the *Annals of Internal Medicine*, a prestigious journal read by 100,000 internists, suggesting that all 17 million diabetics, regardless of their cholesterol levels, should be on long-term statin drugs to lower heart attack and stroke risk. In the first place, the reason diabetics have such a high incidence of arteriosclerosis is that the disease from its onset is associated with a dramatic increase in free radical production, which oxidizes the LDL cholesterol in their bodies. The only reason statin drugs lower risk at all is because they have some antioxidant and anticoagulant properties. Still, safer and more powerful antioxidants are available as supplements and in healthy diets."[84]

Chronic, recurrent infections are endemic to diabetics, and by taking statins that lower their immunity even further, diabetics are increasing their risk of developing cancer and other serious diseases. Statins can lead to liver failure. They can also cause nerve damage, making walking painful and causing pain in your limbs.

Statins are known to damage muscles, which can be fatal. You'll notice symptoms like muscle pain, weakness, muscle tenderness, and fatigue.[85]

One study has concluded that taking statin cholesterol-lowering drugs results in decreased attention and delayed reflexes, which make it difficult to perform simple tasks like driving. The researchers noted that the lower a person's cholesterol, the worse they were. There are other studies that report difficulty thinking and memory loss as extreme as suspecting the onset of Alzheimer's.[86] When I talk about creating a healthy, solid brain, let me make it perfectly clear that cholesterol is imperative for *normal* brain function, so taking statins works against this goal.

Surgery: As much as I shy away from the very notion of doctors and drugs, the field of surgery does fascinate me with its astonishing advancements and miraculous possibilities. Many people will go through life without having a single surgery—though that's becoming rare. If you have to have surgery to have the best possible result, if it's elective, then you have time to get in the best shape possible. If it's the result of an accident, then you should have an advance plan with your family and friends to bring you food, water, supplements, green juice, raw milk, theraputic fats (Activator X, GLA, cod liver oil, red palm oil, and coconut oil), organic self-care products, and anything else you need to protect yourself from the known toxins of the hospital environment.

Toxic Doctors: I said this in *Death by Supermarket*, and I will repeat it here: I have many doctor friends, some very close friends, and I respect and admire doctors in many ways. I've had spectacular experiences under enlightened doctors' care. I'm lucky to have relationships with enlightened doctors because traditional medicine is toxic and so are the doctors who inflexibly adhere to the so-called "standard of care." Traditional medicine has strayed far away from prevention and healing, and the doctors who practice this medicine don't understand or want to know about balancing the entire person, mind, body, and spirit. Rather these doctors practice compartmentalized medicine (called "specializing") so that each organ and system is treated as an individual entity rather than an integrated whole. The treatment is comparable to duct taping (OTCs or long-term prescription drugs) or hitting a problem/symptom with a sledgehammer (radiation/surgeries/procedures). Toxic doctors categorize women as "hysterical" if they can't figure out what is causing a health problem. They have put the vast majority of American men and women over the age of forty on an accelerated aging path with dangerous nutritional advice and cocktails of drugs. They stonewall any evidence that eating a historically eaten diet including cholesterol and saturated fat is healthy, and refuse to even consider that the low-fat diet was a mistake. Toxic doctors, for example, don't understand the dangers posed by monosodium glutamate in hospital food, of heavily vaccinating an infant, of prescribing unproven drugs, and so on.

If you feel that your doctor isn't receptive to your desire to seek wellness through the integration of mind, body, and spirit, and belittles or condescends to you, find an enlightened doctor. You can find enlightened doctors by Googling "integrative physician" in your area. Many doctors are coming over to the light and want to partner with you on your health.

Vaccinations: Mainstream science has pretty much attributed the remarkable fall in infectious diseases to the development of vaccinations, but the truth is that improved public health measures and nutrition have played a much bigger role in the decline of infectious disease. There are a growing number of scientific studies that demonstrate serious dangers in our present vaccine policy, including altered brain development, seizures, and a loss of brain cell connections, called synapses. These studies all point to over-vaccination as a real and present danger to kids and, in certain instances, adults.

Consider that we exist in a toxic stew of our polluted environment and we have toxic nutrition, and then add chemical additives in vaccines as well as whatever infectious organism is being targeted by a given vaccine. These combined poisonous stressors lower a person's threshold to defend and detoxify. A typical vaccine could include aluminum, mercury, hydrolyzed proteins, MSG, oils, and many complex molecules known as immune adjuvants. Aluminum, mercury, hydrolyzed protein, and MSG are known to be directly toxic to the brain.

Alzheimer's disease, Parkinson's disease, Lou Gehrig's disease, autism spectrum disorders, and Gulf War Syndrome are just a few of the "injuries" that are thought to be linked to vaccines. There are major factors to consider when looking at vaccination injuries. One is a possible genetic weakness in a person's (or baby's) ability to metabolize a certain toxin, and the other is the cumulative effects or synergic toxicity of many agents.

There is substantial research linking Gulf War Syndrome and autism to the administration of too many vaccines over too short a period of time. Gulf War veterans are a prime example of the dangers of the cumulative effects of toxins because they were also exposed to pesticides, aspartame breakdown products, combat stress, high intake of food-based excitotoxins (MSG and aspartame), possible exposure to released nerve agents, and exposure to contaminated vaccines. And aside from Gulf War Syndrome, Pentagon officials have reluctantly admitted to a 200 percent increased incidence of amyotrophic lateral sclerosis, or Lou Gehrig's disease (ALS) in Gulf War veterans. [87]

We do know that vaccines should not be given to individuals with impaired immunity for fear of triggering immune attacks on the central nervous system, such as peripheral neuropathy (nerve injuries), multiple sclerosis, encephalitis, and allergic encephalomyelitis (inflammation of the brain and spinal cord). These conditions are autoimmune disorders where the immune system attacks specific components of the brain and spinal cord by mistake. Normally, an immune attack on viruses and other organisms occurs rapidly and is quickly terminated. With a weakened immune system, you have a more prolonged attack that leaves the surrounding healthy cells and tissues soaked in destructive free radicals and these free radicals with time can flood the entire body.

Vaccinations, if too numerous and spaced too close together, act like a chronic illness, flooding the entire body with free radicals.

According to Dr. Hugh Fudenberg's research (one of the biggest names in immunology), those who had five or more flu shots during the period of his study (1970 to 1980) had ten times the risk of developing Alzheimer's disease than did those who either did not get the vaccine or got it only one or two times. He suggests two reasons: mercury and aluminum in the vaccines are directly toxic to brain cells and overstimulate the brain's immune system. The more vaccines given, the greater the risk of substantial harm. And to top this off, the mercury in vaccines accumulates in the brain and is very difficult to remove.

So how do we protect ourselves from disease? Dr. Weston Price, the dentist I talked about earlier, writes about immunity in his book *Nutrition and Physical Degeneration*. He traveled the world for ten years looking for the key to optimal health. In 1935 he was researching in Africa where he encountered over thirty tribes of primitive people: Dr. Price writes of the stunning contrast between the pampered but sickly Europeans and the primitive but rugged Africans. "Very few of the many Europeans with whom we came in contact had lived in central Africa for as much as two years without serious illness or distinct evidence of physical stress." He vividly describes the constant exposure to the disease-carrying vectors jiggers, mosquitoes, and ticks. "We had to be most careful not to touch the hides with which the natives protected their bodies from the cold at night and from the sun in the daytime without thorough sterilization following any contact. There was a grave danger from the lice that infected the hair of the hides. We dared not enter several districts because of the dreaded tsetse fly and the sleeping sickness it carries." He wondered at the apparent health of the natives until he learned of the unique immunity they had developed and which was largely transmitted to their offspring. Dr. Price examined whole villages where every person had contracted typhus fever and was immune. "One also wonders why people with such resistance to disease are not able to combat the degenerative diseases of modern civilization. When they adopt modern civilization they then become susceptible to several of our modern degenerative processes, including tooth decay."[88]

If Dr. Price thought those Europeans suffered from poor immune systems then, he would be astounded today. With the saturation of antibiotics in food, as well as the rabid chemical hand and household disinfectants, our sanitized bodies are prime targets for hosts to take up residence. The best we can do is to beef up our immune systems by mimicking the dietary habits of Dr. Price's primitive people, and by avoiding toxic exposure (including hand sanitizers!), and by chelating our toxic loads.

I'm not preaching no drugs, no vaccines, no surgeries. All I'm saying is to be prudent as you only have one precious body and *you* are the gatekeeper, not your doctor. If you must be vaccinated, space out the shots, so that you can rest and repair in between as you would with any toxic assault. One of the more common reasons for immune dysfunction is nutritional deficiency, even deficiency of a single nutrient. Over-vaccination depletes vitamin A, the carotenoids, vitamin C (as ascorbate), vitamin E, and the minerals selenium and zinc. Vitamin E (natural E), selenium, zinc, vitamin C, and flavonoids (from fruits and vegetables) are critical for normal immune function but are very common deficiencies, especially after middle age. If deficiency of only selenium impairs cellular immunity, then additional nutritional deficiencies can have devastating effects on the immune system. Studies show that nutritional depletion, even of one or two nutrients, dramatically increases vaccine complications.[89]

If Receiving a Vaccination, Avoid These Immune Suppressants

Factory-food products (contain MSG, soy, and aspartame)
Fluoride (city water, soy, toothpaste, and mouthwash)

Processed vegetable oils (corn, safflower, sunflower, peanut, soybean, canola oils)

Sweetened drinks, even fruit drinks

Toxic chemicals, personal care products, and household products[90]

Thimerosal: Manufacturers of vaccines use thimerosal, which is 49.6 percent mercury, as a preservative to prevent the growth of microorganisms. Thimerosal can interfere with the developing nervous system of an infant or child. Thimerosal has been reduced to trace amounts in vaccines used on children six and under, but it's still extensively used in many flu vaccinations, along with aluminum.

Gardasil Vaccine: I decided to investigate Gardasil after seeing a young girl on CNN who was suffering from an autoimmune condition, the onset of which occurred just months after receiving a Gardasil vaccine. She wiped away her tears and glumly said, there was, "No way of knowing if Gardasil was to blame."

Gardasil supposedly protects against *some*, not all of the cancer-causing forms of the sexually transmitted human papilloma virus (HPV). Merck's efforts in lobbying the FDA resulted in the fast-tracking of Gardasil to the market. And so now American girls and young women are taking part in a massive, potentially lethal experiment of a vaccine that contains four types of HPV proteins, aluminum neurotoxins (associated with multiple sclerosis, Alzheimer's disease, and Parkinson's disease), polysorbate-80 (linked to infertility in mice), and sodium borate (the main ingredient in roach killer).

Merck put millions of dollars into convincing state legislatures to mandate Gardasil to schoolgirls as young as eleven. Eighteen states were swept into the debate. Lobbying parents have stood in the way of forcing girls to be vaccinated if they want to continue attending school.[91]

As of this writing there have been fifty-three U.S. reports of death among females who have received Gardasil although, according to the CDC, scientists have been unable to find evidence that the deaths were caused by the vaccine. One woman died within three hours of receiving the vaccine. Seven women died in less than two days. One twenty-year-old woman died just four days after receiving Gardasil. Eleven women died less than a week after receiving the vaccine. Of the adverse effects reported to the Vaccine Adverse Event Reporting System (VAERS) during the last three years, Gardasil was linked to 76 percent of the "did not recover" events for girls and women between the ages of six and twenty-nine.

Gardasil was responsible for 78.5 percent of all "disabled" events and 75 percent of all deaths linked to vaccines (same age group), during that time.

Adverse Reactions of Gardasil

- Anaphylactic shock
- Autoimmune disorders
- Blindness or temporary interruption of vision
- Chest pains
- Coma
- Drop in blood pressure
- Facial warts, warts on hands and feet
- Fainting
- Genital wart outbreak, even in patients who had tested negative for HPV and genital warts prior to vaccination
- Grand mal seizures
- Guilliane Barre Syndrome (an inflammatory disorder of the nerves that can lead to paralysis)
- Hearing loss
- Heart palpitations
- Inability to concentrate (brain fog)
- Loss of consciousness
- Memory loss
- Migraines
- Miscarriages
- Numbness
- Paralysis
- Seizures
- Spontaneous abortion
- Symptoms of chemically induced menopause (including facial hair, disruption of menses, drastic mood swings, hormone imbalance, painful menstruation, and polycystic ovarian syndrome)[92]

Robert Ball, director of the FDA's office of biostatistics and division of epidemiology says, "We're monitoring the safety of the HPV vaccine very carefully, and the only adverse event that causes some concern is fainting after the vaccine." According to the FDA, there is no link between Guillain-Barre syndrome and Gardasil vaccination; the incidents that have occurred are pure coincidence.

Cervical cancer used to be the leading cause of cancer death for women in the United States, but in the past forty years, cervical cancer and subsequent death has decreased because of the Pap test. There are more than a hundred types of HPVs, but only ten to thirty of these strains lead to cervical cancer. In 90 percent of women infected, HPV clears up on its own within two years, at which point cervical cells go back to normal.[93] It's only when the HPV virus lingers for many years that these abnormal cells turn into cancer. So the vast majority of abnormal Pap tests do not result in cancer. Even abnormal Pap tests clear by themselves without treatment 40 percent of the time. And out of the remaining cases only 1 percent actually progress to cancer.

This type of cancer usually develops in the late twenties to midthirties, but the (very limited) protection period of Gardasil is estimated to be only five years. So a ten-year-old who gets her first series of shots will need four additional booster shots to make it to her thirties. Merck's Gardasil HPV vaccine was released on the consumer market when cervical cancer was already on a steady decline.[94]

But what about HPV? At least 50 percent of sexually active men and women acquire genital HPV infection at some point in their lives. However, what we are not told on the glossy commercials is that a healthy immune system typically fights off HPV. Primarily the girls and women who are infected with HPV who go on to develop cervical cancer are those who are immunocompromised (i.e., infected with HIV or have had an organ transplant).

Factors That Increase Risk of Cervical Cancer Associated with HPV

Compromised immune system

Douching

Not using condoms

Nutritional deficiencies, especially vitamin A and folate, zinc, selenium, calcium, and iron, which are all associated with eating factory-food products

Oral contraceptives

Smoking

Merck is now facing two major lawsuits. Merck and the FDA are denying the allegations. For more information go to truthaboutgardasil.org.

X-rays and CT Scans: CT scans pose long-term cancer risks and radiation overdose.[95] For each millirem of radiation we receive, our risk of dying from cancer is increased by about one chance in four million. Health physicists generally agree on limiting exposure to about one hundred mrem per year from all sources (medical X-rays generally deliver less than ten mrem).[96] It's also worth noting here that a round-trip cross-country airline flight delivers the same amount of radiation as a chest X-ray. So if you fly a lot, adjust your antioxidant intake accordingly—and don't eat airline snacks.

appendix eight:

Carbohydrate Counter

The goal is to become so educated about carbs that you don't need to really calculate, you just know how much carb to eat per meal. The Carbohydrate Counter is your reference until you get a running idea of carbs. I've calculated 15 grams of carb in the following carb selections. Fifteen grams is how much someone who is overweight with type 2 diabetes would eat per meal and snack. For goodness sake, don't go this low in your carb portions if you are not obese with type 2 diabetes. You'll damage your metabolism and defeat the purpose of reading this book.

Dairy

Cottage cheese 1 cup
Kefir 1 cup
Yogurt 1 cup
Whole milk 1 cup

Fruit

Apple 1 small
Apples (dried) 3 rings
Applesauce (unsweetened) ¾ cup
Apricots 2 medium
Apricots (dried) 7 halves
Avocados ½
Bananas ½ medium
Bananas (dehydrated) 1 tbs
Blackberries ¾ cup
Blueberries ¾ cup
Boysenberries 1 cup

Carambola (sliced) 1½ cups
Cherries (with pits) 1 cup
Crabapples (sliced) ¾ cup
Cranberries (unsweetened) 1 cup whole
Currants 2 tbs
Dates 2 medium
Figs (fresh) 2 medium
Figs (dried) 1 medium
Gooseberries 1 cup
Grapefruit ½ large
Grapes 15 grapes
Guavas 1½ fruit
Kiwi fruit 1 large
Kumquats 5
Lemons 3 medium
Limes 2 medium
Loquats 5 large
Mangos ½ medium
Melons (cantaloupe) 1 cup (cubes)
Melons (casaba/cubed) 1½ cups
Melons (honeydew) 1 cups (diced)
Mulberries 1 cup
Nectarines 1 medium

Oranges 1 medium
Tangerines 2 small
Papayas ½ cup
Passion fruit 3
Peaches 1 medium
Peaches (dried) 2 halves
Pears ½ large
Pears (dried) 1 half
Persimmons (native) 2 medium
Pineapple ¾ cup
Plantains (cooked) ⅓ cup
Plums 2 fruits
Pomegranates ½ fruit
Prunes 3 prunes
Raisins (dark/golden) 2 tbs
Raspberries 1 cup
Rhubarb 7 stalks
Strawberries 1½ cups
Sun-dried tomatoes ⅙ ounce
Tamarinds 15 fruits
Tomatoes (green and red) 1 medium
Tomatillos 1 large
Watermelon (diced) 1¼ cups

Starchy Veggies

Acorn squash ½ cup
Artichokes 1
Beets 1 cup
Butternut squash ⅔ cup
Carrots 1 cup
Corn ½ cup

Green peas ½ cup
Jerusalem artichokes ½ cup
Leeks 1 cup
Lima beans ½ cup
Lotus root ½ cup
Okra 1 cup

Parsnip ⅔ cup
Potato ½ medium
Rutabagas (raw) ¼ large

Sweet potato or yam ½ medium
Turnips ½ cup

NOTE: *All selections are cooked unless noted.*

Grains

Amaranth ½ cup
Barley ½ cup
Brown rice ⅓ cup
Buckwheat ⅓ cup
Buckwheat groats ⅓ cup
Bulgur ⅓ cup
Corn grits ½ cups
Couscous farina ⅓ cup
Durum wheat 1½ tbs
Millet ½ cup
Oats ½ cup
Polenta ½ cup

Popcorn (air popped) 3 cups
Quinoa 1½ tbs
Rye 1½ tbs
Semolina (whole grain) 1½ tbs
Sorghum (whole grain) 1½ tbs
Tapioca 1½ tbs
Wheat (whole grain) 1½ tbs
Wheat bran (uncooked) ⅓ cup
Wheat germ ¼ cup
Wild rice ½ cup

NOTE: *All selections are cooked unless noted.*

Whole Grain Flour and Meals

Acorn flour ⅛ cup
Almond meal ½ cup
Almond powder ½ cup
Amaranth flour ⅛ cup
Arrowroot flour scant ⅛ cup
Brown rice flour scant ⅛ cup
Buckwheat flour scant ⅛ cup
Carob flour scant ⅛ cup
Corn flour scant ⅛ cup
Cornmeal scant ⅛ cup

Oat bran flour scant ⅛ cup
Peanut flour 1½ oz
Pecan flour 1 ounce
Potato flour scant ⅛ cup
Rye flour 3/4 ounce
Semolina flour scant ⅛ cup
Semolina scant ⅛ cup
White all-purpose flour scant ⅛ cup
Whole wheat flour scant ⅛ cup

NOTE: *Measured dry.*

Legumes

Adzuki beans ¼ cup

Black beans ⅓ cup

Broadbeans (fava beans) ½ cup

Chickpeas (garbanzo) ⅓ cup

Cowpeas (black-eyed peas) ½ cup

Cranberry (Roman) beans ⅓ cup

French beans ⅓ cup

Great Northern beans ⅓ cup

Garbanzo beans ⅓ cup

Hyacinth beans ⅓ cup

Hominy ½ cup

Kidney beans ⅓ cup

Lentils ⅓ cup

Lupins 1 cup

Moth beans ⅓ cup

Mung beans ⅓ cup

Mungo beans (dry) ½ cup

Navy beans ⅓ cup

Pigeon peas ½ cup

Pink beans ⅓ cup

Pinto beans ⅓ cup

Pumpkin 1 cup

Split peas ⅓ cup

White beans ⅓ cup

Yellow beans ⅓ cup

Some Very Interesting Facts About Nuts

Nuts contain protein and carbs, so you can't just eat them indiscriminately or you'll put on fat like a squirrel preparing for winter. Equally important to know is that nature has imbued nuts with toxins to keep predators from decimating the entire crop. If you've ever downed a bunch of nuts with a glass of wine and ended up with a tummy ache and blamed it on the wine, it was actually the nuts.

If you're going to eat a lot of nuts, you need to rid them of their toxins. Put nuts in a large bowl and cover with water and a couple of pinches of sea salt. Cover with a plate and leave the nuts at room temperature for eight hours (cashews get too soggy, so only soak them for six hours). Drain and place the nuts on a stainless steel cookie sheet and dehydrate at 150° for twelve to twenty-four hours—or use a dehydrator.

Nuts, Nut Butters, and Seeds

Acorns ¼ cup

Almonds ½ cup

Almond butter ½ cup

Almond paste 2 tbs

Amaranth seed 2 tbs

Brazil nuts (butternuts) ⅔ cup

Cashews ⅓ cup

Cashew butter ¼ cup

Chinese chestnuts ¼ cup

Coconut cream ½ cup

Coconut liquid 2 cups

Coconut meat 1 cup

Coconut milk 1 cup

European chestnuts ¼ cup

Filberts or hazelnuts ¾ cup

Ginkgo nuts ¼ cup

Hickory nuts ½ cup

Japanese chestnuts ⅜ cup

Lotus seeds ¾ cup

Macadamia nuts ¾ cup

Peanut butter ¼ cup

Peanuts ½ cup

Pecans ⅔ cup

Pine nuts ½ cup

Pistachio nuts ½ cup

Pumpkin and squash kernels ½ cup

Pumpkin and squash seeds ¼ cup

Safflower kernels ¼ cup

Sesame butter (tahini) ¼ cup

Sesame seed kernels ½ cup

Sunflower seed butter ¼ cup

Sunflower seed kernels ½ cup

Walnuts 1 cup

Watermelon seed kernels 12 tbs

NOTE: *Nuts contain protein, fat, and carbs. All selections are raw unless otherwise noted.*

Sugar (equal to 15 grams of carb)

Maple Sugar and Blackstrap Molasses: contains minerals (1 tbs)

Unrefined Honey: contains healthy enzymes and antioxidants (1 tbs)

Sucanant or Rapadura: Dehydrated cane sugar juice, which contain minerals (3 tbs)

Stevia Rebaudiana: South American herb that is two hundred times sweeter than sugar but does not trigger an insulin response or have any calories or carbs.

acknowledgments

After writing six books in the health genre, I decided to be a novelist for the rest of my life. I thought I would never write another health book again. It was during talks on my novel *Karma*, however, that women began asking me about my personal program and inspired me to write my program down. I have those many women—most who I don't know—to thank for the inspiration for this book.

I would never have written a single word about health if I hadn't been interested in health and real food in the first place. My influence was my grandma, Stella, who doled out supplements at a time when it was totally kooky and out there, made me real food to eat, and gave me Adelle Davis's books to read. My next influence was Heini Baumgartner, a Swiss German hitchhiker who I met in Tokyo who ultimately continued my introduction to real, whole living foods.

I have to credit my sister Nadine Saubers, R.N. who introduced me to running a very long time ago and launched my passion for exercise. Nadine is also responsible for a great deal of research in this book as well as the original design of my website, blog, and Facebook pages, and for providing comic relief during the crash writing of this manuscript.

So many people influenced and helped me in my own thrilling journey. I'm deeply indebted to Allen Thomashefsky, M.D., Amy Hazard, L.A.c., Billy Asad, Carolyn Grothe, M.S., M.F.T., Cathy Quinn, Ph.D., Christopher K. Germer, Ph.D., David Allen, M.D., David Magone, Derek Thiele, Eric Golowski, Genet Jeanjean, M.A.,M.Ed., Grazzy Macedo, Jeremy E. Kaslow, M.D., C.C.N., Jitka Gunaratna, Kaayla Daniel, Ph.D., C.C.N., Khenpo Migmar, Tseten Rinpoche, Lynne Begier, Maoshing Ni, L.A.c., D.O.M., Michele Nichols, Natalie Orfalea, Olga Pikalova, Rebecca Pocheo, Russell L. Blaylock, M.D., C.N.N., Scott Blossom, L.A.,c., Stephen G. Gilligan, Ph.D., Steve Dwelley, and Vidu Gunaratna.

The most significant person in my life and career is John Davis, my best friend, brilliant career strategist, adviser, and coach who deserves the credit for getting me to realize that I had something important to contribute. Everything I've accomplished I owe to John.

endnotes

1 Felix Grün and Bruce Blumberg, "Minireview: The Case for Obesogens," *Molecular Endocrinology* 23 (8): 1127-1134 (2009), http://mend.endojournals.org/cgi/content/full/23/8/1127, accessed Nov. 4, 2010.
2 Felix Grün and Bruce Blumberg, "Minireview: The Case for Obesogens," *Molecular Endocrinology* 23 (8): 1127-1134 (2009), http://mend.endojournals.org/cgi/content/full/23/8/1127, accessed Nov. 4, 2010.
3 Evan Osnos, Profiles, "The Next Incarnation," *The New Yorker*, October 4, 2010, p. 63.
4 Sharon Begley, "The Depressing News About Antidepressants," *Harman Newsweek LLC* (January 29, 2010), http://www.newsweek.com/2010/01/28/the-depressing-news-about-antidepressants.html, accessed Nov. 5, 2010.
5 Adele Davis, *Let's Eat Right To Keep Fit* (New York: Harcourt, Brace and Company, Inc. 1954), p. 249.
6 Morando Soffritti et al., "First Experimental Demonstration of the Multipotential Carcinogenic Effects of Aspartame Administered in the Feed to Sprague-Dawley Rats," (Nov. 17, 2005), http://www.sweetpoison.com/pdf/Soffritti_et_al_in_EHP.pdf. Accessed Nov. 3, 2010.
Morando Soffritti et al., "First Experimental Demonstration of the Multipotential Carcinogenic Effects of Aspartame Administered in the Feed to Sprague-Dawley Rats," (Nov. 17, 2005), http://www.sweetpoison.com/pdf/Soffritti_et_al_in_EHP.pdf, accessed Nov. 3, 2010.
French Food Safety Agency, "Opinion on a Possible Link Between the Exposition to Aspartame and the Incidence of Brain Tumors in Humans," (May 7, 2002), http://www.aspartame.org/pdf/AFSSA-Eng.pdf, accessed Nov. 3, 2010.
7 Russell L. Blaylock, MD, "The Connection Between MS And Aspartame,"(June 7, 2004) http://www.rense.com/general53/ms.htm, accessed Nov. 3, 2010.
8 Marcelle Pick, OB/GYN NP, "Sugar Substitutes and the Potential Danger of Splenda," (October 14, 2010), http://www.womentowomen.com/healthyweight/splenda.aspx, accessed Nov. 3, 2010.

9   Robban Sica, MD, "MSG - The Slow Poisoning of America," (May 27, 2007), http://www.beating-cancer-gently.com/msg.html, accessed Nov. 3, 2010.
10 Russell L. Blaylock, M.D. *Excitotoxins: The Taste That Kills* (Santa Fe, New Mexico: Health Press, 1977), pp. 255-256.
11 Jeff Nield, "U.S. Farmers Planting Less GMO Soy," (March 12, 2009), http://www.treehugger.com/files/2009/03/us-farmers-planting-less-gmo-soy.php, accessed Nov. 3, 2010.
12 http://www.mamashealth.com/Heart_stat.asp, accessed Nov. 5, 2010.
13 http://www.health-report.co.uk/saturated_fats_health_benefits.htm#3.
14 Y. Koga et al, "Recent Trends in Cardiovascular Disease and Risk Factors in the Seven Countries Study: Japan," *Lessons for Science from the Seven Countries Study*, H. Toshima et al, eds, (New York, Springer: 1994) 63-74. Thomas J. Moore. *Lifespan: What Really Affects Human Longevity*, 1990, New York: Simon and Schuster.
15 B. A. Watkins et al, "Importance of Vitamin E in Bone Formation and in Chrondrocyte Function," Purdue University, Lafayette, IN, AOCS Proceedings, 1996; B. A. Watkins, and M. F. Seifert, "Food Lipids and Bone Health," *Food Lipids and Health*, R. E. McDonald and D. B. Min, eds, p 101, (New York, Marcel Dekker, Inc: 1996).
16 A. A. Nanji, et al, *Gastroenterology*, Aug 1995, 109(2):547-54; Y. S. Cha, and D. S. Sachan, *Journal of the American College of Nutrition*, Aug 1994, 13(4):338-43; H. L. Hargrove, et al, *FASEB Journal*, Meeting Abstracts, Mar 1999, #204.1, p A222.
17 M. L. Garg, et al, *FASEB Journal*, 1988, 2:4:A852; R. M. Oliart Ros, et al, "Meeting Abstracts," *AOCS Proceedings*, May 1998, 7, Chicago, IL.
18 G. H. Dahlen, et al, *Journal of Internal Medicine*, Nov 1998, 244(5):417-24; P. Khosla, and K. C. Hayes, *Journal of the American College of Nutrition*, 1996, 15:325-339; B. A. Clevidence, et al, *Arteriosclerosis, Thrombusis, and Mascular Biology*, 1997, 17:1657-1661.
19 J. J. Kabara, *The Pharmacological Effects of Lipids*, The American Oil Chemists Society, Champaign, IL, 1978, 1-14; L. A. Cohen, et al, *Journal of the National Cancer Institute*, 1986, 77:43.
20 U. Ravnskov, *Journal of Clinical Epidemiology*, Jun 1998, 51:(6):443-460.
21 H. Kaunitz, C.S. Dayrit, "Coconut Oil Consumption and Coronary Heart Disease." *Philippine Journal of Internal Medicine*, 1992;30:165-171. I.A. Prior, F. Davidson, C.E. Salmond, Z. Czochanska, "Cholesterol, Coconuts, and Diet on Polynesian Atolls: a Natural Experiment: the Pukapuka and Tokelau Island Studies", *American Journal of Clinical Nutrition*, 1981;34:1552-1561.
22 http://www.health-report.co.uk/saturated_fats_health_benefits.htm#38.
23 Mark Hyman, MD, "Cholesterol: Wrong Target for Primary Prevention of Cardiovascular Disease?" (Nov. 19, 2009), http://ultrawellnesscenter.com/files/2010/05/Cholesterol-AT.pdf, accessed Nov. 8, 2010.
24 Edward Howell, *Food Enzymes for Health and Longevity*, 2nd Ed. (Twin Lakes, WI: Lotus Press, 1994), pp. 17-21.

25 Russell L. Blaylock, M.D., CCN, "How Vaccines Can Damage Your Brain," (Feb. 26 2008), http://articles.mercola.com/sites/articles/archive/2008/02/26/how-vaccines-can-damage-your-brain.aspx, accessed Nov. 10, 2010.
26 R.J. Wurtman, J.J. Wurtman, "Brain Serotonin, Carbohydrate-craving, Obesity and Depression," *Obesity Reviews*, Vol. 3 Suppl. 4 (1995): pp. 477S-480S.
27 www.mediacurves.com.
28 http://www.newsweek.com/2010/01/28/the-depressing-news-about-antidepressants.html, accessed Nov. 9, 2010.
29 Email from Stephen G. Gilligan, Ph.D., Tuesday, September 7, 2010, 5:25 a.m.
30 http://www.eeginfo.com/research/addiction_main.html, accessed Nov. 18, 2010.
31 Ron Schmid, *The Untold Story of Milk* (Washington, D.C.: New Trends Publishing, Inc. 2003), pp. 193-229.
32 Elaine F. Weiss, "Thwarting Cancer Before It Strikes," *Johns Hopkins Magazine* (April 2000) Website: http:// www.jhu.edu/~jhumag/0400web/48.html. Accessed Nov. 18, 2004.
33 Ron Schmid, *The Untold Story of Milk* (Washington, D.C.: New Trends Publishing, Inc. 2003), pp. 203-204.
34 C. Ip et al., "Conjugated Linoleic Acid. A Powerful Anti-carcinogen from Animal Fat Sources," *Cancer*, Vol.74 No.3 suppl (1994): pp. 1050-4. A. Aro et al., "Inverse Association between Dietary and Serum Conjugated Linoleic Acid and Risk of Breast Cancer in Postmenopausal Women," *Nutrition and Cancer*, Vol.38 No. 2 (2000): pp. 151-7. Z. Wu, L.D. Satter, M.W. Pariza, "Paddocks Containing Red Clover Compared with all Grass Paddocks Support High CLA Levels in Milk." *U.S. Dairy Forage Research Center* (1997).
35 Erik R. Olson et al., "Inhibition of Cardiac Fibroblast Proliferation and Myofibroblast Differentiation by Resveratrol," *American Journal of Physiology-Heart and Circulatory Physiology*, Vol. 288 (2005): pp. H1131-H1138. Zou et al., 'Effect of Red Wine and Wine Polyphenol Resveratrol on Endothelial Function in Hypercholesterolemic Rabbits,' *International Journal of Molecular Medicine*, Vol.11 No.3 (2003): pp. 317–320.
36 http://www.johnleemd.com/store/estrogen_dom.html Reprinted with permission from *What Your Doctor May Not Tell You about Menopause*, by John R. Lee, M.D. and Virginia Hopkins.
37 http://www.ncbi.nlm.nih.gov/pmc/articles/PMC1033362/pdf/medhist00159-0005.pdf.
38 http://www.naturalnews.com/022751_Wyeth_women_the_FDA.html.
39 Susan Davis, "Testosterone Deficiency in Women." *Journal of Reproductive Medicine* 2001;46:291-296, http://www.usdoctor.com/testtwo.htm, accessed Dec. 2, 2010.
40 Dixie Meyer, (2007). "Selective Serotonin Reuptake Inhibitors and Their Effects on Relationship Satisfaction." *Family Journal* 15 (4):392–397.
41 Srinivansan S. Pillay, M.D., *Life Unlocked: 7 Revolutionary Lessons to Overcome Fear* (New York, Rodale, 2010) pp. 16–17

42 Roger Ekirch, *At Day's Close: Night in Times Past*, (New York: W.W. Norton & Company, 2005).
43 Book Review by Christopher K. Germer on *The Compassionate Mind: A New Approach to Life's Challenges*, by Paul Gilbert. (Constable and Robinson, Ltd. London, 2009; Oakland, CA: New Harbinger, 2010). Email from Dr. Germer, August 5, 2010.
44 http://www.meditationandpsychotherapy.org/faculty.html.
45 http://ccare.stanford.edu/node/25,www.psych.stanford.edu/~psyphy/pdfs/Hutcherson_08_2.pdf,www.unc.edu/peplab/publications/fredricksonfinkel08.pdf, http://www.sciencedaily.com/releases/2008/10/081007172902.htm.
46 http://psyphz.psych.wisc.edu/web/News/Meditation_Alters_Brain_WSJ_11-04.htm.
47 http://www.yogatreesf.com/teachers/scott_blossom.htm.
48 Rebecca Mead, "The Yoga Bums," *The New Yorker*, p 38, August 14, 2000.
49 http://www.kpjayi.org/.
50 http://www.bikramyoga.com/BikramYoga/about_bikram_yoga.php.
51 Anon. "Health Risks of Genetically Modified Foods." *Lancet*, Vol.353 No. 9167 (1999): p.181.
52 Ronnie Cummins, "Hazards of Genetically Engineered Foods and Crops: Why We Need A Global Moratorium." Organic Consumers Association. http://www.organicconsumers.org/ge/gefacts.pdf, accessed Nov. 20, 2010.
53 B.N. Ames, I. Elson-Schwab, E.A. Silver, "High-dose Vitamin Therapy Stimulate Variant Enzymes with Decreased Coenzyme-binding Affinity (increased Km): Relevance to Genetic Disease and Polymorphisms." *American Journal of Clinical Nutrition* 2002;75:616–58.
54 Y. Sato et al., "Dietary Carotenoids Inhibit Oral Sensitization and the Development of Food Allergy," *Journal of Agricultural Food Chemistry* 58:12 (2010 Jun 23): 7180-6.
55 Linus Pauling Institute, "Micronutrient Research for Optimum Health," Aug. 9, 2010 http://lpi.oregonstate.edu/infocenter/othernuts/coq10/, accessed Nov. 20, 2010.
56 http://milestonegroupnj.com/?p=142; http://www.abajournal.com/news/article/high-functioning_alcoholic_lawyers_may_defy_stereotypes, Legal Profession Assistance Conference, "Drug and Alcohol Abuse & Addiction in the Legal Profession," (2010) Nov. 19, 2010 <http://www.benchmarkinstitute.org/t_by_t/mcle/sa.pdf>.accessed Nov. 19, 2010.
57 M. Ben Amar (2006). "Cannabinoids in Medicine: A Review of Their Therapeutic Potential," *Journal of Ethnopharmacology* 105 (1–2): 1–25.
58 F. Grotenhermen, (2002). "Review of Therapeutic Effects." *Cannabis and Cannabinoids: Pharmacology, Toxicology and Therapeutic Potential*. (New York, NY : Haworth Press. p. 124).
    University of Bath (1 August 2005). "Cannabis-based Drugs Could Offer New Hope for Inflammatory Bowel Disease Patients."
    E.B. Russo (February 2004). "Clinical Endocannabinoid Deficiency (CECD): Can This Concept Explain Therapeutic Benefits of Cannabis in Migraine, Fibromyalgia,

Irritable Bowel Syndrome and Other Treatment-resistant Conditions?." *Neuro Endocrinology Letters* 25 (1-2): 31–9.

J. Zajicek, P. Fox , H. Sanders et al. (November 2003). "Cannabinoids for Treatment of Spasticity and Other Symptoms Related to Multiple Sclerosis (CAMS study): Multicentre Randomised Placebo-controlled Trial." *Lancet* 362 (9395): 1517–26. doi:10.1016/S0140-6736(03)14738-1.

"Spinal Cord Injury and Disease." *Therapeutic Uses of Marijuana*. Medical Marijuana Information Resource Centre. Retrieved 9 August 2009.

M. Maurer, V. Henn, A. Dittrich, A. Hofmann (1990). "Delta-9-tetrahydrocannabinol Shows Antispastic and Analgesic Effects in a Single Case Double-blind Trial." *European Archives of Psychiatry and Clinical Neuroscience* 240 (1): 1–4.

R.W. Kogel, P.B. Johnson, R. Chintam, C.J. Robinson, B.A. Nemchausky, (October 1995). "Treatment of Spasticity in Spinal Cord Injury with Dronabinol, a Tetrahydrocannabinol Derivative." *American Journal of Therapeutics* 2 (10): 799–805.

M. Ben Amar (April 2006). "Cannabinoids in Medicine: A Review of Their Therapeutic Potential." *Journal of Ethnopharmacology* 105 (1–2): 1–25.

S.D. McAllister, R.T. Christian, M.P. Horowitz, A. Garcia, P.Y. Desprez (November 2007). "Cannabidiol as a Novel Inhibitor of Id-1 Gene Expression in Aggressive Breast Cancer Cells." *Molecular Cancer Therapeutics* 6 (11): 2921–7.

L.J. Morel, B. Giros, V. Daugé (June 2009). "Adolescent Exposure to Chronic Delta-9-Tetrahydrocannabinol Blocks Opiate Dependence in Maternally Deprived Rats". *Neuropsychopharmacology* 34 (11): 2469–76. PhysOrg.com (7 July 2009).

W.N. Raby, K.M. Carpenter, J. Rothenberg et al. (July 2009). "Intermittent Marijuana Use is Associated with Improved Retention in Naltrexone Treatment for Opiate-dependence." *The American Journal on Addictions* 18 (4): 301–8.

Tod H. Mikuriya (6 October 1999). "Dependency and Cannabis."

59 "Descriptions of Allowable Conditions under State Medical Marijuana Laws," *The U.S. Government Accountability Office* (GAO), Appendix IV, November 2002.

60 Neil Osterweil, (24 May 2006). "ATS: Marijuana Smoking Found Non-Carcinogenic." *MedPage Today*.

Marc Kaufman, (26 May 2006). "Study Finds No Cancer-Marijuana Connection." *Washington Post*.

61 American Thoracic Society (21 May 2007). "Marijuana Worsens COPD Symptoms in Current Cigarette Smokers." Press release.

62 Donald P. Tashkin, (14 April 2009). "Does Smoking Marijuana Increase the Risk of Chronic Obstructive Pulmonary Disease?" (PDF). CMAJ (Toronto: Canadian Medical Association) 180 (8): 797–8.

63 Julius Goepp, MD, "Enhanced Antioxidant Protection Against Heart Disease, Cancer, Allergies, and More," *Life Extension Magazine* (April 2009), http://www.lef.org/magazine/mag2009/apr2009_Quercetin_01.htm, accessed Aug. 9, 2010.

64 Kristie Leong M.D., "The Hidden Dangers of Fake Nails," January 28, 2008, *Associated Content, Inc*. Shine, Accessed 7/15/10, <http://www.associatedcontent.com/article/557507/the_hidden_dangers_of_fake_nails.html?cat=69>.

65 M. Santibez Margello et al., "Occupational Risk Factors in Alzheimer's Disease: a Review Assessing the Quality of Published Epidemiological Studies," *Occupational and Environmental Medicine*, 2007;64:723–732, BMJ Publishing Group Ltd, Accessed 7/15/10, http://www.epa.gov/radiation/understand/health_effects.html.
66 DW Staff, "German Study Says Condoms Contain Cancer-causing Chemical," DW-WORLD.DE, 5/29/04, Accessed 7/15/10, http://www.dw-world.de/dw/article/0,,1220847,00.html.
67 Sumana Reddy, M.D., "Latex Allergy," Copyright 1998 by the American Academy of Family Physicians, accessed 7/14/10, http://www.aafp.org/afp/980101ap/reddy.html.
68 Aetna InteliHealth Inc., "Proper Use of a Condom," *The Trusted Source*, 1996–2010, accessed 7/14/10, <http://www.intelihealth.com/IH/ihtIH/c/8776/28837/213508.html?d=dmtContent>.
69 http://www.huffingtonpost.com/samuel-s-epstein/how-to-sunbathe-safely_b_258454.html.
70 http://www.independent.co.uk/news/science/mobile-phone-use-raises-childrens-risk-of-brain-cancer-fivefold-937005.html, http://www.articlesbase.com/diseases-and-conditions-articles/swedish-study-links-brain-damage-to-cell-phone-radiation-394802.html, accessed Dec. 2, 2010.
71 http://articles.mercola.com/sites/articles/archive/2008/10/18/scientists-warn-congress-about-cell-phones-and-cancer.aspx, accessed Nov. 20, 2010.
72 Juliana Mazzeo, MS, CDN, "Acid Blockers and Malnutrition - the Myth of Hyperacidity, 2005, http://www.nymedicalnutrition.com/images/pdf/acid%20blockers%20and%20malnutrition.pdf, accessed Nov. 20, 2010.
73 Juliana Mazzeo, MS, CDN, "Acid Blockers and Malnutrition - the Myth of Hyperacidity, 2005, http://www.nymedicalnutrition.com/images/pdf/acid%20blockers%20and%20malnutrition.pdf, accessed Nov. 20, 2010.
74 Juliana Mazzeo, MS, CDN, "Acid Blockers and Malnutrition - the Myth of Hyperacidity, 2005, http://www.nymedicalnutrition.com/images/pdf/acid%20blockers%20and%20malnutrition.pdf, accessed Nov. 20, 2010.
75 Culley et al., "General Anesthetic-induced Neurotoxicity," *Current Opinion in Anesthesiology* 20:408–413.ß (2007), 409.
76 AIDS InfoNet. Fact Sheet 556, "Mitochondrial Toxicity," July 9, 2009, The Body is a Service of Body Health Resources Corporation, http://www.thebody.com/content/art6071.html, accessed July, 14, 2010.
77 Chen Yumin et al., "Collateral Damage in Cancer Chemotherapy: Oxidative Stress in Nontargeted Tissues," *MI*, June 2007 vol. 7 no. 3 147–156.
78 David M. Nudell, MD, Mara M. Monoski, Larry I. Lipshultz, MD, "Common Medications and Drugs: How They Affect Male Fertility," *Urologic Clinics of North America* - Volume 29, Issue 4 (November 2002), http://www.mdconsult.com/das/article/body/227470511-2/jorg=journal&source=&sp=12611256&sid=0/N/327203/1.html?issn=0094-0143, accessed Nov. 20, 2010.

79 MitoAction.org, "Table of Reported Drugs with Mitochondrial Toxicity," Mito Action, 2010, Accessed 7/15/10, http://www.mitoaction.org/files/Mito%20Toxins%20Chart.pdf.
80 John R. Lee, M.D., "Are Mammograms Worth It?," http://www.virginiahopkinstestkits.com/mammogramsdrlee.html.
Maggie Mahar, "Truth Squad—Medical Reporting on Mammograms," http://www.healthwatchersnews.com/2009/12/truth-squad—medical-reporting-on-mammograms/.
Virginia Hopkins, "Mammogram Controversy – Follow the Money," http://www.healthwatchersnews.com/2009/11/mammogram-controversy-follow-the-money/.
81 S. L. Baker, "New Study: 85% of Big Pharma's New Drugs are 'Lemons' and Pose Health Risks to Users" Aug. 18, 2010, *Natural News*, Sept. 4, 2010, http://www.naturalnews.com/029506_Big_Pharma_lemons.html.
82 News: Analysis & Commentary, "Hooked on the Cash From Cholesterol," *Bloomberg BusinessWeek*, July 26, 2004, http://www.businessweek.com/magazine/content/04_30/b3893048_mz011.htm, accessed Aug. 9, 2010.
83 Russell L. Blaylock, M.D., *The Blaylock Wellness Report*, Vol. 1, No. 3 (August 2004): 3.
84 Russell L. Blaylock, M.D., *The Blaylock Wellness Report*, Vol. 1, No. 3 (August 2004): 3.
85 Russell L. Blaylock, M.D., *The Blaylock Wellness Report*, Vol. 1, No. 3 (August 2004): 4.
86 Russell L. Blaylock, M.D., *The Blaylock Wellness Report*, Vol. 1, No. 3 (August 2004): 3–4.
87 Russell L. Blaylock, M.D., *The Blaylock Wellness Report*, Vol. 1, No. 1 (May 2004): 3.
88 Weston A. Price, *Nutrition and Physical Degeneration*. 6th Ed. (La Mesa, CA: Price-Pottenger Nutrition Foundation, 1939-2003), pp. 131–133.
89 Russell L. Blaylock, M.D., *The Blaylock Wellness Report*, Vol. 6, No. 7 (July 2009): 9.
90 Russell L. Blaylock, M.D., *The Blaylock Wellness Report*, Vol. 1, No. 1 (May 2004): 8.
91 Terry J. Allen, "HPV Vaccine: Betting on a Mercky Record," *In These Times* (February 27, 2007) Aug. 9, 2010 http://www.inthesetimes.com/article/3057/ http://www.sourcewatch.org/index.php?title=Gardasil.
92 Norma Erickson, "What Are the Reported Adverse Reactions for Gardasil?" *AMVaccines Examiner* (March 15, 2010) http://www.examiner.com/x-40801-Vaccines-Examiner~y2010m3d15-What-are-the-reported-adverse-reactions-for-Gardasil. Tegan N. Millspaw, "Examining the FDA's HPV Vaccine Records," *Judicial Watch* (June 30, 2008), http://www.judicialwatch.org/documents/2008/JWReportFDAhpvVaccineRecords.pdf, accessed Aug. 9, 2010.
93 "Genital HPV Infection—CDC Fact Sheet" (November 24, 2009) http://www.cdc.gov/std/hpv/stdfact-hpv.htm, accessed Aug. 9, 2010.
94 Gwendolyn V. Kelly, MD, Laura Spinelli, MD, "Sex, Science, and Vaccines: The Decline of Cervical Cancer," Martha Jefferson Hospital (Spring 2006) http://www.marthajefferson.org/clinicalfront/website_spring_06/cervical.php, accessed Aug. 9, 2010.

95 Marilynn Marchione, "CT Scans Pose a Growing Danger to Americans: Experts Call for Increased Regulation to Improve Safety," msnbc.com, Associated Press, http://www.msnbc.msn.com/id/37881079, accessed July 15, 2010.

96 EPA, "Radiation Protection," February 23, 2010, http://www.epa.gov/radiation/understand/health_effects.html#otherlongterm, accessed July 15, 2010.

index

A

aaomed.org, 229
N-acetyl cysteine (NAC), 92
Activator X, 41, 53, 77, 91, 104, 168
acupuncture, 92, 93–95
addictions
   acupuncture for, 93–95
   ending, 81–95
adenosine triphosphate (ATP), 14
adrenal burnout
   causative factors, 191–192
   recovery from, 195–196
   stages of, 191–195
   stress and, 190
   symptoms of, 195
adrenal fatigue, 111
adrenal gland, stress and, 190
adrenal hormones, 162
adrenaline, 211, 215
adrenaline rush, 88, 191
aerobic exercise, 212
aging
   anti-aging strategies, 110–111
   muscle mass and, 212
   overview, 18–21
   signs of, 10, 40
   weight loss and, 9–21
aging, accelerated, 10–21
   adrenal burnout and, 194
   coffee and, 104
   dehydration and, 130
   insulin and, 33
   prescription drugs and, 124–125
agitation, sleep and, 181–182
agn (fire), 118
akasha (space), 118
alcohol, insomnia and, 184
alcoholics, body weight in, 83
Alcoholics Anonymous, 90
alcoholism, 90–91
Allen, David, 153
allergies
   "blasters," 113
   desensitization to, 99–100
   to foods, 99–100
   soy and, 29
   triggers, 29
alpha waves, 92–93, 190, 205
Alzheimer's disease, 156
American Cancer Society (ACS), 85–86

American College for the Advancement in Medicine, 128
amino acids
   essential, 38–39
   from food, 39
   human metabolism and, 38–39
   neurotransmitter production and, 78
amnesia, sleeping pills and, 185
amygdala, 201, 205
anabolic steroids, 161
anaerobic exercise, 212
anti-aging strategies, 110–111
antidepressants, 5
   dependence on, 194
   efficacy of, 91
   use of, 3, 5, 147
antioxidants
   athlete intake of, 90
   intake of, 92
   in multivitamins, 107
   supplements, 106–107
anxiety, causes of, 196
appearance, physical, 2
apu (water), 118
arsenic, tap water, 135
arteries, caffeine and, 87
Asad, Billy, 223–224
asanas (postures), 219
Ashtanga, 218–219
aspartame
   free radical generation by, 12, 79
   marketing of, 23–24
   metabolic syndrome and, 25
   metabolites of, 23–24
   multiple sclerosis and, 24–25
   obesity and, 25, 33
aspirin, 114
athletes, nutrition for, 214
attention deficit disorder (ADD), 28, 73, 76, 93
attitudes, negative, 187
autoimmune diseases, 13, 27, 42, 102, 103, 138
autonomic nervous system, 203
Awakening the Buddha Within (Das), 188
ayur (life), 117
Ayurvedic medicines, 115, 117–119
Ayurvedic therapy, 133–134

B

B-complex vitamins, 107–108
babies, brain-related problems, 73
bananas, glycemic index of, 136
Bandhas, 219
bathing, relaxation and, 179
beans, coumestans in, 27–28
beauty, relativity of, 2
bed yoga, 179
bedrooms, 179–181
bedtimes
   consistency in, 182, 183
beef, enzymes in, 40
beer, raw (live), 137
Begier, Lynne, 223
belly fat, 82, 83
Benson, Herbert, 189–190
Benson-Henry Institute (BHI), 189
beta waves, 92, 190, 205
beverages, 133. *see also green tea; green veggie juice; herbal teas*
The Bhagavad Gita, 217
Bi-Est patch, 157
bicarbonate, 135

bioidentical hormone replacement (BHRT), 58, 92
  choice of, 152–154
  considerations, 146
  detox lifestyle and, 125
  overview of, 141–170
biomodulation, micro-dose, 202–205
biotin, 136
birth defects, caffeine and, 87
black salt, 56
Blaylock, Russell L., 17, 79
blood pressure, caffeine and, 87
blood sugar
  balanced, 75
  caffeine and, 87
  exercise and, 214–215
Blossom, Scott, 217
body, goal checklist for, 7
body weight
  mental adjustment to, 3–4
  optimal, 2, 34
  overweight/obese, 63–64
  too thin, 62–63
bone mass, 210
bovine spongiform encephalopathy (BSE), 39
brain
  calming of, 174
  caring for, 73–80
  cholesterol and, 49
  common problems with, 73
  composition of, 76
  decreasing inflammation in, 80
  dietary supplements for, 77–79
  estrogen and health of, 156
  hormones and, 164
  meditation and, 201
  metabolic rate of, 79
  overload, 172
  principles for health of, 75
  protection from inflammation, 79
  repair of, 91–92
  saturated fats and, 46
  sleep and repair of, 172
  stimulants and, 81–82
  wind down time, 177
brainwaves, 92–93, 190
breast cancer, 153
breathing
  exercise and, 213
  pranayama, 223
  ujjayi pranayama, 219
Buddha, 188–189
Buddhism, 187–188, 198–201
bupropion (Wellbutrin, Zyban), 85
butterfat, 138

C

cadmium, 135
caffeine, 33, 87–88, 134
calcium, 27, 46, 135
calorie restriction, 30–31
Camellia sinesis, 134
cancer
  anticancer supplements, 113
  cell growth, 135
Candida (yeast), 100
canker sores, 227
canola oil, 32
CAPOs. *see Concentrated Animal Feeding Operations (CAPOs)*
carbo-loading, 214–215
carbohydrates
  counter, 294–298
  protein ratio with, 58–59
  refined, 34

carbohydrates continued
  set point and, 56–58, 62–68
  snacks and, 60–61
carbon bond saturation, 42
carbon dioxide gas, 135
carbon water filters, 132
carcinogens, cigarette, 84
catechins, 134
celiac disease, 102
cellulite, development of, 40
chelation therapy, 126, 127–128
children. *see babies; kids*
Chinese medicines, 115–117
chlorine, tap water, 132
cholesterol, 48–52
  benefits of, 50
  dietary, 40–41
  foods laden with, 52
  therapeutic value of, 48–52
cholorella, 106
Choudhury, Bikram, 222
cigarettes, carcinogens in, 84
circadian rhythms
  darkened bedrooms and, 180
  light exposure and, 183
  regulation of, 164, 165, 175
Coca Cola, 12, 13
coconut milk, 133–134
coconut oil, 47–48
coconut shell filter systems, 132
coconut water, 133
cod liver oil, 43, 44, 45, 91
coffee, 83, 104
The Compassionate Mind (Gilbert), 197
Concentrated Animal Feeding Operations (CAPOs), 23, 39
confidence, health and, 2, 5

conjugated linoleic acid (CLA), 138
constipation, 97, 126
contentment system, 197
Cortef, 163
CortiSlim, 49
cortisol, 49. *see also hydrocortisone*
  energy release and, 215
  excess of, 193
  exercise and, 212
  morning levels of, 209
  release of, 192
  stimulant action and, 83
cortisone. *see hydrocortisone*
coumestans, 27–28, 143

D

Dalai Lama, 23–24
Daniel, Kaayla T., 27
Das, Suyra (Lama), 188
Davis, Adelle, 105
dehydration, 130, 176
dehydroepiandrosterone (DHEA), 163–164
  cholesterol and, 49
  exercise and, 211
  release of, 192
delta waves, 92
dendrites, 79
depression, brain health and, 74. *see also antidepressants*
detox lifestyle, 91, 121–129
DHEA (dehydroepiandrosterone), 163–164
  cholesterol and, 49
  exercise and, 211
  release of, 192
diabetes, type 2, 16–17, 84

diet
    enzymatic foods in, 68–69
    low-fat, 31–32, 40–41
    optimal metabolism and, 61–62
    supplements, 96–120
diet, balanced, 9–10, 34, 36–72
    brain health and, 74–75
    digestion of, 59
    inflammation and, 79
    meals per day, 59–60
    principles of, 37
dieting
    extreme, 30–31, 89
    famine and, 33
    malnutrition and, 4
diketopiperazine, 24
2.3-dimercaptosuccinic acid (DMSA), 128
diuresis, caffeine and, 87
DNA
    oxidation of, 15
    repair enzymes, 79
    vulnerability of, 79
docosahexaenoic acid (DHA), 44
dopamine, 76, 207
doshas (life forces), 118
drishti, 219
drug addiction, 90–91
drug addicts, 83
drug companies, 86
drug hormones, 146–151
drugs, 19. *see also pharmaceutical drugs*
dryer sheets, 13
Dwelley, Steve, 218

E

eatwild.com, 71
eggs, 48–49, 136

eicosapentaenoic acid (EPA), 44
electrolytes, 131
emphysema, smoking and, 84
endocrine disruptors, 27–28
endocrine system
    aging and, 11–12
    balanced diet and, 57
    saturated fats and, 46
endorphins, 77, 94, 177–178, 207
endurance, exercise and, 211
energy levels, 193–194
Enig, Mary, 41–42
environment, toxins in, 122–123, 261–265
enzymatic foods, 68–69
Epstein, Samuel, 86
Ericksonian hypnotherapy, 205–206
Escherischia coli O157:H7, 40
essential fatty acids (EFAs), 43–44
    exercise and, 216
    function of, 77
    in protein smoothies, 136
    saturated fats and, 46
    sources of, 77
estradiol, 156
estriol, 156
estrogen dominance, 142–145
estrogen receptors, 149
estrogens, 151, 154–157, 186
    deficiency of, 154–156
estrone, 156
ethylenediaminetetraacetic acid (EDTA), 128
excitotoxins, 24–25, 28
exercise
    aerobic, 212
    anaerobic, 212
    anti-aging qualities of, 208

exercise continued
  basic principles, 209–210
  breathing and, 213
  consistency of, 209
  daily, 92
  endurance and, 211
  extreme, 89–90
  by fitness level, 229–230
  flexibility and, 210
  free radicals production and, 214
  in heat, 225–226
  hormones and, 211–212
  insomnia and, 184
  interval training, 213
  lactic acid and, 135
  nutrition and, 214–216
  over exercising, 227–228
  psychology of, 231
  regular, 207–231
  strength and, 210
  in the sun, 227
  training and, 211
  variety of, 216–217

F

facelifts, 204
factory-produced food
  inflammation and, 79
  sex drive and, 22–23
  toxins in, 233–237
fashion industry, 1
fats
  in a balanced diet, 10
  detox lifestyle and, 126
  dietary, 40–41, 214
  exercise and loss of, 208–209
  from food, 41–43
  healthy, 52
  increase of, 14
  metabolism of, 56–57, 58, 107
  miscellaneous healthy, 52–53
  monounsaturated, 45–46
  oxidized, 42
  polyunsaturated, 43–45
  rancid, 42
  saturated, 42, 46–52
  vegetarians and, 53
fatty acids, 41–42. *see also essential fatty acids (EFAs)*
fear, stress and, 205
fibrocystic breast disease, 87
fight-or-flight response, 189
fish, wild-caught, 38–40
fitness, exercise and, 209–210, 229–230
flax, marketing of, 44–45
flaxseed, 27–28
flea collars, 13
fleur de sel de Guérande, 56
flexibility, exercise and, 210
fluoride, 26–28, 79
folate, solubility of, 106
food. *see also diet, balanced; factory-produced food; nutrition*
  cooked, 70
  current state checklist, 18–19
  factory-produced, 22–35
  free-range, 38–40
  home-grown, 71
  locally-grown, organic, 69–70
  raw, 70
  real, living, 36–72
  sensitivities, 99–100
  sleep and, 175
Food and Drug Administration (FDA)

approval of CAPOs by, 23
approval of MSGs, 25
on BHRT, 153
on environmental toxins, 122
on hormone replacement, 146
Recommended Daily Intakes, 105
formaldehyde, 23
Four square cigarettes, 84
free radicals
  aging and, 12–14
  antioxidants and, 106–107
  creation of, 33
  exercise and, 214
  generators of, 13–14
  impact on DNA by, 79
  mitochondrial damage, 14
  stimulants and, 82
free-range food, 38–40

G

gamma amino butyric acid (GABA), 77
gamma-linolenic acid (GLA), 45, 77
gardening, home-grown food, 71
gastroesophageal reflux disease (GERD), 98
gastrointestinal (GI) tract
  cholesterol and health of, 49
  fixing problems with, 103–104
  healing of, 109
  health status and, 96
  pH of, 97–98
  problems ignored too long, 99
  problems related to, 98
  symptoms of problems with, 97
Gauloise cigarettes, 84
Gautama, Siddhartha, 188. *see also Buddha*

gender, personal choices and, 3
GERD. *see gastroesophageal reflux disease (GERD)*
Germer, Christopher K., 187, 198–200, 208
getprolo.com, 229
Gilbert, Paul, 197
Gilligan, Stephen, 205–206
glucagon, exercise and, 211
glutamate, 26–27, 28
gluten intolerance, 101–102
glycemic index, 59
glycogen, storage of, 50
GMO Monsanto Round-Up Ready soy, 26
goals, 5–8
goiters, 145
goitrogens, soy and, 28
green tea, 92, 134
green veggie juice, 79, 106, 126
grocery shopping, 70–72
Grothe, Carolyn, R., 205, 206
growth hormone (GH)
  human (hGH), 165–167, 186, 208, 215
  recombinant bovine (rBGH), 137
growth hormone-releasing factor, 167
Gunaratna, Jitka, 94
Guoin, Ken, 131

H

hair analysis, 128
happiness, 5–8
Hatha yoga, 217–218
Hathayoga Pradìpika(Svatmarama), 218
Hawaiian sea salt, 56
HDL-cholesterol, 48, 150

healing
  supplements and, 108
  sympathetic nervous system and, 203
health
  current state checklist, 20
  definition of, 1–4
heart, health of, 111–112
heart disease, 84
heart rates
  exercise and, 212
  target rates, 211, 212
heartburn, 87, 109. *see also gastroesophageal reflux disease (GERD)*
heat, exercise in, 225–226
heat exhaustion, 226
heavy metal toxicity, 127–128
herbal teas, 134, 257–260
herbivores, 38
herbs
  description of, 238–256
  examples of, 55
  medicinal, 114
heroin, 90
herpes virus, 112, 227
Hi-Lite cigarettes, 84
high-fructose corn syrup, 153
home-care products, 123–124, 273–276
homeopathic medicine, 119–120
hormonal imbalance, 11–12, 33
hormone replacement therapy, 3, 27–28
hormones
  anti-aging, 110–111
  exercise and, 211–212
  heart health and, 112
human chorionic gonadotropin (HCG), 160, 184

hunter-gatherer ways, 70–72
hydration, 130, 176–177
hydrocortisone, 162–163. *see also cortisol*
5-hydroxy tryptophan (5-HTP), 78
hyperactivity, 28
hypnosis, 92
hypnotherapy, 205–206
hyponatremia, 131
hypothyroidism, 195
  diagnosis of, 145–146
  soy and, 27, 28
  symptoms of, 145–146
hysterectomies, 147

I

IBS. *see irritable bowel syndrome (IBS)*
immune system, 47, 100–101, 112
incentive systems, 197
inflammation
  aging and, 17–18, 125
  brain health and, 75
  brain protection from, 79
  causative factors, 17–18
  detox lifestyle and, 126
  disease and, 125
  EFA reduction of, 216
  omega-6 and, 45
  reduction of, 79
  supplements decreasing, 80
insomnia, 173–186
insulin
  function of, 15, 57, 214–215
  levels of, 15–16
  stimulant action and, 83
  stimulants and levels of, 82
insulin resistance, 15–17, 38
Internet, shopping via, 71

interstitial cystitis, 78
interval training, 213
irritable bowel syndrome (IBS), 103
isoflavones, 27, 143
Iyengar, B.K.S., 217, 220
Iyengar yoga, 220

J

Japanese diet, 26
Jayasuriya, Anton, 94
Jois, K. Pattabhi (Guruji), 217, 218
juicers, 140
juicing, benefits of, 139–140

K

kapha (water and earth), 118–119
Karma (Deville), 90
Kaslow, Jeremy E., 203–204
Kegel, Arnold, 220
Kegel exercises, 220
Kent cigarettes, 84
Kest, Brian, 224
kids, brain-related problems, 73
Kikrim yoga, 222–223
knitting, 178
kosher salt, 56
Krishnamacharya, Tirumalai, 217, 220

L

lactic acid, 136
lactose intolerance, 138
lamb, enzymes in, 40
lauric acid, 134
LDL-cholesterol, 45–46, 51
lead, tap water, 135

leaky gut syndrome, 100–101
Lee, John, 143
Life (Richard), 171
Life Unlocked (Pillay), 181, 205
lifestyle
    current state checklist, 19
    detoxification and, 121–129
lignans, 27–28, 143
linoleic acid (omega-6), 43–44
linolenic acid (omega-3), 34–44
lipid hypothesis, 40–41, 41
lipid peroxidation, 12
lipids. *see fats*
Listeria monocytogenes, 40
liver, sugar release from, 37–38, 50
low-fat diets, 31–32
Lp(a), 47
lung cancer, 83, 84
lungs, saturated fats and, 46

M

"mad cow disease," 39
Madannathons, 223
magnesium, 77, 78
magnetism, personal, 4–5
Magone, David, 221–222
malaria, symptoms of, 117
malnutrition
    brain health and, 74
    dieting and, 4
    sex-drive and, 22–23
manganese, 26–27, 28
MAO inhibitors, 78
Marlboro cigarettes, 84
Mayo Clinic, 32
meals
    number of, 59–60
    sample, 62–68

meat
  in a balanced diet, 10
  grass-fed, 71
  humanely-raised, 38–40
  omega-6 in, 45
meditation
  amygdala and, 201
  brainwaves and, 190
  Buddhist, 187–188
  daily practice of, 201–202
  Metta, 198–201
Mediterannean diet, 31–32
melanomas, 169, 227
melatonin, 164–165, 165, 175, 186
mentors, finding, 225
mercury, 79
metabolic breakdown, 11
metabolic syndrome, 25
metabolism, optimal, 61–62
Metta (loving kindness), 199
Metta meditation, 198–201
micro-dose biomodulation, 202–205
micronutrients, 53–55
milk, raw (live), 137–138
mind, goal checklist for, 6–7
The Mindful Path to Self-
  Compassion (Germer), 187, 200
mineral water, 134–135
minerals
  function of, 104–106
  supplements with, 108
Minnesota Semi Starvation Surgery, 22, 33
mitochondria
  degeneration of, 14–15
  free radical damage to, 24–25
  function of, 14
  restoration of, 110

monosodium glutamate (MSG), 25–26, 33, 79
mood disorders, 74
morphine, 114
moxabustion, 116
MSG. *see monosodium glutamate (MSG)*
mulabanda, 219, 220
multiple sclerosis, 24–25, 138
multivitamins, 92, 107. *see also Specific vitamins*
muscle, exercise and, 208–209
music, relaxation and, 178

N

Narcotics Anonymous, 90
National Institutes of Health
  Women's Health Institute (WHI), 147, 150
neural therapy, 202–205
neurofeedback therapy, 92–93
  brain health and, 92
neurotransmitters
  brain depletion of, 92
  dietary fats and, 40
  function of, 76–77
  production of, 78
  sleep and, 175
Newsweek, 91
Ni, Maoshing, 117
niacin, solubility of, 106
Nichols, Michele, 218
nicotine, effects of, 83–86
noise pollution, 180–181
nonsteroidal anti-inflammatory drugs (NSAIDs), 100–101
nutrition. *see also diet; food*
  brain health and, 75
  exercise and, 214–216

O

obesity
  aspartame and, 25
  reasons for, 33–35
  sample meals for, 63–64
obesogens, 34
oils
  polyunsaturated, 42–43, 77
  toxins related to, 121
omega-3 fatty acids, 42, 43–45, 77
omega-6 fatty acids, 43–45, 77
1-800-CALLMOM, 196–198
oral contraceptives, 151–152
organic food
  benefits of, 70–71
  detox lifestyle and, 126–127
  economics of, 70–71
orgasms, effects of, 178
osteoporosis, 46, 84
over-the-counter drugs, 126
oxytocin, 170

P

Pacheco, Rebecca, 225
Pacific Islander diets, 47
pain
  acupuncture for, 93–95
  meditation and, 202
  quality of life and, 202
pancreas, insulin resistance and, 16
parasympathetic nervous system, 203
pasteurization, 137
Patañjali, 217
peas, coumestans in, 27–28
Pellegrino, 134
penicillin, molds and, 114
penicillin G, 137
peristalsis, 98
pesticides, 79
pets, 178
pH
  GI tract, 97–98
  homeostatic, 135, 139
pharmaceutical drugs
  hangover effect, 185
  overprescription, 124–125
  side-effects of, 114
  toxins in, 124–125, 277–293
phosphoric acid, 135
phytates, 28
phytoestrogens, 27–28, 33, 143
phytonutrients, 139, 140
Pilates, 210
The Pill, 151–152
Pillay, Srinivasan, 181, 205
pineal gland, 164
pitta (fire and water), 119
plastic water bottles, 266
plastics, 27, 266
platelet-rich plasma (PRP), 229
polyphenols, 140
post-exertional malaise, 227
potassium, 227
prakriti (constitution), 118
prana, 115
PranaVayu yoga, 221–222
pranayama (breathing), 223
pregnenolone, 49, 159–160
Premarin, 146–149, 154
PremPro, 147, 154, 156
prescriptions, overboard with, 124–125
Price, Weston A., 9–10, 41, 47
prithvi (earth), 118
probiotics, 126–127

procaine (Novocain), 204
progesterone, 157–159
progesterone replacement, 143
progestins, 149–151
prolotherapy, 228–229
protease inhibitors, 28
protein smoothies, 135–136
proteins
    carbohydrate ratio with, 58–59
    dietary, 214
    metabolism of, 107
    snacks and, 60–61
Provera (medroxyprogesterone acetate), 147, 150, 156
Prozac, warnings, 78
pubococygeus muscles, 220
purging, 89

Q

Qi, 94, 115, 117
Qigong, 116
quinine, 114

R

rawusa.org, 138
reading, sleep and, 179
real food, 36–72
recombinant bovine growth hormone (rBGH), 137
Recommended Daily Intake (RDI), 105
relaxants, natural, 186
The Relaxation Response (Benson), 189
REM (rapid eye movement) sleep, 185
resource-seeking system, 197

riboflavin, solubility of, 106
rice, 136
RICE acronym, 228
Richard, Keith, 171

S

Salmonella spp., 40, 136
salt
    dietary, 55–56
    intake of, 216
    sea salt, 56
Samadhi (enlightened state), 199–200
scars, 204
scents, 13
scraping, 116
sea algae, 216
sea salt, 56
Secrets of Longevity (Ni), 117
self-care products, toxins, 123, 266–272
self-compassion
    emotional healing and, 199
    training for, 201
    transformation and, 3
self-compassion meditations, 75, 92, 186, 187–206
self-confidence, health and, 5
self-esteem, 74
self-soothing system, 196–198
Selye, Hans, 190
seniors, brain-related problems, 73
sermorelin, 167
serotonin
    disposal of, 89
    function of, 77
    production of, 49
set point, carbs and, 56–58, 62–68

sex
  endorphin release and, 177–178
  health and, 2
  life balance and, 118
  mulabanda and, 220
  oxytocin and, 170
sex drive, 22–23
sexy, definition of, 4–5
Shadow Yoga, 218
Shavasana (corpse pose), 179
sleep
  brain health and, 75
  brainwaves in, 93
  conditions for, 173–186
  deprivation, 172–173
  growth hormone production of, 166
  healing and, 195–196
  requirements for, 171–186
  scheduling of, 182
  wake-up times and, 184
sleep hygiene protocols, 173–174
sleeping pills, 185
smoking
  addiction to, 83–86
  body weight in, 83
  quitting, 84–86
snacks, 59–61
snoring, 180
sodas, consumption of, 135
somatic cell counts (SCC), 137
soothing system, 197–198
soy, 26–28
spirit, goal checklist for, 8
spirulina, 106
Splenda (sucralose), 23–24, 25
sports injuries, 228–230
SSRIs (selective serotonin reuptake inhibitors), 89

stimulants
  addictive, 82
  brain health and, 75, 81–82
  insomnia and, 184
  stress responses and, 82–83
strength, exercise and, 210
stress
  addiction to, 88
  avoidance of, 119
  causes of, 204
  emotional, 88
  fear and, 205
  inflammation and, 79
  physiological response to, 190
  triggers, 82–83
stress hormones, 16
sugar
  cholesterol and, 51
  dietary, 215–216
  energy and, 30
  free radical oxidation and, 37
  insomnia and, 184
sunblocks, 168
sunlight, vitamin D_3 and, 92
supplements
  allergy blasters, 113
  anti-aging strategies, 110–111
  anticancer, 113
  antioxidants in, 107
  antiviral, 112
  for brain nutrition, 77–79
  description of, 238–256
  detox lifestyle and, 125–126
  dietary, 96–120
  digestive, 109
  GI tract healing and, 109
  GI tract problems and, 104
  heart health and, 112

supplements continued
  minerals in, 108
  mitochondrial restoration and, 110
  shopping for, 105–106
survival mechanisms, 205
Svatmarama, Svami, 218
sympathetic nervous system, 203
synapses, 76, 79

T

tap water, 131
tapas (purification through burning), 224
taste buds
  desensitization of, 30
  rebooting, 29–30
taste receptors, 30
teas, 134
teeth, caffeine and, 87
television shows, 74
testosterone, 160–161
testosterone replacement, 161
thermoregulation, 33
theta waves, 92–93
Thomashefsky, Allen, 228–229
thyroid-binding globulin (TBG), 145, 149
thyroid gland, 144–145
thyroid-releasing hormone (TRH), 144
thyroid-stimulating hormone (TSH), 145
thyroxine (T4), 144, 145, 146
tobacco, oxidative effects, 84
toxins
  effects of, 122
  environmental, 122–123, 261–265
  in factory foods, 233–237

  home-care products and, 273–276
  medical, 277–293
  oil-related, 121
  self-care products and, 266–272
  sources of, 121
training, exercise and, 211
trans fats, 41
triglycerides, 50, 51, 58
trihalomethanes, 135
triiodothyronine (T3), 144, 146
trypsin, 136
tryptophan, 78, 165
  foods containing, 175–176
  melatonin production and, 175
Tseten, Migmar, 222
type A personalities, 177

U

uddiyana bandha, 219
ujjayi pranayama, 219
ultraviolet B (IVB) exposure, 169, 227
urinalysis, heavy metal levels, 128
Utthita Hasta Padangustasana, 224–225

V

vaccines, 79
valium, 185
varenicline (Chantix), 86
vata (space and air), 118
vayu (air), 118
veda (knowledge), 117
vegan diets, 53, 215
vegans, 53
vegetable oils, 76
vegetables
  fresh, organic, 53–55
  nonstarchy, 53–54

vegetarian diets, 53, 215
veggie juices, 138–139
vinyasa yoga, 221
viral infections, 112
visualization, 6
vitamin A, 44, 106, 138
vitamin B_6, 77, 78, 106
vitamin B_{12}, 106
vitamin C, 106
vitamin D_3, 167–169
   in butter fat, 138
   cholesterol conversion to, 49
   in cod liver oil, 44
   deficiencies, 27, 168, 227
   detox lifestyle and, 126–127
   hypervitaminosis, 227
   solubility of, 106
   sunlight and, 92
   supplementation, 169
   toxicity of, 169
vitamin E, 46, 106
vitamin F, 43, 227
vitamin K, 106
vitamins (micronutrients)
   depletion of, 151
   function of, 104–106
   solubility of, 106
vomiting, 89

W

wake-up times, 184
walking, 177
water
   body content of, 130
   bottled, 131
   purification systems, 131–133
   tap, 131
weight gain, 173

weight loss, 9–21, 32
weight management, 57–58, 223–224
WesThroid, 146
whey, cold-pressed, 136
white noise machines, 180
white tea, 134
wine, benefits of, 140
workaholics, 88
Wyeth, 154

X

xenoestrogens
   environmental, 143
   obesity and, 33
   sources of, 143
xenohormones
   description of, 27
   plastic water bottles and, 27, 131, 266

Y

Yang, Yin and, 116
yeast *(Candida),* 100
Yin and Yang, 116
Yin yoga, 220
yoga, 179
   benefits of, 190
   as exercise, 217
   flexibility and, 210
   interval training and, 213
   weight management and, 223–224

Z

zealotry, 80
Zoloft, warnings, 78